Section Five — Probability and Statistics

Probability 125
Equal and Unequal Probabilities 126
Listing Outcomes 127
   Warm-Up and Practice Questions 128
Venn Diagrams 130
Types of Data 132
Line Graphs and Pictograms 133
   Warm-Up and Practice Questions 134
Bar Charts 136
Pie Charts 138
   Warm-Up and Practice Questions 139
Mean, Median, Mode and Range 141
Frequency Tables 142
Averages from Frequency Tables 143
Scatter Graphs 144
   Warm-Up and Practice Questions 145
Revision Summary 147

Section Six — Exam Practice

Mixed Practice Tests 148
Practice Exam:
   Practice Paper 1 158
   Practice Paper 2 168

Answers 178
Index 190

Published by CGP

From original material by Richard Parsons.

Editors:
Alex Billings, Ellen Burton, Dan Chesman, Sarah George, Shaun Harrogate,
Tom Miles, Claire Plowman, Rosa Roberts and Caley Simpson

With thanks to Sammy El-Bahrawy and Glenn Rogers for the proofreading.
With thanks to Alastair Duncombe for the reviewing.

ISBN: 978 1 78908 244 9

Printed by Elanders Ltd, Newcastle upon Tyne.
Clipart from Corel®

Calculating Tips

KS3 Maths — you're going to love it. There's plenty of learning to be done and plenty of fun to be had. But first, here are some tips that will help you on your way to maths glory.

Don't Be Scared of **Wordy Questions**

For the 'real-life' questions you've first got to work out what the question's asking you to do.

> 1) **Read** the question **carefully**.
>   Think **what bit of maths** you might need to answer it.
>
> 2) **Underline** the **BITS YOU NEED** to answer the question
>   — you might not have to use **all** the numbers they give you.
>
> 3) Write out the question **IN MATHS** and answer it,
>   showing all your **working** clearly.

 **EXAMPLE:** **Ben's Bakery is branching out into mini pastries. All the mini pastries will weigh 50% as much as a normal pastry. If a croissant normally weighs 200 g, how much will a mini croissant weigh?**

The "50%" tells you this is a percentages question (covered on page 28).

You need 200 g (the normal weight) and 50% (the percentage).
It doesn't matter what the shop is called or what the pastry is.

You want to work out 50% of 200 g, so: 50% of 200 g = 0.5 × 200 = 100 g

Don't forget the units in your final answer — this is a question about weight in grams, so the units will be g.

Working with **Units**

When you have a question involving units it's usually best to do the calculations without the units. Then you can add the units back in at the end — careful you don't forget about them.

Money questions always crop up — you'll have to keep an eye on the units and the decimal places.

 **EXAMPLE:** **Nicola buys a new jacket for £30. After 2 months she sells the jacket for a 5% profit. How much profit does she earn on the jacket in a) pounds, and b) pence?**

1) This percentages question is asking you to find 5% of £30.   0.05 × 30 = 1.5

2) The question uses pounds (£30), so 1.5 means 1.5 pounds.
   Answers in pounds should always be given to 2 decimal places.
   You might need to fill in the 2nd decimal place with a 0, like this: £1.50

3) Part b) asks for the answer in pence. £1 = 100p.
   So to change pounds into pence — times by 100:   1.50 × 100 = 150p

---

 EXAM TIP ## Underline the parts of the question you need...

Don't be put off by 'real-life' questions — once you've worked out what calculation you need to do you can ignore the wordy bits. Just remember to include the units in your answer.

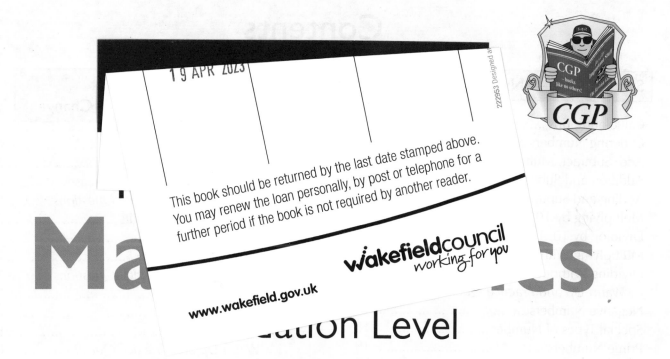

Ma ...tics

...ation Level

This CGP book is packed with crystal-clear notes and examples for every key topic
on the KS3 Maths curriculum — perfect if you're working at a foundation level.

But it doesn't end there. We've also included plenty of practice questions and
mixed-topic tests (with answers) to make sure you've got to grips with it all.

Once you've worked through that lot, you should be ready for the practice exam
at the end of the book — it'll test you on everything you've learned at KS3!

How to access your free Online Edition

This book includes a free Online Edition to read on your PC, Mac or tablet.
You'll just need to go to **cgpbooks.co.uk/extras** and enter this code:

0232 1036 9676 7110

By the way, this code only works for one person. If somebody else has used
this book before you, they might have already claimed the Online Edition.

Complete

Revi... ...ctice

7000000384980

<u>Everything</u> you need for the whole course!

Contents

Section One — Numbers

Calculating Tips 2
Ordering Numbers and Place Value.............. 5
Add, Subtract, Multiply and Divide............... 7
Addition and Subtraction............................. 9
Adding and Subtracting Decimals................ 10
Multiplying by 10, 100, etc. 11
Dividing by 10, 100, etc. 12
Multiplying Without a Calculator................. 13
Dividing Without a Calculator 14
Warm-Up and Practice Questions 15
Negative Numbers...................................... 17
Special Types of Number 18
Prime Numbers 19
Multiples, Factors and Prime Factors............ 20
LCM and HCF 21
Warm-Up and Practice Questions 22
Fractions, Decimals and Percentages 24
Fractions.. 25
More Fractions.. 27
Percentages 28
Warm-Up and Practice Questions 29
Rounding Numbers 31
Accuracy and Estimating............................ 33
Powers... 34
Square Roots and Cube Roots 35
Warm-Up and Practice Questions 36
Revision Summary 38

Section Two — Algebra and Graphs

Algebra — Simplifying 39
Algebra — Multiplying................................ 40
Formulas... 42
Making Formulas From Words 43
Solving Equations 44
Warm-Up and Practice Questions 46
Number Patterns and Sequences.................. 48
Warm-Up and Practice Questions 50
X and Y Coordinates 52
Straight Line Graphs 53
Plotting Straight Line Graphs...................... 56
Warm-Up and Practice Questions 57
Reading Off Graphs 59
Travel Graphs 60
Conversion Graphs 61
Warm-Up and Practice Questions 62
Revision Summary 64

Section Three — Ratio, Proportion and Rates of Change

Ratios 65
Proportion Problems................................... 66
Percentage Increase and Decrease.............. 68
Warm-Up and Practice Questions 69
Metric and Imperial Units........................... 71
Conversion Factors 72
Reading Timetables 74
Warm-Up and Practice Questions 75
Maps 77
Scale Drawings 79
Speed 80
Warm-Up and Practice Questions 82
Revision Summary 84

Section Four — Geometry and Measures

Symmetry 85
Quadrilaterals... 86
Triangles and Regular Polygons................... 87
Congruence 88
Similarity 89
Warm-Up and Practice Questions 90
Perimeter and Area 92
Areas 93
Area of Compound Shapes 94
Circles 95
Circle Questions 96
Warm-Up and Practice Questions 97
3D Shapes 99
Nets and Surface Area 100
Volume.. 102
Warm-Up and Practice Questions 103
Lines and Angles..................................... 105
Measuring Angles.................................... 106
Five Angle Rules 107
Parallel Lines 109
Interior and Exterior Angles...................... 110
Warm-Up and Practice Questions 112
Transformations 114
Enlargements 116
Warm-Up and Practice Questions 117
Triangle Construction............................... 119
Constructions 121
Warm-Up and Practice Questions 122
Revision Summary 124

Calculating Tips

Here are a few tips to help you out with your calculations. They might seem a bit unusual and a little bit tricky, but learn them you must. They'll come in really handy later on.

BODMAS

<u>B</u>rackets, <u>O</u>ther, <u>D</u>ivision, <u>M</u>ultiplication, <u>A</u>ddition, <u>S</u>ubtraction

<u>BODMAS</u> tells you the <u>ORDER</u> in which operations should be done:
Work out <u>Brackets</u> first, then <u>Other</u> things like squaring,
then <u>Divide</u> / <u>Multiply</u> groups of numbers before <u>Adding</u> or <u>Subtracting</u> them.

If you've got multiplications and/or divisions next to each other (like $12 \div 6 \times 4$), just work from left to right. The same thing applies to additions and/or subtractions next to each other too.

EXAMPLES:

1. Work out $4 + 6 \div 2$

1) Follow BODMAS —
   do the <u>division</u> first...

   $4 + 6 \div 2$
   $= 4 + 3$

2) ...then the <u>addition</u>: $= 7$

If you don't follow the order of BODMAS, you get:
$4 + 6 \div 2 = 10 \div 2 = 5$

2. Calculate $10 - 2^3$

1) The cube is an '<u>other</u>'
   so that's first:

   $10 - 2^3$
   $= 10 - 8$

2) Then do the <u>subtraction</u>: $= 2$

3. Find $(8 - 2) \times (3 + 4)$

1) Start by working out the <u>brackets</u>: $(8 - 2) \times (3 + 4)$

2) And now the <u>multiplication</u>: $= 6 \times 7$
   $= 42$

Hidden Brackets in Fractions

This is a bit of a funny one — when you have a <u>fraction</u> with <u>calculations on the top</u> or <u>bottom</u> you have to imagine they're <u>in brackets</u> and do them first.

EXAMPLE:

Work out $\dfrac{16}{6 + 6 \div 3}$.

1) Imagine the bottom of the fraction is <u>in brackets</u>. $\dfrac{16}{(6 + 6 \div 3)}$

2) Now follow <u>BODMAS</u> to do the calculation. $= \dfrac{16}{(6 + 2)} = \dfrac{16}{8} = 2$

EXAMPLE:

Work out $\dfrac{20 \times 5}{4 + 2 \times 3}$.

1) Imagine the top and bottom are <u>both in brackets</u>. $\dfrac{(20 \times 5)}{(4 + 2 \times 3)}$

2) Now follow <u>BODMAS</u> to do the calculation. $= \dfrac{100}{(4 + 6)} = \dfrac{100}{10} = 10$

You've got to get your operations in the right order...

BODMAS is very important — make sure you learn what it stands for. Remember that it applies to every calculation, so you need to use it whenever there's more than one operation.

Calculating Tips

Ever wondered what all those <u>fancy buttons</u> on your calculator do? Well you're about to find out. Careful though — reaching for your calculator isn't always the best option.

Calculators

Make sure you know the important features on your calculator and how to use them.

SHIFT (OR 2ND FUNC)

Press this <u>first</u> if you want to use something written <u>above</u> a button (e.g. the pi (π) button).

SQUARE, CUBE AND ROOTS

E.g. **4** **x^2** gives <u>4 squared</u> = <u>16</u>.
And **$\sqrt[3]{}$** **27** gives the <u>cube root</u> of <u>27</u> = <u>3</u>.

FRACTIONS

E.g. for $\frac{1}{4}$ press **1** **▤** **4** .
(If you have a button that looks like **$a\frac{b}{c}$** instead, use it in the same way.)
For $1\frac{3}{5}$ press **1** **▤** **3** **▤** **5** (you might have to press shift first).

To <u>cancel down a fraction</u>, enter it and press **=** .

Pressing the **▤** or **S⇔D** button also <u>switches</u> an answer between a <u>fraction</u> and a <u>decimal</u>.

3.6

THE ANSWER

Before you jot down 3.6, think about <u>what it means</u>. E.g. in a money question, it might mean <u>£3.60</u>.

BRACKETS

Calculators use <u>BODMAS</u> (see p.3), so if there's part of a question you want the calculator to do <u>FIRST</u> then <u>put brackets in</u> to tell it so.

MEMORY (STO, RCL & M+)

E.g. for $\frac{840}{12 \times 8}$:

Press **12** **×** **8** **=** and then **STO** **M+** to store the bottom line in the memory.

Then press **840** **÷** **RCL** **M+** **=** , and the answer is 8.75.

The 'Ans' button gives the number you got when you <u>last pressed</u> the '=' button.

PI (π) (See page 95.)

The calculator stores the number for <u>pi</u> (= 3.141...). If it's <u>above</u> another button as shown here, press the **shift** button <u>first</u>.

With great power comes great responsibility — so here is some advice about using your calculator.

<u>DON'T</u> reach straight for your calculator. If you put a big calculation into your calculator all in one go you're quite likely to get the wrong answer.

<u>DO</u> show all your working — you're more likely to get the right answer by doing it in stages than doing it all in one go.

Calculators are handy but don't forget to show your working...

Your calculator might be a little bit different to the one shown above — no need to panic though. Just make sure you can do all of the above functions on your own calculator and you'll be flying.

Section One — Numbers

Ordering Numbers and Place Value

A nice easy page here — it's all about reading, writing and ordering whole numbers.

Split **Big Numbers** into **Columns** and **Parts**

1) First, you need to know the names of all the columns. E.g. for the number 3 232 594:

MILLIONS	HUNDRED-THOUSANDS	TEN-THOUSANDS	THOUSANDS	HUNDREDS	TENS	ONES
3	2	3	2	5	9	4

2) You can then split any number up into its parts, like this:

	3 000 000	Three million
	200 000	Two hundred thousand
	30 000	Thirty thousand
Line up the	2 000	Two thousand
columns so you	500	Five hundred
can read the	90	Nine tens (ninety)
numbers clearly.	4	Four ones

→ These add together to make 3 232 594.

Look at **Big Numbers** in Groups of **Three**

To read or write a BIG number, follow these steps:

1) Start from the right-hand side of the number →

2) Moving left, ←, put a space every 3 digits to break it up into groups of 3.

3) Now going right, →, read each group of three as a separate number, as shown.

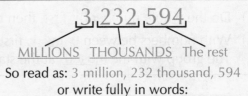

MILLIONS THOUSANDS The rest
So read as: 3 million, 232 thousand, 594
or write fully in words:
Three million, two hundred and thirty-two thousand, five hundred and ninety-four.

Ordering Numbers

EXAMPLE: **Put these numbers in order from smallest to largest:**

53 17 9 1729 754 3 548 88 2321

1) First put them into groups, the ones with fewest digits first:

1-digit	2-digit	3-digit	4-digit
9 3	53 17 88	754 548	1729 2321

2) Then just put each separate group in order of size:

3 9	17 53 88	548 754	1729 2321

The digits of a number are the individual values (0-9) that are written in each place value column.
E.g. in 623, the digits are 6, 2 and 3.

Splitting big numbers into groups of three is key...

Once you've split a big number into groups of three, just remember to add 'thousand' or 'million' onto the end of the group to say how big it is, e.g. 163 000 is one hundred and sixty-three thousand.

Ordering Numbers and Place Value

You need to be able to put decimal numbers in order too. Again, it's all about the columns. After the decimal point, the columns are called decimal places.

Split Decimals into Decimal Places

1) The decimal places have names too. E.g. for the number 173.753:

HUNDREDS	TENS	ONES	DECIMAL POINT	TENTHS	HUNDREDTHS	THOUSANDTHS
1	7	3	.	7	5	3

2) You can split up decimals into parts too:

With decimals, line up the decimal points.

100.000	One hundred
70.000	Seven tens (seventy)
3.000	Three ones
0.700	Seven tenths
0.050	Five hundredths
0.003	Three thousandths

→ These add together to make 173.753.

Putting Decimals in Order of Size

1) Do the whole number bit first, then the bit after the decimal point.
2) With numbers between 0 and 1, first group them by the number of 0s at the start. The group with the most 0s at the start comes first.

EXAMPLE: Write these numbers in order, from smallest to largest:

0.1   9.01   0.53   0.0011   0.027   0.023   0.0023   2.6

1) Do the whole-number bit first. Most of these decimals don't have a whole number bit.

0.1   0.53   0.0011   0.027   0.023   0.0023   2.6   9.01

2) The rest of the decimals are between 0 and 1, so group them by the number of 0s at the start.

2 initial 0s	1 initial 0	no initial 0s	
0.0011 0.0023	0.027 0.023	0.1 0.53	2.6 9.01

3) Once they're in groups, just order them by comparing the first non-zero digits.
(If the first non-zero digits are the same, look at the next digit along instead.)

0.0011   0.0023   0.023   0.027   0.1   0.53   2.6   9.01

Ordering decimals can seem strange at first, but stick with it...

Ordering whole numbers is the easy part — it gets a bit more complicated when you come to ordering decimals. Learn the rules on this page and you'll be ordering decimals in no time.

Add, Subtract, Multiply and Divide

These operations are the building blocks of maths — you have to use them all the time, so it's important that you know how they work.

Using Opposite Operations

Adding and Subtracting

Start off with a number, add any number to it and then subtract the same number — you'll be back to the number you started with. This comes in handy when checking your answer.

 **Simon has 26p and steals 14p from his sister Emma. How much money does Simon have now?**

Add the two amounts together to get the total.

26 + 14 = 40p

Check your answer by using the opposite operation — you should get the amount you started with.

40 − 14 = 26p ✓

Multiplying and Dividing

Multiplying and dividing are opposite operations too. Start off with a number, multiply it by any number and then divide by the same number — you'll be back to the number you started with.

 **Michelle has 3 bags each containing 4 coconuts. She empties all of the coconuts into a box. How many coconuts are in the box?**

Multiply the two numbers together to get the total.

3 × 4 = 12 coconuts

Check your answer by using the opposite operation — you should get the number of bags you started with.

12 ÷ 4 = 3 bags ✓

Use opposite operations to check your answers...

Many people find subtraction and division harder than addition and multiplication, but with opposite operations it's easy to check your answer and make sure you haven't made a mistake. Opposite operations also come up in lots of other places too, so it's worth learning them now.

Add, Subtract, Multiply and Divide

Here are a couple of <u>handy tricks</u> for addition and multiplication calculations — learn them and they'll make your life so much easier.

Patterns in Calculations

Addition

You can make <u>addition</u> questions easier by using opposite operations. If you <u>add</u> something to one number you have to <u>subtract</u> the same amount from the other number.

$$+4 \begin{array}{c} 46 + 54 \\ 50 + 50 \end{array} -4 \quad \begin{array}{l} = 100 \\ = 100 \end{array}$$

EXAMPLE: **Jameela has 18 chocolate mice and Tyrone has 37. How many chocolate mice do they have in total?**

<u>Adding 2</u> to 18 makes it an easier number to work with. Just remember to <u>subtract 2</u> from the other side.

$$+2 \begin{array}{c} 18 + 37 \\ 20 + 35 \end{array} -2 \quad \begin{array}{l} = 55 \\ = 55 \end{array}$$

Multiplication

The same goes for <u>multiplication</u> questions. If you <u>multiply</u> one number by something you have to <u>divide</u> the other number by the same number.

$$\begin{array}{c} \times 2 \\ \times 2 \end{array} \begin{array}{c} 14 \times 8 \\ 28 \times 4 \\ 56 \times 2 \end{array} \begin{array}{c} \div 2 \\ \div 2 \end{array} \quad \begin{array}{l} = 112 \\ = 112 \\ = 112 \end{array}$$

EXAMPLE: **How many 20 g bags of crisps have the same weight as three 120 g bags of crisps?**

Here the total weight of the crisps doesn't matter. You can just use <u>opposite operations</u> until you have 20 g × ....

$$\begin{array}{c} \div 2 \\ \div 3 \end{array} \begin{array}{c} 120\ g \times 3 \\ 60\ g \times 6 \\ 20\ g \times 18 \end{array} \begin{array}{c} \times 2 \\ \times 3 \end{array}$$

Opposite operations can make calculations easier...

Try these calculations by making the numbers easier to work with: 13 + 27, 69 + 26, 15 × 6, 22 × 5. Remember to write down what you are doing to each side. (Answers below.)

(Ans: 40, 95, 90, 110)

Addition and Subtraction

You ought to know how to do sums with just a <u>pen and paper</u> — so put away those calculators.

Adding

1) <u>Line up</u> the <u>units columns</u> of each number.

2) Add up the columns from <u>right to left</u> starting with the <u>units</u>: $2 + 1 + 6 = \underline{9}$.
   Write a 9 at the bottom of the units column.

3) Add up the <u>next column</u>: $4 + 3 + 7 = \underline{14}$.
   Write a '$\underline{4}$' at the bottom of the tens column and <u>carry over</u> the '$\underline{1}$' to the next column.

4) Add up the final column, including anything carried over: $3 + 2 + 0 \underline{+ 1} = \underline{6}$.

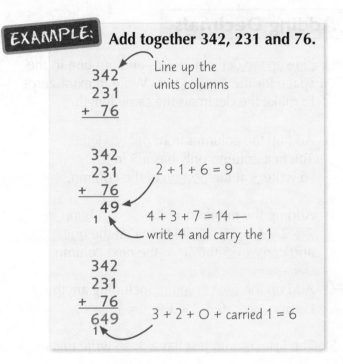

EXAMPLE: **Add together 342, 231 and 76.**

```
  342     Line up the
  231     units columns
+  76
```

```
  342
  231     2 + 1 + 6 = 9
+  76
   49
  1        4 + 3 + 7 = 14 —
           write 4 and carry the 1
```

```
  342
  231
+  76
  649      3 + 2 + 0 + carried 1 = 6
  1
```

Subtracting

EXAMPLE: **Zaara the zebra used to weigh 372 kg. Her current weight is 324 kg. How much weight has she lost (in kg)?**

```
  372     Line up the units columns
– 324     2 is smaller than 4,
          so you can't do 2 – 4
```

```
  6 12
  3̶7̶2
– 324     Borrow 10 from
          the tens column
```

```
  6 12
  3̶7̶2
– 324     12 – 4 = 8
    8
```

```
   6 12
   3̶7̶2
 – 324    6 – 2 = 4
   048
          3 – 3 = 0
```

So Zaara has lost 48 kg.

1) Line up the <u>units columns</u> of each number.

2) Going <u>right to left</u>, take the <u>bottom</u> number away from the <u>top</u> number.
   Here the top number (2) is <u>smaller</u> than the bottom number (4), so <u>borrow 10</u> from the next column along. The '7' in the tens column becomes '6'.

3) You now have $2 + 10 = \underline{12 \text{ units}}$, so you can do the subtraction: $12 – 4 = \underline{8}$. Write the 8 at the <u>bottom</u>.

4) Subtracting the numbers in the <u>next column along</u> gives $6 – 2 = \underline{4}$, so write 4 at the <u>bottom</u>.

5) In the <u>last column</u>, $3 – 3 = \underline{0}$.

EXAM TIP

Make sure each number is in the right column...

Subtractions can be tricky. Once you've done a subtraction question, check your answer by adding it to the number you subtracted. You should get back to the number you started with.

Adding and Subtracting Decimals

The <u>methods</u> for adding and subtracting <u>decimals</u> are <u>just the same</u> as the ones on the last page. But instead of lining up the units, always make sure you <u>line up the decimal points</u>.

Adding Decimals

1) <u>Line up the decimal points</u> and put one in the space for the <u>answer</u> too. Write in extra zeros to make the decimals the same length.

2) Add up the columns from <u>right to left</u>. The first column only has a 5 in it, so write <u>5</u> at the <u>bottom</u> of the column.

3) Add up the numbers in the <u>next column along</u>: 7 + 2 + 6 = <u>15</u>. Write the '5' at the <u>bottom</u> and <u>carry over</u> the '1' to the next column.

4) Add up the <u>next column</u>, including anything <u>carried over</u>: 0 + 2 + 1 <u>+ 1</u> = <u>4</u>.

5) The <u>last column</u> just has a <u>3</u>, so write this in.

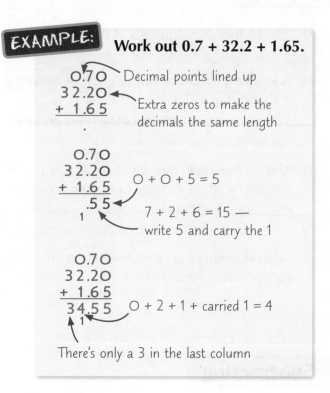

EXAMPLE: **Work out 0.7 + 32.2 + 1.65.**

Decimal points lined up

Extra zeros to make the decimals the same length

0 + 0 + 5 = 5

7 + 2 + 6 = 15 —
write 5 and carry the 1

0 + 2 + 1 + carried 1 = 4

There's only a 3 in the last column

Subtracting Decimals

1) At first, this question doesn't look like it has any <u>decimals</u> in it. But we need both numbers in <u>pounds</u> — so it becomes <u>£5.00 – £0.91</u>.

2) Set it out as usual, making sure you <u>line up the decimal points</u> and put one in for the <u>answer</u>.

3) Look at each column from <u>right to left</u>, taking away the <u>bottom number from the top</u>.

4) <u>Borrow 10</u> from the <u>next column along</u> if you need to, as with whole numbers.

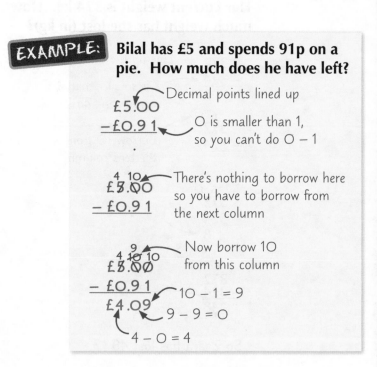

EXAMPLE: **Bilal has £5 and spends 91p on a pie. How much does he have left?**

Decimal points lined up

0 is smaller than 1, so you can't do 0 − 1

There's nothing to borrow here so you have to borrow from the next column

Now borrow 10 from this column

10 − 1 = 9

9 − 9 = 0

4 − 0 = 4

Always line up the decimal points...

Decimal questions look tough, but if you remember to line up the decimal points they are exactly the same as whole number questions. Don't forget about the carried or borrowed numbers either.

Multiplying by 10, 100, etc.

Learn a few simple rules on this page and you'll be able to multiply any number by 10, 100, 1000, etc.

1) To **Multiply** Any Number by **10**

Move the decimal point <u>ONE</u> place <u>BIGGER</u> and if it's needed, <u>ADD A ZERO</u> on the end.

E.g. $1.6 \times 10 = 1\,6$

$6213 \times 10 = 6\,2\,1\,3\,0$

$672.12 \times 10 = 6\,7\,2\,1\,.2$

2) To **Multiply** Any Number by **100**

Move the decimal point <u>TWO</u> places <u>BIGGER</u> and <u>ADD ZEROS</u> if necessary.

E.g. $3.5 \times 100 = 3\,5\,0$

$78 \times 100 = 7\,8\,0\,0$

$3.7734 \times 100 = 3\,7\,7\,.3\,4$

3) To **Multiply** by **1000** or **10 000**, the same rule applies:

Move the decimal point so many places <u>BIGGER</u> and <u>ADD ZEROS</u> if necessary.

E.g. $99.67 \times 1000 = 9\,9\,6\,7\,0$

$1.729 \times 10\,000 = 1\,7\,2\,9\,0$

You always <u>move</u> the <u>DECIMAL POINT</u> this much:
<u>1 place for 10</u>,   <u>2 places for 100</u>,
<u>3 places for 1000</u>,   <u>4 for 10 000</u>,   etc.

4) To **Multiply** by Numbers like **20, 300, 8000** etc.

<u>MULTIPLY</u> by <u>2</u> or <u>3</u> or <u>8</u> etc. <u>FIRST</u>,
then move the decimal point so many places <u>BIGGER</u> (↘)
according to how many zeros there are.

EXAMPLE: **Calculate 110 × 500.**

1) First <u>multiply by 5</u>... $110 \times 5 = 550$
2) ...then move the decimal point <u>2 places</u>. $550 \times 100 = 55000$

Moving a decimal point to the right makes a number bigger...

Nothing too strenuous on this page. The key thing to remember is that you move the decimal point so many places across according to how many zeros are in the number you're multiplying by.

Dividing by 10, 100, etc.

This page tells you how to do the opposite of the previous page. Remember — when you multiply by 10, 100, 1000, etc. you move the decimal point to the right... here, you move it to the left.

1) To **Divide** Any Number by **10**

Move the decimal point <u>ONE</u> place <u>SMALLER</u> and if it's needed, <u>REMOVE ZEROS</u> after the decimal point.

E.g. $32.2 \div 10 = 3.22$

$6541 \div 10 = 654.1$

$4200 \div 10 = 420.0 = 420$

2) To **Divide** Any Number by **100**

Move the decimal point <u>TWO</u> places <u>SMALLER</u> and <u>REMOVE ZEROS</u> after the decimal point.

E.g. $333.8 \div 100 = 3.338$

$160 \div 100 = 1.60 = 1.6$

$1729 \div 100 = 17.29$

3) To **Divide** by **1000** or **10 000**, the same rule applies:

Move the decimal point so many places <u>SMALLER</u> and <u>REMOVE ZEROS</u> after the decimal point.

E.g. $6587 \div 1000 = 6.587$

$978 \div 10\ 000 = 0.0978$

You always <u>move</u> the <u>DECIMAL POINT</u> this much:
<u>1 place for 10</u>,   <u>2 places for 100</u>,
<u>3 places for 1000</u>,   <u>4 for 10 000</u>,   etc.

4) To **Divide** by Numbers like **40, 300, 7000** etc.

<u>DIVIDE</u> by <u>4</u> or <u>3</u> or <u>7</u> etc. <u>FIRST</u>, then move the decimal point so many places <u>SMALLER</u> (i.e. to the left 🠔).

EXAMPLE: **Calculate 180 ÷ 200.**

1) First <u>divide by 2</u>... $180 \div 2 = 90$
2) ...then move the decimal point <u>2 places smaller</u>. $90 \div 100 = 0.9$

Moving a decimal point to the left makes a number smaller...

Knowing how to divide by multiples of 10, 100, 1000, etc. will make harder topics like percentages (see page 24) so much easier. So make sure you learn the rules of how it's done.

Multiplying Without a Calculator

Multiplying with a calculator is easy. The real challenge comes when you don't have a calculator.
There are lots of methods you can use — three popular ones are shown below.
Just make sure <u>you can do it</u> using whichever method <u>you prefer</u>...

The **Traditional Method**

EXAMPLE:

a) Work out 32 × 18

Split it into <u>separate</u>
<u>multiplications</u>, then
add up the results in
<u>columns</u> (right to left).

```
    3 2
  × 1 8
  2 5₁6  ── This is 8 × 32
  3 2 0  ── This is 10 × 32
  5 7 6
```
This is 256 + 320

b) Work out 272 × 52

```
    2 7 2
  ×    5 2
    5₁4 4  ── This is 272 × 2
  1 3₃6₁0 0  ── This is 272 × 50
  1 4,1 4 4
```
This is 544 + 13 600

Other Methods

Here are a couple more methods you can use.

This method's got lots of
different names — you might
know it as lattice multiplication
or Chinese multiplication.

EXAMPLE:

Work out 48 × 33.

The Grid Method

1) <u>Split up</u> each number into its <u>units</u> and <u>tens</u>
   (and <u>hundreds</u> and <u>thousands</u> if it has them).
   48 = 40 + 8 and 33 = 30 + 3

2) Draw a grid, with the
   'bits' of the numbers
   round the outside.

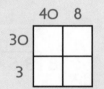

3) <u>Multiply</u> the bits
   round the edge to
   fill <u>each square</u>.

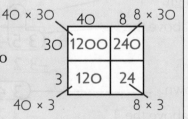

	40	8
30	1200	240
3	120	24

40 × 30   40   8   8 × 30
40 × 3   8 × 3

4) Finally, <u>add up</u>
   the numbers in
   the squares.

```
    1200
     240
     120
  +   24
    1584
```

The 'Gelosia' Method:

1) Arrange the calculation
   as shown and do 4
   <u>easy multiplications</u>
   to <u>fill up the grid</u>...

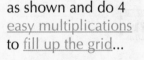

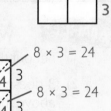

4 × 3 = 12   8 × 3 = 24

4 × 3 = 12   8 × 3 = 24

2) Then just <u>add up along the diagonals</u>
   (going <u>right to left</u>) to get the answer.

1 5 8 4

You might need to <u>carry</u> a
number over when adding up.

All that multiplication and not a calculator in sight...

Work out 25 × 17, 84 × 34 and 19 × 78 using the method you like best. (Answers below.)

(Ans: 425, 2856, 1482)

Dividing Without a Calculator

OK, time for some dividing without a calculator — ready for another challenge?

Dividing **Whole Numbers**

There are two common ways to do division — long division and short division.
Here are some examples of both methods at work. Learn the method you find easier.

Short Division

You'll find it helpful to write out the first few multiples of the number you're dividing by.

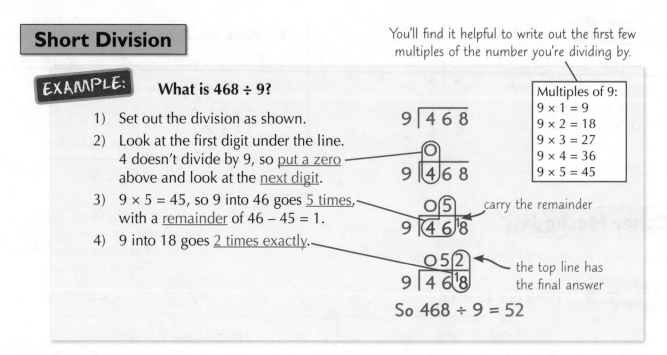

EXAMPLE: **What is 468 ÷ 9?**

1) Set out the division as shown.

2) Look at the first digit under the line.
   4 doesn't divide by 9, so put a zero
   above and look at the next digit.

3) 9 × 5 = 45, so 9 into 46 goes 5 times,
   with a remainder of 46 − 45 = 1.

4) 9 into 18 goes 2 times exactly.

Multiples of 9:
9 × 1 = 9
9 × 2 = 18
9 × 3 = 27
9 × 4 = 36
9 × 5 = 45

carry the remainder

the top line has
the final answer

So 468 ÷ 9 = 52

Long Division

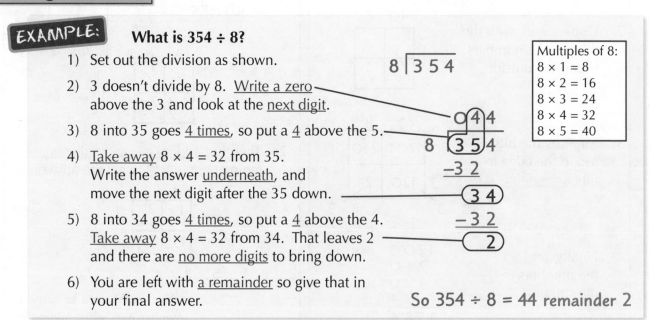

EXAMPLE: **What is 354 ÷ 8?**

1) Set out the division as shown.

2) 3 doesn't divide by 8. Write a zero
   above the 3 and look at the next digit.

3) 8 into 35 goes 4 times, so put a 4 above the 5.

4) Take away 8 × 4 = 32 from 35.
   Write the answer underneath, and
   move the next digit after the 35 down.

5) 8 into 34 goes 4 times, so put a 4 above the 4.
   Take away 8 × 4 = 32 from 34. That leaves 2
   and there are no more digits to bring down.

6) You are left with a remainder so give that in
   your final answer.

Multiples of 8:
8 × 1 = 8
8 × 2 = 16
8 × 3 = 24
8 × 4 = 32
8 × 5 = 40

So 354 ÷ 8 = 44 remainder 2

Try out both methods of dividing to see which you prefer...

A lot of people think that short division is better because it can be quick — but it's no good getting a quick answer if it's not the right answer. Take your time and use whichever method you like the most.

Warm-Up and Practice Questions

These warm-up questions will test whether you've learnt the facts properly. Go back over any bits you don't know, then there will be no nasty surprises when it comes to the practice questions.

Warm-Up Questions

Only use your calculator in question 1.

1) Using BODMAS, work out $(11 - 9) \times (3 \times 2)^2$. Then try it on your calculator.

2) Write these numbers out fully in words: a) 9 905 285   b) 6 054 203

3) Write < or > between each of the following pairs of numbers to make a true statement:
   a) 34   47   b) –2   –6   c) 1.4   0.8   d) –1.2   0.4

4) Put these numbers in order from smallest to largest:
   13.54   3.42   0.55   0.004   8.63   1.23   0.032

5) Find the missing numbers: a) 96 + 67 = 100 + ...   b) 8 × 21 = 2 × ...

6) Work out   a) 113 + 645 + 39   b) 1239 – 387

7) Alia bought 3 items with prices £11.74, £7.12 and £0.76. What was the total cost?

8) Carry out the following multiplications and divisions:
   a) 4.9 × 100   b) 1729 × 10   c) 3.33 ÷ 10   d) 85.21 ÷ 1000

9) Work out   a) 55 × 18   b) 150 × 22   c) 502 × 35

10) Work out   a) 128 ÷ 8   b) 504 ÷ 7   c) 552 ÷ 12

Practice Questions

Once you've managed to get through the warm-ups, you can have a go at these practice questions. Here's a worked example to start you off, and then you're on your own for some more practice.

1   Keisha has 26 boxes of coloured pencils and each box contains 15 pencils.

   a)   How many pencils are there altogether?

$$
\begin{array}{r}
2\,6 \\
\times\,1\,5 \\
\hline
1\,3^3O \\
2\,6\,O \\
\hline
3\,9\,O
\end{array}
$$

← This is 5 × 26

← This is 10 × 26

...........390...........
[2 marks]

   b)   Keisha wants to separate the pencils into boxes of 7 pencils.
        How many boxes would she completely fill?

7 × 1 = 7
7 × 2 = 14   ← Write out the first few multiples of 7
7 × 3 = 21
7 × 4 = 28   O 5 5 remainder 5
7 × 5 = 35   7) 3 9⁴O

.........55......... boxes
[2 marks]

Practice Questions

2   Use BODMAS to work out the values of the following calculations.

a) $5 + 6 \times (7 - 5)$

....
[2 marks]

b) $\dfrac{57 + 3}{4 \times 5 - 10}$

....
[2 marks]

3   Put each set of numbers in order of size, starting with the smallest.

a)   48   572   309   6479   517   7

....
[2 marks]

b)   0.4   0.303   0.43   0.31   0.44   0.043

....
[2 marks]

4   Jack has £6.37 in his wallet. On his birthday, his grandma gives him £25.

a)   How much money does he have altogether?

£.............................
[2 marks]

b)   He spends £8.90 on a new computer game. How much does he have left?

£.............................
[2 marks]

Negative Numbers

Numbers less than zero are <u>negative</u>. You can <u>add</u>, <u>subtract</u>, <u>multiply</u> and <u>divide</u> with them.

Adding and Subtracting with Negative Numbers

Use the <u>number line</u> for <u>addition</u> and <u>subtraction</u> involving negative numbers:

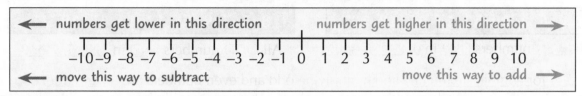

← numbers get lower in this direction   numbers get higher in this direction →

–10 –9 –8 –7 –6 –5 –4 –3 –2 –1 0 1 2 3 4 5 6 7 8 9 10

← move this way to subtract   move this way to add →

EXAMPLES:

What is –3 + 5?   Start at –3 and move 5 places in the positive direction:

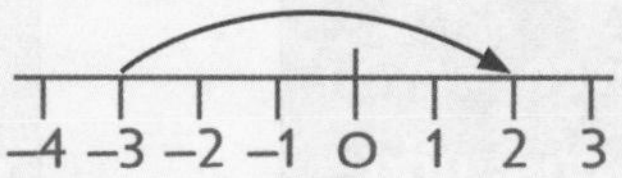

–4 –3 –2 –1 0 1 2 3

So –3 + 5 = 2

Work out 3 – 6   Start at 3 and move 6 places in the negative direction:

–4 –3 –2 –1 0 1 2 3 4

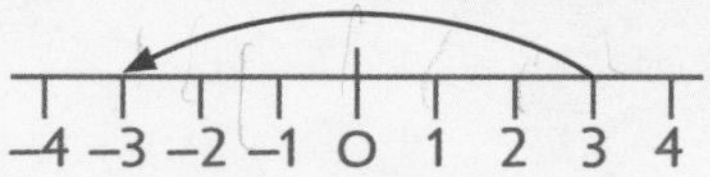

So 3 – 6 = –3

Find –1 – 5   Start at –1 and move 5 places in the negative direction:

–6 –5 –4 –3 –2 –1 0

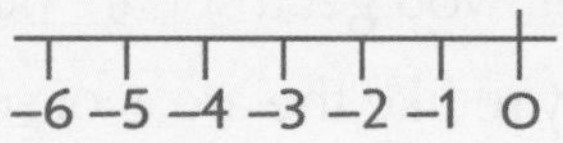

So –1 – 5 = –6

Use These Rules for Combining Signs

These rules are <u>ONLY TO BE USED WHEN</u>:

+	+	makes	+
+	–	makes	–
–	+	makes	–
–	–	makes	+

1) Multiplying or dividing

EXAMPLES:

┌ (invisible + sign)

Find: a) -3×5 – + makes –   so $-3 \times 5 = -15$

       b) $-18 \div -3$ – – makes +   so $-18 \div -3 = 6$

2) Two signs appear next to each other

EXAMPLES: **Work out:**   a) $3 - -9$ – – makes +   so $3 - -9 = 3 + 9 = 12$

                  b) $2 - -8 + -12$ – – makes +   and   + – makes –

                                  so $2 - -8 + -12 = 2 + 8 - 12 = -2$

Are you positive you've learnt all about negative numbers?

Always start a calculation by combining signs — if they're the same it makes + and if they're different it makes –. Then it's just a straightforward add, subtract, multiply or divide question.

Special Types of Number

Whole numbers can be put into special groups with different properties. Here are a few of them.

Even and Odd Numbers

EVEN numbers all divide by 2

| 2 | 4 | 6 | 8 | 10 | 12 | 14 | 16 | 18 | 20 ... |

All EVEN numbers END in 0, 2, 4, 6 or 8

ODD numbers don't divide by 2

| 1 | 3 | 5 | 7 | 9 | 11 | 13 | 15 | 17 | 19 | 21 ... |

All ODD numbers END in 1, 3, 5, 7 or 9

These rules for adding, subtracting and multiplying odd and even numbers are always true. Try them out with some random odd or even numbers. The answer will give you the rule.

Adding
odd + odd = even
even + even = even
odd + even = odd

Subtracting
odd − odd = even
even − even = even
odd − even = odd
even − odd = odd

Multiplying
odd × odd = odd
even × even = even
odd × even = even

Square Numbers

1) When you multiply a whole number by itself, you get a square number.
2) They're called square numbers because they're like the areas of squares.
3) You have to know the first few off by heart.

$1 \times 1 = 1$ $2 \times 2 = 4$ $3 \times 3 = 9$

1^2	2^2	3^2	4^2	5^2	6^2	7^2	8^2	9^2	10^2	11^2	12^2
1	4	9	16	25	36	49	64	81	100	121	144
(1×1)	(2×2)	(3×3)	(4×4)	(5×5)	(6×6)	(7×7)	(8×8)	(9×9)	(10×10)	(11×11)	(12×12)

Cube Numbers

1) When you multiply a whole number by itself, then by itself again, you get a cube number.
2) They're called cube numbers because they're like the volumes of cubes.
3) It's useful to know these cube numbers off by heart.

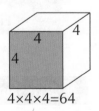

$1 \times 1 \times 1 = 1$ $2 \times 2 \times 2 = 8$ $3 \times 3 \times 3 = 27$ $4 \times 4 \times 4 = 64$

1^3	2^3	3^3	4^3	5^3	10^3
1	8	27	64	125	1000
(1×1×1)	(2×2×2)	(3×3×3)	(4×4×4)	(5×5×5)	(10×10×10)

Learn the first twelve square numbers...

It's handy to be able to recognise square and cube numbers, so make sure you learn the ones on this page. Don't forget that even numbers always divide by two — useful when simplifying calculations.

Prime Numbers

There's one more special type of number you need to know about — the prime numbers...

PRIME Numbers Don't Divide by Anything

Prime numbers are all the numbers that only come up in their own times table:

| 2 | 3 | 5 | 7 | 11 | 13 | 17 | 19 | 23 | 29 | 31 | 37 | ... |

The only way to get ANY PRIME NUMBER is: 1 × ITSELF

E.g.   The only numbers that multiply to give 3 are 1 × 3
        The only numbers that multiply to give 19 are 1 × 19

EXAMPLE: **Show that 18 is not a prime number.**

Just find another way to make 18 other than 1 × 18:   3 × 6 = 18

18 divides by other numbers apart from 1 and 18, so it isn't a prime number.

Five Important Facts

1) 1 is NOT a prime number.
2) 2 is the ONLY even prime number.
3) The first four prime numbers are 2, 3, 5 and 7.
4) Prime numbers end in 1, 3, 7 or 9 (2 and 5 are the only exceptions to this rule).
5) But NOT ALL numbers ending in 1, 3, 7 or 9 are primes, as shown here:
    (Only the circled ones are primes.)

② ③ ⑤ ⑦
⑪ ⑬ ⑰ ⑲
21 ㉓ 27 ㉙
㉛ 33 ㊲ 39
㊶ ㊸ ㊼ 49
51 ㊾ 57 ㊾
㊱ 63 ㊷ 69

How to FIND Prime Numbers — a very simple method

1) All primes (above 5) end in 1, 3, 7 or 9 — ignore any numbers that don't end in one of those.
2) To find which of them ACTUALLY ARE primes you only need to divide each one by 3 and 7.
    If it doesn't divide exactly by either 3 or 7 then it's a prime.

— This works for primes up to 120.

EXAMPLE: **Find all the prime numbers in this list:**   **51, 52, 53, 54, 55, 56, 57, 58, 59**

1) Get rid of anything that doesn't end in 1, 3, 7 or 9:   51, 52, 53, 54, 55, 56, 57, 58, 59

2) Now try dividing 51, 53, 57 and 59 by 3 and 7:

    51 ÷ 3 = 17 so 51 is NOT a prime number

    53 ÷ 3 = 17.666... and 53 ÷ 7 = 7.571... so 53 is a prime number

    57 ÷ 3 = 19 so 57 is NOT a prime number

    59 ÷ 3 = 19.666... and 59 ÷ 7 = 8.428... so 59 is a prime number

    So the prime numbers in the list are 53 and 59.

A number is prime if it only divides by 1 and itself...

Remember — 1 is not a prime number, it's the only exception to the rule.

Multiples, Factors and Prime Factors

Make sure you know about prime numbers (p.19) before you try to find prime factors.

Multiples and Factors

The MULTIPLES of a number are just the values in its times table.

EXAMPLE: **Find the first 5 multiples of 12.**

You just need to find the first 5 numbers in the 12 times table: 12   24   36   48   60

The FACTORS of a number are all the numbers that divide into it exactly. Here's how to find them:

EXAMPLE: **Find all the factors of 28.**

Increasing by 1 each time

1 × 28
2 × 14
3 ×
4 × 7
5 ×
6 ×
7 × 4

So the factors of 28 are:
1, 2, 4, 7, 14, 28

1) Start off with 1 × the number itself, then try 2 ×, then 3 × and so on, listing the pairs in rows.

2) Try each one in turn. Cross out the row if it doesn't divide exactly.

3) Eventually, when you get a number repeated, stop.

4) The factors are the numbers you haven't crossed out.

Finding Prime Factors — The Factor Tree

Any whole number can be written as a string of prime numbers all multiplied together — this is called a prime factorisation. The easiest way to find a prime factorisation is using a factor tree.

EXAMPLE: **Find the prime factorisation of 40.**

40
4   10
②   ②   ②   ⑤

So 40 = 2 × 2 × 2 × 5
      = 2³ × 5

You could split 40 into 2 and 20 or 5 and 8 instead
— you'll always get the same prime factorisation.

1) Start with the number at the top, and split it into factors as shown.

2) Every time you get a prime, ring it.

3) Keep going until you can't go further (i.e. you're just left with primes), then write the primes out in order.

4) (Optional) Group numbers that are the same into powers (i.e. 2 × 2 × 2 = 2³).

The prime factorisation of a number is always the same, no matter how you split it up.
Every number has a unique prime factorisation — no two are the same.

Any number can be written as a product of prime factors...

If this is all new to you, have another read through it — especially prime factorisation.
Then scribble down a two-digit number and try to find its prime factorisation.

LCM and HCF

Here are two big fancy names for you — but don't be put off, they're both <u>easy</u>.

LCM — 'Lowest Common Multiple'

'<u>Lowest Common Multiple</u>' sounds a bit complicated, but all it means is this:

> The <u>SMALLEST</u> number that will <u>DIVIDE BY ALL</u> the numbers in question.

METHOD:
1) <u>LIST</u> the <u>MULTIPLES</u> of <u>ALL</u> the numbers.
2) Find the <u>SMALLEST</u> one that's in <u>ALL the lists</u>.
3) That's the LCM.

EXAMPLE: Find the lowest common multiple (LCM) of:

a) 3 and 4

Multiples of <u>3</u>: 3, 6, 9, (12) 15, ...
Multiples of <u>4</u>: 4, 8, (12) 16, ...

So the LCM of 3 and 4 is 12.

b) 9 and 12

Multiples of <u>9</u>: 9, 18, 27, (36) 45, 54, 63, ...
Multiples of <u>12</u>: 12, 24, (36) 48, 60, 72, ...

So the LCM of 9 and 12 is 36.

HCF — 'Highest Common Factor'

'<u>Highest Common Factor</u>' — all it means is this:

> The <u>BIGGEST</u> number that will <u>DIVIDE INTO ALL</u> the numbers in question.

METHOD:
1) <u>LIST</u> the <u>FACTORS</u> of <u>ALL</u> the numbers.
2) Find the <u>BIGGEST</u> one that's in <u>ALL the lists</u>.
3) That's the HCF.

EXAMPLE: Find the highest common factor (HCF) of 12 and 30.

Factors of <u>12</u> are: 1, 2, 3, 4, (6) 12
Factors of <u>30</u> are: 1, 2, 3, 5, (6) 10, 15, 30

So the <u>highest common factor</u> (HCF) of 12 and 30 is 6.

List the multiples or factors when finding LCMs and HCFs...

Be careful when you're listing the factors of a number — make sure you use the proper method (as shown on p.20). This way you're much less likely to miss one or make a silly mistake.

Warm-Up and Practice Questions

It's time to face the music — try these warm-up questions to see how much you've learnt.
When you feel like you're ready you should move on to the tougher practice questions.

Warm-Up Questions

1) Work out: a) –6 + 11   b) –5 – 10   c) –3 × –6   d) 21 ÷ –7   **Try these <u>without</u> using a calculator.**

2) On Friday the temperature in Negaton was –5 °C and the temperature in Tiverville was –19 °C. What was the difference in temperature between Negaton and Tiverville?

3) Which of the following numbers are odd? 53, 61, 123, 74, 90, 872, 712, 7305, 5012

4) Find the first two numbers that are both square numbers and cube numbers.

5) Write down all the prime numbers from this list: 49, 63, 38, 73, 77, 18, 39, 83

6) Find: a) the first 8 multiples of 9,   b) all the factors of 36.

7) Express 60 as a product of its prime factors.

8) Find the lowest common multiple (LCM) of 3 and 7.

9) Find the highest common factor (HCF) of 32 and 48.

Practice Questions

Take a look at the worked question below and see if you can follow the working. Once you've read through it carefully you can have a go at the practice questions on the next page.

1   The factors of a number are all the numbers that divide into it.

a)   Find all the factors of the following numbers.

22   1, 2, 11, 22

41   1, 41

33   1, 3, 11, 33

110   1, 2, 5, 10, 11, 22, 55, 110

[4 marks]

b)   Which of the four numbers above is prime? Give a reason for your answer.

41 is the only prime number. It is the only number from the list where the factors are just 1 and itself.

[2 marks]

c)   What is the HCF of 22, 33 and 110?

Look at the lists above to find the highest number which is a factor of 22, 33 and 110.

11

[1 mark]

Practice Questions

2   Factor trees allow you to find the prime factors of a number.

a)   Complete the factor tree.

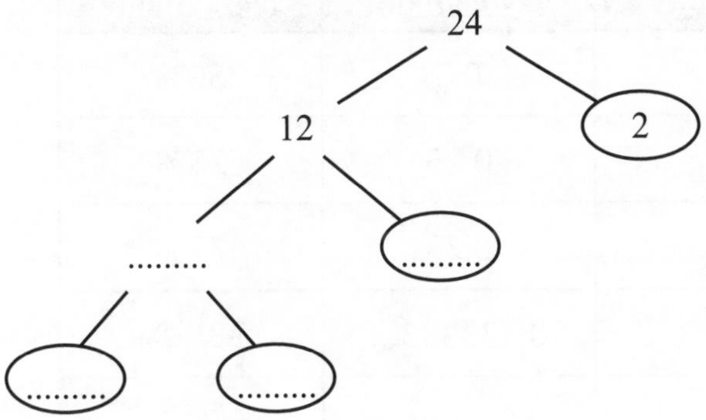

```
                          24
                       /      \
                    12          (2)
                   /   \
             (.....)    (.....)
              /    \
         (.....)   (.....)
```

[2 marks]

b)   Write down the prime factorisation of 24.

....

[1 mark]

3   In a football league, teams get 3 points for a win, –3 points for a loss and 0 points for a draw. The table below shows the points for 5 teams in the league.

Team	Number of points
Ringford Rovers	–3
Woodgreen Wanderers	3
Fleeting Footers	12
Steventon Scorers	–6
Trybridge Tigers	–9

a)   Which of these teams is lowest in the league?

....

[1 mark]

b)   The Steventon Scorers play the Woodgreen Wanderers and win.
How many points do the Steventon Scorers have now?

....

[1 mark]

c)   How many points do the Ringford Rovers need to equal the score of the Fleeting Footers?

....

[1 mark]

Fractions, Decimals and Percentages

Fractions, decimals and percentages are <u>three different ways</u> of describing when you've got <u>part</u> of a <u>whole thing</u>. They're <u>closely related</u> and you can <u>convert between them</u>.

This table shows the really common conversions which you ought to know straight off:

Fractions with a 1 on the top (e.g. $\frac{1}{2}$, $\frac{1}{3}$, $\frac{1}{4}$, etc.) are called <u>unit fractions</u>.

Fraction	Decimal	Percentage
$\frac{1}{2}$	0.5	50%
$\frac{1}{4}$	0.25	25%
$\frac{3}{4}$	0.75	75%
$\frac{1}{3}$	0.333333...	$33\frac{1}{3}\%$
$\frac{2}{3}$	0.666666...	$66\frac{2}{3}\%$
$\frac{1}{10}$	0.1	10%
$\frac{2}{10}$	0.2	20%
$\frac{1}{5}$	0.2	20%
$\frac{2}{5}$	0.4	40%

O.3333... and O.6666... are known as '<u>recurring</u>' <u>decimals</u> — the same pattern of numbers carries on repeating itself forever.

The more of those conversions you learn, the better — but for those that you <u>don't know</u>, you must <u>also learn</u> how to <u>convert</u> between the three types. These are the methods:

Fraction $\xrightarrow{\text{Divide}}$ Decimal $\xrightarrow{\times \text{ by } 100}$ Percentage

E.g. $\frac{7}{20}$ is $7 \div 20$ $= 0.35$ e.g. 0.35×100 $= 35\%$

Fraction $\xleftarrow[\text{The awkward one}]{}$ Decimal $\xleftarrow[\div \text{ by } 100]{}$ Percentage

<u>Converting decimals to fractions</u> is a bit more awkward.
The digits after the decimal point go on the top, and a <u>power of 10</u> on the bottom — with the same number of zeros as there were decimal places.

$0.6 = \frac{6}{10}$ $0.3 = \frac{3}{10}$ $0.7 = \frac{7}{10}$ etc.

$0.12 = \frac{12}{100}$ $0.78 = \frac{78}{100}$ $0.05 = \frac{5}{100}$ etc.

These can often be <u>cancelled down</u> — see the next page.

Practise converting between fractions, percentages and decimals

Learn the conversions in the table at the top of the page off by heart. Work out any other conversions using the four methods for converting — decimals to fractions is the tricky one.

Fractions

This page tells you how to deal with fractions <u>without your calculator</u>.

Equivalent Fractions

$\frac{1}{4}$ ...is equivalent to... $\frac{4}{16}$

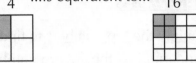

1) <u>Equivalent</u> fractions are <u>equal in size</u>...
2) ...but the <u>numbers</u> on the top and bottom are <u>different</u>.
3) To get from one fraction to an equivalent one — <u>MULTIPLY top and bottom</u> by the <u>SAME NUMBER</u>:

$$\overset{\times 2}{\frac{1}{2} = \frac{2}{4}} \qquad \overset{\times 5}{\frac{3}{4} = \frac{15}{20}} \qquad \overset{\times 100}{\frac{1}{5} = \frac{100}{500}}$$
$$\underset{\times 2}{} \qquad \underset{\times 5}{} \qquad \underset{\times 100}{}$$

Cancelling Down

1) You sometimes need to <u>simplify</u> a fraction by '<u>cancelling down</u>'.
2) This means <u>DIVIDING top and bottom</u> by the <u>SAME NUMBER</u>.
3) To get the fraction <u>as simple as possible</u>, you might have to do this <u>more than once</u>:

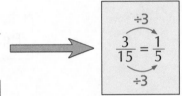

$$\frac{3}{15} = \frac{1}{5} \qquad \overset{\div 3}{}$$

$$\overset{\div 10 \quad \div 2}{\frac{20}{40} = \frac{2}{4} = \frac{1}{2}}$$
$$\underset{\div 10 \quad \div 2}{}$$

Ordering Fractions

<u>Ordering fractions</u> — first you just have to make the bottom numbers (denominators) of the two fractions <u>equal</u> by finding <u>equivalent fractions</u>. Then <u>compare</u> the size of the top numbers (numerators).

EXAMPLE: **Which is bigger, $\frac{2}{3}$ or $\frac{3}{4}$?**

1) Look at the <u>bottom numbers</u> of the fractions: <u>3</u> and <u>4</u>.
2) Think of a number they will <u>both go into</u> — try <u>12</u>.
3) Change each fraction (make <u>equivalent</u> fractions) so the <u>bottom number is 12</u>.
4) Now check which is bigger by looking at their <u>top numbers</u>.

$$\overset{\times 4}{\frac{2}{3} = \frac{8}{12}} \qquad \overset{\times 3}{\frac{3}{4} = \frac{9}{12}}$$
$$\underset{\times 4}{} \qquad \underset{\times 3}{}$$

9 is <u>bigger</u> than 8,

so $\frac{3}{4}$ is bigger than $\frac{2}{3}$.

Always cancel down fractions as far as possible...

A question might ask you to simplify a fraction or give your answer in its simplest form. Don't be put off — all it means is cancel the fraction down until you can't cancel any further.

Fractions

When dealing with fractions, <u>always</u> simplify your answer as much as possible.

Multiplying

1) <u>Multiply</u> the <u>top numbers</u> to find the <u>numerator</u>...

2) ...and <u>multiply</u> the <u>bottom numbers</u> to find the <u>denominator</u>.

$$\text{E.g. } \frac{3}{5} \times \frac{4}{7} = \frac{3 \times 4}{5 \times 7} = \frac{12}{35}$$

Dividing

1) Turn the 2nd fraction <u>UPSIDE DOWN</u>...

2) ...and then <u>multiply</u>, as shown above.

$$\text{E.g. } \frac{3}{4} \div \frac{1}{3} = \frac{3}{4} \times \frac{3}{1} = \frac{3 \times 3}{4 \times 1} = \frac{9}{4}$$

Adding and Subtracting

1) If the <u>bottom numbers</u> are the <u>same</u>, add or subtract the <u>TOP NUMBERS ONLY</u>, leaving the bottom number <u>as it is</u>.

$$\text{E.g. } \underline{\text{adding}}: \frac{2}{6} + \frac{1}{6} = \frac{2+1}{6} = \frac{3}{6} = \frac{1}{2} \qquad \text{and } \underline{\text{subtracting}}: \frac{5}{7} - \frac{3}{7} = \frac{5-3}{7} = \frac{2}{7}$$

2) If the bottom numbers are <u>different</u>, you have to <u>make them the same</u> using <u>equivalent fractions</u> (see previous page).

EXAMPLE: Work out $\frac{1}{4} + \frac{5}{12}$.

1) Look at the <u>denominators</u> of the fractions: **4 and 12**

2) They are both <u>factors of 12</u> so change $\frac{1}{4}$ so that the <u>denominator</u> is <u>12</u>. $\frac{1}{4} = \frac{3}{12}$

3) Now <u>add the fractions</u> — simplify your answer if possible. $\frac{3}{12} + \frac{5}{12} = \frac{8}{12} = \frac{2}{3}$

What fraction of this page have you learnt?

When adding or subtracting fractions, remember that the denominators of the fractions always have to be the same. When you're multiplying or dividing, the denominators don't have to be the same.

More Fractions

One last page on fractions — starting with what happens when you have a fraction greater than 1.

Mixed Numbers

Mixed numbers have an integer part and a fraction part.
Improper fractions are where the top number is bigger than the bottom number.

EXAMPLES:
1. Write $3\frac{4}{5}$ as an improper fraction.

1) Think of the mixed number as an addition: $\quad 3\frac{4}{5} = 3 + \frac{4}{5}$

2) Turn the integer part into a fraction: $\quad 3 + \frac{4}{5} = \frac{15}{5} + \frac{4}{5} = \frac{15+4}{5} = \frac{19}{5}$

2. Write $\frac{23}{3}$ as a mixed number.

1) Divide the top number by the bottom. $\qquad 23 \div 3 = 7$ remainder 2
2) The answer gives the whole number part. $\qquad \frac{23}{3} = 7\frac{2}{3}$
3) The remainder goes on top of the fraction.

You can add, subtract, multiply and divide mixed numbers by turning them into improper fractions and then using the rules on the previous page.

Adding: $\quad 1\frac{5}{7} + 3\frac{1}{7} = \frac{12}{7} + \frac{22}{7} = \frac{34}{7} = 4\frac{6}{7}$ $\qquad$ Subtracting: $\quad 5\frac{1}{3} - 1\frac{2}{3} = \frac{16}{3} - \frac{5}{3} = \frac{11}{3} = 3\frac{2}{3}$

Multiplying: $\quad 3\frac{1}{2} \times \frac{1}{4} = \frac{7}{2} \times \frac{1}{4} = \frac{7}{8}$ $\qquad$ Dividing: $\quad \frac{2}{3} \div 2\frac{2}{3} = \frac{2}{3} \div \frac{8}{3} = \frac{2}{3} \times \frac{3}{8} = \frac{6}{24} = \frac{1}{4}$

Finding a **Fraction of** Something

Multiply the 'something' by the TOP of the fraction, and divide it by the BOTTOM.
It doesn't matter which order you do these two steps in — just start with whatever's easiest.

E.g. $\frac{9}{20}$ of £360 = £360 $\div$ 20 $\times$ 9 = £162 $\qquad$ In other words, £162 is $\frac{9}{20}$ of £360.

You can write one number as a fraction of another number just by putting the first number over the second and cancelling down. This works if the first number is bigger than the second number too — you'll just end up with a fraction greater than 1.

E.g. 32 is $\frac{32}{44} = \frac{8}{11}$ of 44, and 44 is $\frac{44}{32} = \frac{11}{8}$ of 32.

EXAM TIP

Don't be put off by mixed number calculations...
Mixed number calculations are just the same as normal fraction calculations once you convert to improper fractions — don't forget to turn your answer back into a mixed number.

Percentages

These simple percentage questions shouldn't give you much trouble. Especially if you remember:

> 1) 'Per cent' means 'out of 100', so 20% means '20 out of 100' = $\frac{20}{100}$.
> 2) If a question asks you to work out the percentage OF something you can replace the word OF with a multiplication (×).

'Percentage Of' Questions

If you have a calculator, these questions are easy.

EXAMPLE: **Find 18% of £4.**

1) Translate the question into maths. 18% of £4 = $\frac{18}{100}$ × 4

2) Work it out. [18] [÷] [100] [×] [4] [=] £0.72 = 72p

If you don't have a calculator, you're going to have to do a bit more work.

EXAMPLE: **Find 35% of 120 kg.**

1) First find 10% by dividing by 10.   120 ÷ 10 = 12
2) Then find 5% by dividing 10% by 2.   12 ÷ 2 = 6
3) Make 35% by adding up 10% and 5%.   35% = 10% + 10% + 10% + 5%
                                             = 12 + 12 + 12 + 6 = 42 kg

Writing One Number as a Percentage of Another

To write one number as a percentage of another, divide the first number by the second, then multiply by 100.

EXAMPLE: **Give 36p as a percentage of 80p.**

Divide 36p by 80p, then multiply by 100:   (36 ÷ 80) × 100 = 45%

EXAMPLE: **Farmer Littlewood measured the width of his prized pumpkin at the start and end of the month. At the start of the month it was 80 cm wide and at the end of the month it was 1.4 m wide. Give the width at the end of the month as a percentage of the width at the start.**

1) Make sure both amounts are in the same units   1.4 m = 140 cm
    — convert 1.4 m to cm.
2) Divide 140 cm by 80 cm, then multiply by 100:   (140 ÷ 80) × 100 = 175%

Make sure you know the percentage basics really well...

There are more percentage questions coming up later in the book (p.68), so make sure you learn the basics before you move on. If anything is unclear, have another read through these examples.

Warm-Up and Practice Questions

It's about time you had a bit of practice on fractions, decimals and percentages. Have a go at these warm-up questions first — they'll be a good indication of how much you've learnt.

Warm-Up Questions

Try questions 1-5 <u>without</u> using a calculator.

1) Turn the following decimals into fractions and reduce them to their simplest form.
   a) 0.8   b) 0.3   c) 0.04   d) 0.15

2) Which is greater: a) $\frac{1}{4}$ or 30%?   b) 50% or $\frac{2}{5}$?   c) 0.6 or $\frac{17}{25}$?

3) Cancel these down as far as possible: a) $\frac{20}{28}$ b) $\frac{9}{36}$

4) Which is bigger, $\frac{4}{5}$ or $\frac{2}{3}$?

5) a) $\frac{2}{5} \times \frac{1}{6}$ b) $\frac{3}{7} \div \frac{5}{8}$ c) $\frac{1}{8} + \frac{9}{8}$ d) $2\frac{1}{5} - 1\frac{2}{5}$ e) $\frac{3}{8} + \frac{1}{2}$ f) $\frac{1}{3} + \frac{1}{4}$

6) Find: a) 39% of 505   b) 15% of 340

7) Give: a) 18 m as a percentage of 60 m   b) 1.2 km as a percentage of 480 m

Practice Questions

Have a look at the practice questions below — I've written in the answers for you.
Don't be too jealous though, there's plenty more to keep you going on the next page. Enjoy.

1   Order the following fractions from smallest to biggest: $\frac{2}{3}$ $\frac{1}{2}$ $\frac{1}{6}$

   All of the fractions need to have the same denominator. 2 and 3 both go into 6, so put 6 on the bottom and find the equivalent fractions. Then use the top number to put them in order.

   You multiply the bottom by 2 to make 6, so you need to multiply the top by 2 as well. ⟶ $\frac{4}{6}$ $\frac{3}{6}$ $\frac{1}{6}$

   You multiply the bottom by 3, so multiply the top by 3 too.

   Write your answer with the original fractions in the question, not the equivalent fractions.

   $\frac{1}{6}$ $\frac{1}{2}$ $\frac{2}{3}$
   ....

   [2 marks]

2   Lucy got $\frac{18}{20}$ in her maths test. Saqib got 85% in his. Which student got the higher score?

   You need to write both scores in the same way — it's easiest to write Lucy's score as a percentage.

   First convert the fraction to a decimal. ⟶ $\frac{18}{20}$ is 18 ÷ 20 = 0.9

   0.9 × 100 = 90%   Then convert the decimal to a percentage.

   Lucy
   ....
   [2 marks]

Section One — Numbers

Practice Questions

3   Fill in the missing numbers.

a)

$$\frac{5}{4} = \frac{\boxed{}}{\boxed{}}\frac{\boxed{}}{4}$$

[1 mark]

b)

$$\frac{\boxed{}}{5} = \boxed{2}\frac{3}{5}$$

[1 mark]

4   Callum has 15 hamsters. 6 of his hamsters have brown fur.

a) What percentage of his hamsters have brown fur?

....
[1 mark]

b) 20% of his hamsters have white fur. How many white-furred hamsters does he have?

....
[1 mark]

5   Helen has 21 marbles. $\frac{2}{7}$ of them are blue, $\frac{1}{3}$ are red and the rest are green.
   How many green marbles does Helen have?

....
[2 marks]

Rounding Numbers

You need to be able to use 3 different rounding methods.
We'll do decimal places first, but there's the same basic idea behind all three.

Decimal Places (d.p.)

To round to a given number of decimal places:

> If you're rounding to 2 d.p. the last digit is the second digit after the decimal point.

1) **Identify** the position of the '**last digit**' from the number of decimal places.

2) Then look at the next digit to the **right** — called **the decider**.

3) If the **decider** is **5 or more**, then **round up** the **last digit**.
   If the **decider** is **4 or less**, then leave the **last digit** as it is.

4) There must be **no more digits** after the last digit (not even zeros).

EXAMPLE: **What is 21.84 correct to 1 decimal place?**

$$21.84 = 21.8$$

LAST DIGIT to be written (1st decimal place because we're rounding to 1 d.p.)

DECIDER

The LAST DIGIT stays the same because the DECIDER is 4 or less.

EXAMPLE: **What is 39.7392739 to 2 decimal places?**

$$39 . 7392739 = 39.74$$

LAST DIGIT to be written (2nd decimal place because we're rounding to 2 d.p.)

DECIDER

The LAST DIGIT rounds UP because the DECIDER is 5 or more.

Watch Out for **Pesky Nines**

If you have to round up a 9 (to 10), replace the 9 with 0, and add 1 to digit on the left.

EXAMPLE: **Round 48.897 to 2 d.p.:**

$$48.897 \longrightarrow 48.89 \longrightarrow 48.90 \text{ to 2 d.p.}$$

LAST DIGIT   DECIDER

The question asks for 2 d.p. so you <u>must</u> put 48.90 not 48.9.

EXAM TIP

Always take extra care when the last digit is a 9...

Make sure you always give your answer to the number of decimal places asked for.

Rounding Numbers

Here are the other two rounding methods — they're each slightly different in their own way.

Significant Figures (s.f.)

The <u>1st significant figure</u> of any number is <u>the first digit which isn't a zero</u>.
The <u>2nd, 3rd, etc. significant figures</u> follow straight after the 1st — they're allowed to be zeros.

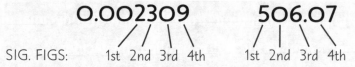

0.002309   506.07

SIG. FIGS: 1st 2nd 3rd 4th   1st 2nd 3rd 4th

To <u>round</u> to a given number of significant figures:

1) Find the <u>last digit</u> — if you're rounding to, say, 3 s.f., then the 3rd <u>significant figure</u> is the last digit.
2) Use the digit to the right of it as the <u>decider</u>, just like for d.p.
3) Once you've rounded, <u>fill up</u> with <u>zeros</u>, up to but <u>not beyond</u> the decimal point.

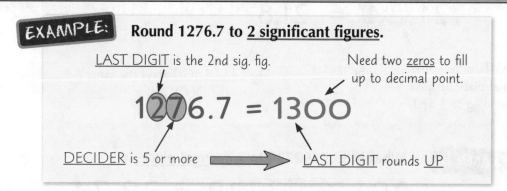

EXAMPLE: **Round 1276.7 to <u>2 significant figures</u>.**

<u>LAST DIGIT</u> is the 2nd sig. fig.   Need two <u>zeros</u> to fill up to decimal point.

1276.7 = 1300

<u>DECIDER</u> is 5 or more ⟹ <u>LAST DIGIT</u> rounds <u>UP</u>

To the Nearest Whole Number, Ten, Hundred etc.

You might be asked to round to the <u>nearest whole number</u>, <u>ten</u>, <u>hundred</u>, <u>thousand</u> or <u>million</u>.

1) Identify the <u>last digit</u>, e.g. for the nearest whole number it's the ones position, and for the 'nearest ten' it's the tens position, etc.
2) Round the last digit and fill in with zeros up to the decimal point.

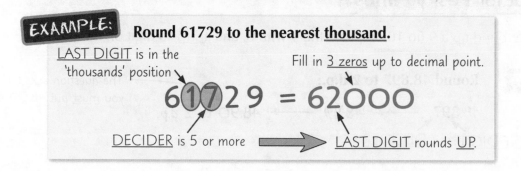

EXAMPLE: **Round 61729 to the nearest <u>thousand</u>.**

<u>LAST DIGIT</u> is in the 'thousands' position   Fill in <u>3 zeros</u> up to decimal point.

61729 = 62000

<u>DECIDER</u> is 5 or more ⟹ <u>LAST DIGIT</u> rounds <u>UP</u>.

Have you figured out how significant this page is?

Lots of rounding for you on this page but it's basically the same thing every time — identify the last digit and then use the digit to the right (decider) to decide if you need to round up or leave it.

Accuracy and Estimating

"Estimate" doesn't mean "take a wild guess", so don't just make something up...

Errors in Rounding

When you round a number using any of the methods on the previous two pages,
your answer won't be exact — it will have some amount of error.

> **The error when rounding is given by ROUNDED VALUE – ACTUAL VALUE.**

EXAMPLE: **What is the error when 478 is given to 1 significant figure?**

1) Round the number to 1 s.f.   478 = 500 (1 s.f.)
2) Subtract the actual value
   from the rounded value.   500 – 478 = 22

EXAMPLE: **What is the error when 3.7643 is given to 2 decimal places?**

1) Round the number to 2 d.p.   3.7643 = 3.76 (2 d.p.)
2) Subtract the actual value
   from the rounded value.   3.76 – 3.7643 = –0.0043

Estimating

> 1) **Round everything off (e.g. to 1 significant figure).**
> 2) **Then work out the answer using these nice easy numbers.**
> 3) **Show all your working.**

EXAMPLE: **Estimate the value of 47 × 22.**

1) Round each number to 1 s.f.   47 × 22 ≈ 50 × 20
2) Do the calculation with
   the rounded numbers.   50 × 20 = 1000

≈ means 'approximately equal to'.

EXAMPLE: **Estimate the value of $\frac{63.2 \times 13}{17}$.**

1) Round each number to 1 s.f. $\frac{63.2 \times 13}{17} \approx \frac{60 \times 10}{20}$
2) Do the calculation with
   the rounded numbers. $= \frac{600}{20} = 30$

Errors can be tricky to get your head around at first...

Choose a calculation with at least one decimal in (e.g. 37.4 × 21.9 + 13) and estimate its
value by rounding to 1 s.f. Then find the error for each of the numbers you rounded.

Powers

You've already seen a few powers on page 18 — well, that's just the tip of the iceberg.

Powers are a very Useful Shorthand

1) Powers are 'numbers <u>multiplied by themselves</u> so many times':

$$2 \times 2 \times 2 \times 2 = 2^4 \text{ ('two to the power 4')}$$
$$4 \times 4 \times 4 \times 4 \times 4 \times 4 = 4^6 \text{ ('four to the power 6')}$$
$$8 \times 8 \times 8 \times 8 \times 8 \times 8 \times 8 \times 8 = 8^8 \text{ ('eight to the power 8')}$$

2) The <u>powers of ten</u> are really easy — the power tells you the number of zeros:

$$10^1 = 10 \qquad 10^2 = 100 \qquad 10^3 = 1000 \qquad 10^4 = 10\,000$$

3) Use the $\boxed{x^\blacksquare}$ button on your calculator to find powers — press $\boxed{9}\ \boxed{x^\blacksquare}\ \boxed{4}\ \boxed{=}$ to get $9^4 = 6561$.

4) Anything to the <u>power 1</u> is just <u>itself</u>, e.g. $4^1 = 4$, $1726^1 = 1726$.

5) Anything to the <u>power 0</u> is 1, e.g. $5^0 = 1$, $102738^0 = 1$.

6) <u>1 to any power</u> is <u>still 1</u>, e.g. $1^{457} = 1$.

The Power Rules

1) When MULTIPLYING, you ADD the powers.

EXAMPLES:

1. Simplify $6^4 \times 6^6$

$6^4 \times 6^6 = 6^{4+6}$
$= 6^{10}$

2. Simplify $2^2 \times 2^3$

$2^2 \times 2^3 = 2^{2+3}$
$= 2^5 = 32$

The two rules only work for <u>powers of the same number.</u>

2) When DIVIDING, you SUBTRACT the powers.

EXAMPLES:

1. Simplify $4^{11} \div 4^4$

$4^{11} \div 4^4 = 4^{11-4}$
$= 4^7$

2. Simplify $y^8 \div y^5$

$y^8 \div y^5 = y^{8-5}$
$= y^3$

Don't be put off by <u>letters</u> — they obey the <u>same rules</u>.

REVISION TIP

Learn all of the rules about powers...

All of the power rules are important, but don't forget the little things — anything to the power 1 is itself, anything to the power 0 is 1 and 1 to any power is still 1.

Square Roots and Cube Roots

Square roots and cube roots are the opposites of squaring and cubing.

Square Roots

'Squared' means 'multiplied by itself': $6^2 = 6 \times 6 = 36$

SQUARE ROOT $\sqrt{}$ is the reverse process: $\sqrt{36} = 6$

The best way to think of it is: | 'Square Root' means 'What Number <u>Times by Itself</u> gives...'

EXAMPLES:

1. What is $\sqrt{81}$?

9 times by itself gives 81 ⟶ $81 = 9 \times 9$
So $\sqrt{81} = 9$

2. What is $\sqrt{7.84}$?

 $\sqrt{}$ 7.84   =   2.8

3. Find <u>both</u> square roots of 100.

$10 \times 10 = 100$, so positive square root = 10

$-10 \times -10 = 100$, so negative square root = -10

<u>All</u> numbers also have a <u>NEGATIVE SQUARE ROOT</u> — it's just the '$-$' version of the normal positive one.

Cube Roots

'Cubed' means 'multiplied by itself and then by itself again': $2^3 = 2 \times 2 \times 2 = 8$

CUBE ROOT $\sqrt[3]{}$ is the reverse process: $\sqrt[3]{8} = 2$

| 'Cube Root' means 'What Number <u>Times by Itself and then by Itself Again</u> gives...'

EXAMPLES: 1. What is $\sqrt[3]{27}$?

3 times by itself and then by itself again gives 27. — $27 = 3 \times 3 \times 3$
So $\sqrt[3]{27} = 3$

2. What is $\sqrt[3]{4913}$?

 $\sqrt[3]{}$ 4913   =   17

Unlike square roots, there is only <u>one answer</u>. Work it out in your head or use a calculator.

<u>Higher roots</u> are found in a similar way — $\sqrt[4]{}$ and $\sqrt[5]{}$ are the <u>reverse processes</u> of 'to the power 4' and 'to the power 5'.

To find these on your calculator, use the $\sqrt[\square]{}$ button: **5**   **32** **=** 2

Square roots have two solutions, cube roots only have one...

These roots can be a bit tricky, but just remember they're the opposite of powers.
If you're stuck on a root question, think — what number times by itself (and by itself again) gives...

Warm-Up and Practice Questions

There's really no point just rushing straight on to the next section — practice really is the best thing you can do to improve your maths skills, so don't neglect it.

Warm-Up Questions

1) Give: a) 16.765 correct to 1 d.p.   b) 6.647895 correct to 3 d.p.   **Only use your calculator in question 11.**
2) Give: a) 7.696 correct to 2 d.p.   b) 11.7998 correct to 3 d.p.
3) Round: a) 2548 to 1 s.f.   b) 36.542 to 2 s.f.   c) 0.05575 to 3 s.f.
4) Give: a) 17.548 to the nearest whole number.   b) 64550 to the nearest hundred.
5) Find the error in rounding when: a) 5.352 is given to 1 d.p.   b) 5230 is given to 1 s.f.
6) Kate buys 78 kg of chocolate cake at a cost of £11.93 per kg. Estimate the total cost.
7) Work out the following calculations: a) $2^3 + 8^2$ b) $3^4 - 5^2$
8) Use power rules to simplify: a) $4^5 \times 4^{11}$ b) $7^9 \div 7^7$
9) Using a combination of power rules, simplify $(7^5 \times 7^{13}) \div 7^6$.
10) Find both square roots of: a) 9   b) 121   c) 169
11) Work out the following to 2 d.p.:   a) $\sqrt{19}$ b) $\sqrt[3]{643}$ c) $\sqrt[5]{1729}$

Practice Questions

It's no good learning all the facts if you can't use your knowledge when it comes to practice questions. These worked examples will show you how to turn that knowledge into answers.

1   Priya runs 100 m in a time of 18.364 seconds.

a)   Calculate the rounding error when she gives her time correct to 1 decimal place.

Round the time to 1 d.p. →   18.364 = 18.4 (1 d.p.)

18.4 − 18.364 = 0.036   ← Subtract the actual value from the rounded value.

..........0.036.......... seconds
[1 mark]

b)   Later, she runs 200 m in a time of 41 seconds correct to 2 significant figures.
Circle which of the numbers below could be her exact time.

40.165 seconds   (41.417 seconds)   41.882 seconds   (40.805 seconds)

This is 40 to 2 s.f.   This is 42 to 2 s.f.

[1 mark]

Practice Questions

2   Given that $5^6 = 15\ 625$, what is 5^5?

....
[1 mark]

3   Evaluate the following to two decimal places.

a) $\sqrt{142}$

....
[1 mark]

b) $\sqrt[3]{82}$

....
[1 mark]

4   Harry is organising a school trip for 154 pupils. The cost of the transport is £614. Harry decides that to cover the cost he must charge pupils £40 each.

Use estimation to check Harry's calculation. Is Harry right?

....
[2 marks]

5   Look at this table:

4^1	4
4^2	16
4^3	64
4^4	256
4^5	1024

a)   Use the table to write down the value of $\sqrt[3]{64}$.

....
[1 mark]

b)   Use the table to help you find the value of $4^2 \times 4^3$.

....
[1 mark]

Revision Summary

Well, that's <u>Section One</u> done — have a go at these questions to see how much you can remember.
- Try these questions and <u>tick off each one</u> when you <u>get it right</u>.
- When you've done <u>all the questions</u> for a topic and are <u>completely happy</u> with it, tick off the topic.

<u>Ordering Numbers and Arithmetic (p.2-14)</u> ☑

Only use your calculator if the question tells you to.

1. Find the value of: a) $4 + 10 \div 2$ b) $(12 \div 3) \times 2$ c) $(8 \times 5) \div 2^2$
2. Write these numbers in words: a) 1 645 100   b) 8 007 182
3. Order these whole numbers from smallest to largest: 12, 564, 874, 911, 19, 87, 81, 98
4. Order these decimals from smallest to largest: 0.02, 1.8, 2.91, 0.09, 0.001, 0.51, 0.9
5. Find the missing numbers: a) $43 + 128 = 50 + \ldots$ b) $20 \times 18 = 2 \times \ldots$
6. Work out: a) $417 + 194$ b) $753 - 157$ c) $(2.3 + 1.123) - 0.75$
7. Find: a) 1.223×100 b) 15.12×1000 c) $6.75 \div 10$ d) $1.24 \div 200$
8. Work out: a) 23×18 b) $306 \div 9$ c) 131×19 d) $672 \div 7$

<u>Types of Number, Factors and Multiples (p.17-21)</u> ☑

9. Work out: a) $-8 + 6$ b) $-4 - 10$ c) -7×-8 d) $81 \div -9$
10. Define: a) even numbers   b) odd numbers   c) square numbers   d) cube numbers
11. Find all the prime numbers between: a) 40 and 50   b) 80 and 90
12. Find: a) the first 5 multiples of 11   b) all the factors of 60
13. Express the following numbers as the product of prime factors: a) 50   b) 36   c) 90
14. Find: a) the LCM of 6 and 8   b) the HCF of 80 and 48

<u>Fractions, Decimals and Percentages (p.24-28)</u> ☑

15. Write: a) 0.6 as a fraction and a percentage   b) 35% as a fraction and a decimal
16. a) Give two fractions equivalent to $\frac{3}{5}$.   b) Simplify $\frac{8}{60}$.   c) Which is bigger, $\frac{3}{10}$ or $\frac{1}{3}$?
17. Work out: a) $\frac{1}{3} + \frac{5}{9}$ b) $\frac{7}{12} - \frac{1}{2}$ c) $\frac{2}{11} \div \frac{3}{10}$ d) $\frac{7}{10} \times \frac{5}{6}$
18. Calculate: a) $\frac{2}{9}$ of 540   b) $\frac{3}{7}$ of 490
19. Use a calculator to find: a) 15% of 78   b) 154% of £86   c) 99% of £99
20. Use a calculator to give 79p as a percentage of £17.89 to 2 d.p.

<u>Rounding and Estimating (p.31-33)</u> ☑

21. Round: a) 164.353 to 1 d.p.   b) 76 233 to 2 s.f.   c) 765 444 to the nearest ten
22. What is the error when 945 is rounded to the nearest hundred?
23. Estimate the value of   a) 38×31 b) $(62 \times 13) + 98$ c) $\dfrac{22.3 \times 54.3}{19.5}$

<u>Powers and Roots (p.34-35)</u> ☑

24. Without using a calculator, work out: a) 10^6 b) 555^1 c) $9^2 - 2^5$
25. Use the power rules to simplify: a) $6^2 \times 6^{11}$ b) $3^9 \div 3^5$ c) $2^{10} \times 2^8$
26. Use a calculator to find: a) $\sqrt{256}$ b) $\sqrt[3]{5.56}$ to 2 d.p.   c) $\sqrt[4]{256}$

Algebra — Simplifying

Algebra really terrifies so many people. But honestly, it's not that bad. The first step is to make sure you <u>understand and learn</u> these <u>basic rules</u> for dealing with algebraic expressions.

Terms

Before you can do anything else with algebra, you must understand what a <u>term</u> is:

> **A TERM IS A COLLECTION OF NUMBERS, LETTERS AND BRACKETS, ALL MULTIPLIED/DIVIDED TOGETHER**

Terms are separated by <u>+ and – signs</u>. Every term has a + or – attached to the <u>front of it</u>.

If there's no sign in front of the first term, it means there's an invisible + sign. ────

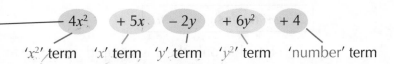

$4x^2 \quad +5x \quad -2y \quad +6y^2 \quad +4$

'x^2' term   'x' term   'y' term   'y^2' term   'number' term

Simplifying or 'Collecting Like Terms'

To <u>simplify</u> an algebraic expression made up of all the <u>same terms</u>, just <u>add</u> or <u>subtract</u> them.

EXAMPLES:

1. Simplify $r + r + r + r$

Just <u>add up</u> all the r's:

$r + r + r + r = 4r$

'r' just means '$1r$'.

2. Simplify $2s + 3s - s$

Again, just <u>combine the terms</u> — don't forget there's a '–' before the last s:

$2s + 3s - s = 4s$

If you have a mixture of <u>different letters</u>, or <u>letters</u> and <u>numbers</u>, it's a bit more tricky. To <u>simplify</u> an algebraic expression like this, you combine '<u>like terms</u>' (e.g. all the x terms, all the y terms, all the number terms etc.).

EXAMPLE: **Simplify $7x + 3 - x - 2$**

number terms

Invisible + sign ─── $\boxed{7x} \boxed{+3} \boxed{-x} \boxed{-2} = \boxed{+7x} \boxed{-x} \boxed{+3} \boxed{-2} = 6x + 1$

x-terms $6x$ $+1$

1) Put <u>bubbles</u> round each term — be sure you capture the <u>+/– sign</u> in front of each.
2) Then you can move the bubbles into the <u>best order</u> so that <u>like terms</u> are together.
3) <u>Combine like terms</u>.

EXAMPLE: **Simplify $4x + y - x + 3y$**

y-terms

Invisible + sign ─── $\boxed{4x} \boxed{+y} \boxed{-x} \boxed{+3y} = \boxed{+4x} \boxed{-x} \boxed{+y} \boxed{+3y} = 3x + 4y$

x-terms $3x$ $+4y$

You can only add or subtract terms if they are 'like terms'...

Be careful you don't add together different terms — remember x^2 and x are different terms.

Algebra — Multiplying

Multiplying algebra is a lot like multiplying numbers, so there's nothing too tricky on this page. Here are a few rules to get you started.

Letters **Multiplied** Together

Watch out for these combinations of letters in algebra that regularly catch people out:

> 1) *abc* means $a \times b \times c$ and $3a$ means $3 \times a$.

The ×'s are often left out to make it clearer.

> 2) gn^2 means $g \times n \times n$.

Note that only the *n* is squared, not the *g* as well.

> 3) $(gn)^2$ means $g \times g \times n \times n$.

The brackets mean that <u>BOTH</u> letters are squared.

> 4) <u>Powers</u> tell you <u>how many</u> letters are multiplied together.
>
> So $r^6 = r \times r \times r \times r \times r \times r$.

Use the **Rules** to **Simplify**

 **EXAMPLES:**

1. **Simplify** $h \times h \times h$

You have 3 *h*'s <u>multiplied together</u>:

$h \times h \times h = h^3$

Careful — h times itself 3 times is h^3, <u>not</u> 3h (3h means h + h + h or 3 × h).

2. **Simplify** $3r \times 2s \times 2$

Multiply the <u>numbers</u> together, then the <u>letters</u> together:

$3r \times 2s \times 2 = 3 \times 2 \times 2 \times r \times s = 12rs$

 The power rules will help you to simplify algebraic expressions

You'll need to know the power rules from page 34 and the rules for multiplying and dividing negative numbers from page 17 for algebra too. If you're a bit rusty on those topics, go back and take another look — they'll come in handy throughout this section.

Algebra — Multiplying

Multiplying out brackets can be a bit tough. No need to panic though — just take it steady and go through each of the examples on this page.

Multiplying Brackets

There are a few <u>key things</u> to remember before you start multiplying out brackets:

1) The thing <u>outside</u> the brackets multiplies <u>each separate term</u> inside the brackets.

2) When letters are multiplied together, they are just written next to each other, e.g. *pq*.

EXAMPLE: **Expand the following:**

a) $2(x + 3)$

$= (2 \times x) + (2 \times 3)$

$= 2x + 6$

b) $y(2y + 5)$

$= (y \times 2y) + (y \times 5)$

$= 2y^2 + 5y$

c) $3t(t - 6)$

$= (3t \times t) + (3t \times -6)$

$= 3t^2 - 18t$

Collecting Like Terms

You might be given <u>more than one</u> single bracket in the same expression, e.g. $3(x + 5) - 6x(x + 3)$. You'll have to <u>expand</u> each bracket separately and then <u>collect like terms</u> to simplify it (see p.39).

EXAMPLE: **Expand $x(x + 6) + y(2y + 3) + x(x + 3)$**

1) <u>Expand</u> each bracket separately.

$x(x + 6)$ + $y(2y + 3)$ + $x(x + 3)$

$= x^2 + 6x$ + $2y^2 + 3y$ + $x^2 + 3x$

2) <u>Group together</u> like terms.

$= x^2 + x^2 + 6x + 3x + 2y^2 + 3y$

3) <u>Simplify</u> the expression.

$= 2x^2 + 9x + 2y^2 + 3y$

Remember to collect like terms after you've expanded...

When you're collecting like terms, you normally write your answer in descending powers — e.g. the x^2 term should come before the x term, and the x term should come before the number term.

Formulas

A <u>formula</u> is a way of giving instructions <u>without</u> using loads of <u>words</u>.
So instead of saying "Square a number, times it by 7 and take away 11", say $N = 7x^2 - 11$.

Substituting Numbers into Expressions

> EXPRESSION — a <u>collection</u> of <u>terms</u> (see p.39). Expressions <u>DON'T</u> have an = sign in them.

Sometimes you'll be given an expression and you'll be asked to substitute some values into it.

 **Substitute $x = 3$ into the expression $10x + 5$.**

Think about what the <u>expression</u> is <u>telling you</u> to do.

Times x by 10 and add 5

Use BODMAS (p.3) to work things out in the right order.

Put the <u>number</u> ($x = 3$) in place of the letter and <u>work out</u> the value.

$3 \times 10 + 5 = 30 + 5$
$= 35$

Substituting Numbers into Formulas

> FORMULA — a <u>rule</u> that helps you work something out (it will have an = sign in it).

Substituting numbers into <u>formulas</u> is just like substituting numbers into expressions.

 **The formula for converting from kilometres (K) to miles (M) is $M = \frac{5}{8}K$.**
Use this formula to convert 16 kilometres (K = 16) into miles.

1) Write out the <u>formula</u> in full.

$M = \frac{5}{8} \times K$

2) Put the number (16) in place of the letter (K).

$M = \frac{5}{8} \times 16$

3) Work out the <u>multiplication</u>.

$M = 10$ so 16 kilometres = 10 miles

The formula for converting between Celsius (C) and Fahrenheit (F) is $F = \frac{9}{5}C + 32$.
If the temperature is 25 °C (C = 25), find the temperature in Fahrenheit.

1) Write out the <u>formula</u> in full.

$F = \frac{9}{5} \times C + 32$

2) Put the number (25) in place of the letter (C).

$F = \frac{9}{5} \times 25 + 32$

3) Work it out in <u>stages</u>.

$F = 45 + 32$
$F = 77$

So 25 °C is equal to 77 °F

Make sure you've put the right numbers into the right places...

Use the formulas for distance and temperature in the examples above to convert:
a) 24 km into miles, b) 40 km into miles, c) 15 °C into °F, d) 50 °C into °F (Answers below.)

(Ans: 15 miles, 25 miles, 59 °F, 122 °F)

Making Formulas from Words

I'll let you in on some useful tricks for making <u>formulas</u> from <u>words</u>. There are <u>two types</u>:

Writing Formulas from Instructions

If you're given <u>instructions about what to do with a number</u> you'll need to be able to write them as a formula. The instructions can be any one of these (where '*x*' stands for a number):

> 1) **Multiply** x 2) **Divide** x 3) **Square or square root** x (x^2 or $\sqrt{x}$)
> 4) **Cube** x (x^3)   5) **Add or subtract a number**

EXAMPLE: To <u>find *y*</u>:

a)   <u>add eight</u> to <u>*x*</u>.

Think about what the instructions are <u>telling you</u> — <u>underline</u> important bits if you need to.

$$x \longrightarrow x + 8 \longrightarrow y = x + 8$$

Start with <u>*x*</u>.   <u>Add 8</u>.   Set the expression <u>equal to *y*</u>.

b)   <u>divide *x* by three</u> and then <u>add four</u>.

$$x \longrightarrow \frac{x}{3} \longrightarrow \frac{x}{3} + 4 \longrightarrow y = \frac{x}{3} + 4$$

Start with <u>*x*</u>.   <u>Divide *x* by 3</u>.   <u>Add 4</u>.   Set the expression <u>equal to *y*</u>.

c)   <u>square *x*</u> and then <u>subtract two</u>.

$$x \longrightarrow x^2 \longrightarrow x^2 - 2 \longrightarrow y = x^2 - 2$$

Start with <u>*x*</u>.   <u>Square *x*</u>.   <u>Subtract 2</u>.   Set the expression <u>equal to *y*</u>.

Making Formulas from Words

Here you'll have to <u>make up a formula</u> by labelling things with letters, e.g. 'c' for '<u>cost</u>'.

   To find the <u>age (*a*)</u> of a barrowbeetle, you <u>divide</u> the number of <u>stripes (*s*)</u> by <u>two</u> and then <u>subtract one</u>. Write a formula for the age of a barrowbeetle.

Pick out the <u>important words</u> — <u>underline</u> them if you need to.

$$s \longrightarrow \frac{s}{2} \longrightarrow \frac{s}{2} - 1 \longrightarrow a = \frac{s}{2} - 1$$

Start with <u>*s*</u>.   <u>Divide *s* by 2</u>.   <u>Subtract 1</u>.   Set the expression <u>equal to *a*</u>.

 Read the question and pick out the information you need...

It might help to <u>underline</u> any bits of the question you think you'll need to use in the formula.

Solving Equations

To solve equations, you must find the value of x (or any given letter) that makes the equation true.

The 'Common Sense' Approach

The trick here is to realise that the unknown quantity 'x' is just a number and the 'equation' is a cryptic clue to help you find it.

EXAMPLE: **Solve the equation $x + 2 = 22$.** ← This just means 'find the value of x'.

This is what you should say to yourself:

'Something + 2 = 22', so that 'something' must be 20. $x = 20$

In other words don't think of it as algebra, but as 'find the mystery number'.

The 'Proper' Way

The 'proper' way to solve equations is to keep rearranging them until you end up with '$x =$' on one side. There are a few important points to remember when rearranging:

Golden Rules

1) Always do the SAME thing to both sides of the equation.
2) To get rid of something, do the opposite.
   The opposite of + is – and the opposite of – is +.
   The opposite of × is ÷ and the opposite of ÷ is ×.
3) Keep going until you have a letter on its own.

EXAMPLES:

1. **Solve $x + 3 = 7$.**

This means 'take away 3 from both sides'.

$$x + 3 = 7$$

The opposite of +3 is –3.

$$(-3) \quad x + 3 - 3 = 7 - 3$$
$$x = 4$$

2. **Solve $x - 2 = 3$.**

$$x - 2 = 3$$

The opposite of –2 is +2.

$$(+2) \quad x - 2 + 2 = 3 + 2$$
$$x = 5$$

3. **Solve $2x = 10$.**

$$2x = 10$$

$2x$ means $2 \times x$, so do the opposite — divide both sides by 2.

$$(\div 2) \quad 2x \div 2 = 10 \div 2$$
$$x = 5$$

4. **Solve $\frac{x}{2} = 4$.**

$$\frac{x}{2} = 4$$

$\frac{x}{2}$ means $x \div 2$, so do the opposite — multiply both sides by 2.

$$(\times 2) \quad \frac{x}{2} \times 2 = 4 \times 2$$
$$x = 8$$

To solve equations, always take it one step at a time...

When you're solving an equation, it's a good idea to write down what you're doing at every stage — put it in brackets next to the equation (like in the examples above).

Section Two — Algebra and Graphs

Solving Equations

You're not done with solving equations yet. Grab a cup of tea and read on...

Solving **Two-Step** Equations

If you come across an equation like $8x - 2 = 14$ (where there's an <u>x-term</u> and a <u>number</u> on the <u>same side</u>), use the same method as before — just do it in <u>two steps</u>:

1) <u>Add or subtract</u> the number first.
2) <u>Multiply or divide</u> to get '$x =$'.

EXAMPLE: **Solve the equation $3x + 2 = 11$.**

$$3x + 2 = 11$$ — The opposite of $+2$ is -2, so subtract 2 from both sides.

(-2) $\quad 3x + 2 - 2 = 11 - 2$

$$3x = 9$$ — The opposite of $\times 3$ is $\div 3$, so divide both sides by 3.

$(\div 3)$ $\quad 3x \div 3 = 9 \div 3$

$$x = 3$$

EXAMPLE: **Solve the equation $\frac{x}{2} - 3 = 4$.**

$$\frac{x}{2} - 3 = 4$$ — The opposite of -3 is $+3$, so add 3 to both sides.

$(+3)$ $\quad \frac{x}{2} - 3 + 3 = 4 + 3$

$$\frac{x}{2} = 7$$ — The opposite of $\div 2$ is $\times 2$, so multiply both sides by 2.

$(\times 2)$ $\quad \frac{x}{2} \times 2 = 7 \times 2$

$$x = 14$$

Equations with an 'x' on **Both Sides**

For equations like $3x + 1 = x - 7$ (where there's an x-term on <u>each side</u>), you have to:
1) Get all the x's on one side and all the <u>numbers</u> on the other.
2) If you need to, <u>multiply or divide</u> to get '$x =$'.

EXAMPLE: **Solve the equation $2x - 7 = x + 3$.**

$$2x - 7 = x + 3$$ — To get the x's on only one side, subtract x from each side.

$(-x)$ $\quad 2x - 7 - x = x + 3 - x$

$$x - 7 = 3$$ — Now add 7 to get the numbers on the other side.

$(+7)$ $\quad x - 7 + 7 = 3 + 7$

$$x = 10$$

Get all the *x*'s on one side and all the numbers on the other...

You can check your answer to questions like these by putting your x-value back into each side of the equation. Both sides should give the same number — if they don't, you've gone wrong.

Warm-Up and Practice Questions

Algebra can seem pretty weird if you're not used to it, but that's why you need to learn the basics really well. Even if you find it easy, it's practice that really fixes things in your brain.

Warm-Up Questions

1) Simplify: a) $a + a + a$ b) $3d + 7d - 2d$ c) $8 - y - 2x + 3y$

2) Expand: a) $x(2x + 3)$ b) $3x(x + 5)$ c) $x(x + 4) - 3(x + 5)$

3) Substitute $x = 4$ into these expressions:

   a) $3x + 3$ b) $5x - 7$ c) $\frac{1}{2}x - 1$

4) An ice cream costs 40p for the cone plus 50p for each scoop of ice cream you have on it. Write a formula for the cost of the ice cream (c pence) in terms of the number of scoops (s).

5) Solve these equations:

   a) $x + 6 = 9$ b) $x - 2 = 9$ c) $9x = 27$

6) Solve these equations:

   a) $2x - 9 = 3$ b) $4x + 7 = 23$ c) $2x - 3 = 3x + 2$ d) $6y - 2 = 4y + 6$

Practice Questions

Now that you've had some practice of these basic algebra techniques, it's time to see how you fare with some exam-style questions. The first one is a worked example to ease you in gently...

1   Bronagh has a square paddling pool. Each side is $x + 1$ metres long. The perimeter of the paddling pool is 24 metres.

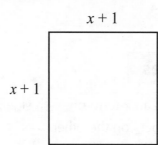

$x + 1$

$x + 1$

a)   Write an equation for the perimeter of Bronagh's paddling pool in the form $ax + b = c$.

        $4(x + 1) = 24$ —————— The perimeter, P, of a square
                                with side length l is $P = 4l$.

     $(4 \times x) + (4 \times 1) = 24$

          $4x + 4 = 24$

                                           $\underline{4x + 4 = 24}$

[1 mark]

b)   Solve your equation to find the value of x.

             $4x + 4 = 24$

    $(- 4)\ \ 4x + 4 - 4 = 24 - 4$

                 $4x = 20$

   $(\div 4)$ $x = 5$

                                         $\underline{x = 5}$

[2 marks]

Practice Questions

2   Simplify the following expressions.

a) $4x - 2y + 3x + y$

....
[1 mark]

b) $-2x + 6x - 5 - 3x^2 + 7x^2$

....
[1 mark]

3   Expand and simplify the following expressions.

a) $4x(2x + 4)$

....
[1 mark]

b) $2(5x - 1) - 7x$

....
[2 marks]

4   Solve:

a) $7k - 3 = 11$

....
[2 marks]

b) $3t + 6 = t + 12$

....
[3 marks]

5   To cook a chicken, it takes 50 minutes for each kilogram it weighs, plus an extra 20 minutes.

a)   Write down a formula for the time T (in minutes) that it takes to cook a chicken that weighs n kg.

....
[1 mark]

b)   How long does it take to cook a 3 kg chicken?

.... minutes
[2 marks]

Number Patterns and Sequences

Sequences are just patterns of numbers or shapes that follow a rule which you need to work out.

Finding **Number Patterns**

The trick to finding the rule for number patterns is to write down what you have to do to get from one number to the next in the gaps between the numbers.
There are 2 main types to look out for:

1) Arithmetic sequences — Add or subtract the same number each time

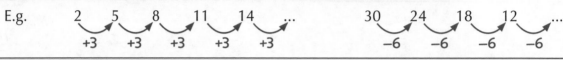

E.g.

2   5   8   11   14   ...   30   24   18   12   ...
   +3   +3   +3   +3   +3   −6   −6   −6   −6

| THE RULE: | 'Add 3 to the previous term' | 'Subtract 6 from the previous term' |

2) Geometric sequences — Multiply or divide by the same number each time

E.g.

2   6   18   54   ...   40 000   4000   400   40   ...
  ×3   ×3   ×3   ×3   ÷10   ÷10   ÷10   ÷10

| THE RULE: | 'Multiply the previous term by 3' | 'Divide the previous term by 10' |

You might get number patterns that follow a different rule — for example, you might have to add or subtract a changing number each time, or add together the two previous terms.
You just need to describe the pattern and use your rule to find the next term.

Shape Patterns

If you have a pattern of shapes, you need to be able to continue the pattern. You might also have to find the rule for the pattern to work out how many shapes there'll be in a later pattern.

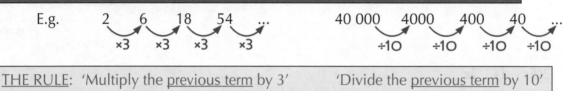

EXAMPLE: **Here are some patterns made of squares.**
   a) Draw the next pattern in the sequence.
   b) Work out how many squares there will be in the 6th pattern.

a) Just continue the pattern — add an extra square to each of the three legs.

b) Set up a table to find the rule:

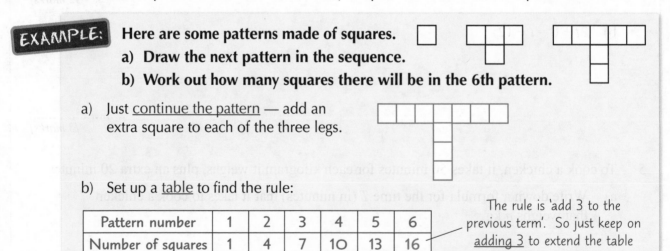

Pattern number	1	2	3	4	5	6
Number of squares	1	4	7	10	13	16

The rule is 'add 3 to the previous term'. So just keep on adding 3 to extend the table until you get to the 6th term.

Always check your rule works for the whole sequence...

When you think you've figured out the rule, check it works for all the terms you've been given.
If it doesn't work for one of them then it's not the correct rule — you'll have to find a different one.

Number Patterns and Sequences

You might have to "find an <u>expression</u> for the <u>nth term</u> of a sequence" — this is a rule with *n* in, like 5*n* – 3. It gives <u>every term in the sequence</u> when you put in different values for *n*.

Finding the **nth Term** of a **Sequence**

This method works for sequences with a <u>common difference</u> — where you <u>add</u> or <u>subtract</u> the <u>same number</u> each time (i.e. the difference between each pair of terms is the <u>same</u>).

EXAMPLE: **Find an expression for the *n*th term of the sequence that starts 2, 8, 14, 20, ...**

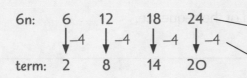

n:	1	2	3	4
term:	2	8	14	20

+6   +6   +6

1) Find the <u>common difference</u>. It's <u>6</u> — this tells you that the sequence is just like the six times table but with some <u>addition</u> or <u>subtraction</u>.

6n:	6	12	18	24

–4   –4   –4   –4

term:	2	8	14	20

2) The six times table is the same as <u>6*n*</u>.

So the expression for the nth term is 6n – 4

3) Work out what you have to <u>add</u> or <u>subtract</u> to get from 6*n* to the term. So it's <u>–4</u>.

n = 1 gives 6n – 4 = 6 – 4 = 2 ✓
n = 2 gives 6n – 4 = 12 – 4 = 8 ✓
n = 3 gives 6n – 4 = 18 – 4 = 14 ✓

4) Put '<u>6*n*</u>' and '<u>–4</u>' together.

5) Check your formula by putting the first few values of *n* back in.

EXAMPLE: **A sequence starts 1, –2, –5, –8...**

When the sequence is decreasing the common difference is negative.

a) Find an expression for the *n*th term of the sequence.

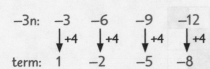

n:	1	2	3	4
Sequence:	1	–2	–5	–8

–3   –3   –3

1) The <u>common difference is negative</u> — so instead of being +3 it's –3 and the expression has <u>–3*n*</u> in it.

–3n:	–3	–6	–9	–12

+4   +4   +4   +4

term:	1	–2	–5	–8

2) To get from <u>–3*n*</u> to the <u>*n*th term</u> in the sequence you need to <u>+4</u>.

So the expression for the nth term is –3n + 4

3) Put <u>–3*n*</u> and <u>+4</u> together.

b) Find the 13th term in the sequence.

n = 13 gives –3n + 4 = (–3 × 13) + 4
                        = –39 + 4 = –35

Put <u>*n* = 13</u> into the expression for the *n*th term.

The *n*th term is in the *n*th position of the sequence...

Have a go at finding the expression for the *n*th term of the sequence that starts 3, 1, –1, –3...
What is the 10th term in this sequence? What about the 100th term? (Answers below.)

(Ans: –2n + 5, –15, –195)

Warm-Up and Practice Questions

Stuff like "find the *n*th term" will sound like complete gibberish if you haven't worked through this section carefully. So try these warm-up questions and check they make sense to you.

Warm-Up Questions

1) Write down the next term in each sequence and find the rule:
   a) 38, 32, 26, ...   b) 1, 4, 16, ...

2) Find an expression for the *n*th term of the following sequences:
   a) 5, 8, 11, 14, ...   b) 3, –2, –7, –12, ...

3) What is the 10th term of the sequence with *n*th term $2n - 5$?

4) a) Draw the next pattern in the sequence of shapes on the right.
    b) How many squares will there be in the 6th pattern?

5) A sequence starts –2, –6, –10, –14.
   a) Find an expression for the *n*th term of the sequence.
   b) Find the 8th term of the sequence.

Practice Questions

Time for some more practice questions. But first, there's a worked example about patterns and sequences — read through it carefully before you have a go at the rest of the practice questions.

1 The diagram shows some floor patterns made up of shaded and unshaded square tiles.

pattern 1

pattern 2

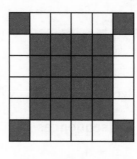

pattern 3

a) Draw the fourth pattern on the blank grid below.

[1 mark]

b) How many shaded tiles will be in the 5th pattern?

There will be a 5 by 5 square of shaded tiles in the middle, and 1 shaded tile in each corner.

(5 × 5) + 4 = 25 + 4 = 29

......29......

[2 marks]

Section Two — Algebra and Graphs

Practice Questions

2   Write the first four terms of a sequence with the *n*th term 5*n* – 6.

.... , ... , ... , ...

[2 marks]

3   Find the *n*th term of the following sequences:

a)   7, 9, 11, 13, …

....

[2 marks]

b)   11, 7, 3, –1, …

....

[2 marks]

4   Look at these patterns of dots.

pattern 1   pattern 2   pattern 3   pattern 4

a)   Draw the next pattern in the sequence.

[1 mark]

b)   How many dots would be in the 8th pattern in the sequence?

....

[2 marks]

X and Y Coordinates

The first thing you'll need to know about graphs is how to <u>read coordinates</u> from them.

Plot **Coordinates** on a **Grid**

1) You draw graphs on a <u>grid</u>, a bit like this one.

2) It's made by two lines crossing — called the <u>axes</u>.

3) The <u>y-axis</u> goes from <u>bottom to top</u>, and the <u>x-axis</u> goes from <u>left to right</u>.

4) They meet at the point with <u>coordinates (0, 0)</u> — this is called the <u>origin</u>.

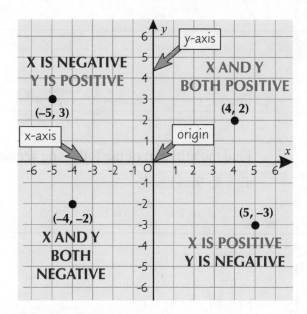

X, Y Coordinates — Getting them in the **Right Order**

1) You must always give <u>coordinates</u> in <u>brackets</u> like this: (x, y)

2) And you always have to be really careful to get them <u>the right way round</u> — x first, then y.

3) Here are <u>three ways</u> you could remember:

$$(x , y)$$

1) The coordinates are always in <u>ALPHABETICAL ORDER</u>, x then y.

2) x is always the flat axis going <u>ACROSS</u> the page.
In other words '<u>x is a...cross</u>' Get it — x is a '×'. (Hilarious isn't it)

3) Remember it's always <u>IN THE HOUSE</u> (→) and then <u>UP THE STAIRS</u> (↑)
so it's <u>ALONG</u> first and <u>then UP</u>, i.e. x-coordinate first, and then y-coordinate.

EXAMPLE: **What are the coordinates of points A, B and C on this graph?**

You need to read off the <u>x-axis</u> to find the <u>first coordinate</u>.

You need to read off the <u>y-axis</u> to find the <u>second coordinate</u>.

A = (3, 3)

B = (−3, 2)

C = (2, −4)

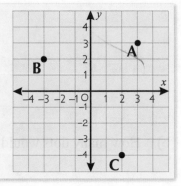

In the house and up the... oh wait, I'm in a bungalow...

Getting the coordinates the right way round is the first step — find the method that works for you.

Straight Line Graphs

Over the next couple of pages you'll learn about all sorts of <u>straight lines</u>.
Here are the most basic ones — horizontal and vertical lines.

Horizontal and Vertical Lines: E.g. x = 3 and y = –2

Vertical lines are always "x = a number"

1) E.g. <u>$x = -5$</u> is a <u>vertical line through '–5'</u> on the x-axis.
2) The <u>y-axis</u> is also the line <u>$x = 0$</u>.

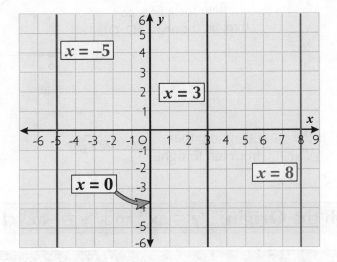

Horizontal lines are always "y = a number"

1) E.g. <u>$y = 3$</u> is a <u>horizontal line through '3'</u> on the y-axis.
2) The <u>x-axis</u> is also the line <u>$y = 0$</u>.

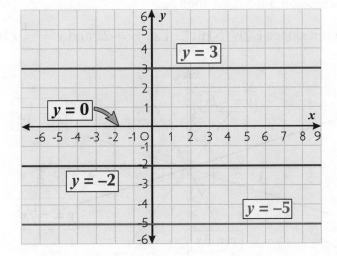

It's easy to spot the equation for a horizontal or vertical line...

If you're asked to work out the equation of a horizontal or vertical line on a graph, just look at the number on the x- or y- axis that it passes through. Don't get them mixed up though — the x-axis is horizontal, but a line with equation 'x = a number' is vertical.

Straight Line Graphs

Here are some more straight line graphs for you to enjoy...

The **Main Diagonals**: "y = x" and "y = –x"

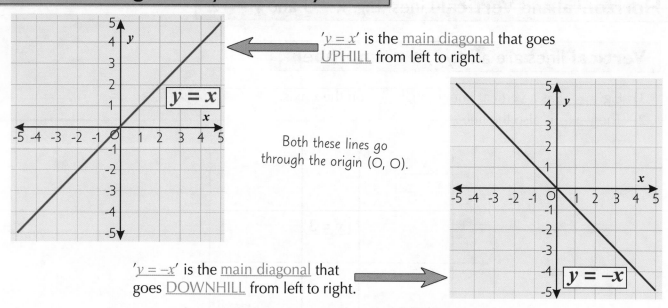

'$y = x$' is the main diagonal that goes UPHILL from left to right.

$y = x$

Both these lines go through the origin (O, O).

'$y = –x$' is the main diagonal that goes DOWNHILL from left to right.

$y = –x$

Other Lines Through the **Origin**: "y = ax" and "y = –ax"

$y = ax$ and $y = –ax$ are the equations for A SLOPING LINE THROUGH THE ORIGIN (where 'a' is just a number).

1) The value of 'a' (known as the gradient) tells you the steepness of the line.

2) The bigger 'a' is, the steeper the slope. E.g. the line $y = 3x$ on the right is steeper than $y = \frac{1}{2}x$, because 3 is bigger than $\frac{1}{2}$.

3) A MINUS SIGN tells you it slopes DOWNHILL. E.g. $y = –2x$ and $y = –\frac{1}{2}x$ both slope downhill.

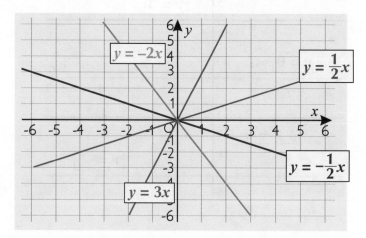

$y = –2x$

$y = \frac{1}{2}x$

$y = –\frac{1}{2}x$

$y = 3x$

Learn the equations for these basic lines before moving on...

These are the some of the easiest straight lines to learn — there are some tougher ones to come. Take a minute to go back through the last two pages and make sure everything makes sense to you.

Straight Line Graphs

You've seen <u>vertical</u> and <u>horizontal</u> straight lines (p.53) and straight lines that pass through the <u>origin</u> (p.54) — now it's time to look at some slightly more complicated straight line equations...

All Other **Straight** Lines

1) Other straight line equations are a little more tricky.

2) The next page shows you how to <u>draw them</u>, but the first step is <u>spotting them</u> in the first place.

3) <u>STRAIGHT LINE EQUATIONS</u> just have 'SOMETHING X, SOMETHING Y, AND A NUMBER' — like in the examples on the right.

4) If an equation has things like $\underline{x^2}$ (or other <u>powers</u>), $\underline{xy}$ or $\frac{1}{x}$, then it's <u>NOT A STRAIGHT LINE</u>.

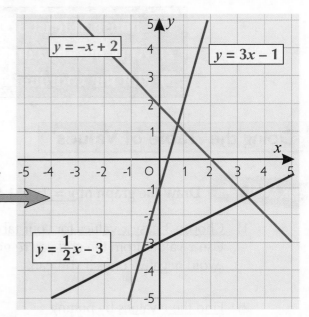

$y = -x + 2$

$y = 3x - 1$

$y = \frac{1}{2}x - 3$

Straight Line Equations don't have any **Extra Bits**

EXAMPLE: **Which of these equations are straight line equations?**

$$y = xy + 3 \qquad\qquad 3y + 3x = 12 \qquad\qquad y = x^2 + 8$$

$$y = 3x + 2 \qquad\qquad y - x - 3 = 2$$

$y = xy + 3$	Contains an $\underline{xy}$ term so <u>isn't</u> a straight line equation.
$3y + 3x = 12$	Only contains $\underline{y}$, $\underline{x}$ and a <u>number</u> so <u>is</u> a straight line equation.
$y = x^2 + 8$	Contains an $\underline{x^2}$ term so <u>isn't</u> a straight line equation.
$y = 3x + 2$	Only contains $\underline{y}$, $\underline{x}$ and a <u>number</u> so <u>is</u> a straight line equation.
$y - x - 3 = 2$	Only contains $\underline{y}$, $\underline{x}$ and <u>numbers</u> so <u>is</u> a straight line equation.

Make sure you can identify straight line equations...

Remember, the equations for straight lines look fairly straightforward — there won't be any funny things like powers, fractions with an x on the bottom, or x's and y's being multiplied together.

Plotting Straight Line Graphs

On this page you get to practise your drawing skills — shame it's only straight line graphs though. They can be difficult to get right, but luckily this method will lead you to the correct answer every time:

> 1) **Choose at least 3 values of x and draw up a table.**
> 2) **Work out the corresponding y-values.**
> 3) **Plot the coordinates, and draw the line.**

Doing the 'Table of Values'

EXAMPLE: **Draw the graph of $\underline{y = 2x + 1}$ for values of x from –3 to 2.**

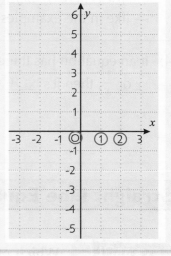

1) Choose 3 easy x-values for your table:
Use x-values from the grid you're given.
Avoid negative ones if you can.

x	O	1	2
y			

2) Find the y-values by putting each x-value into the equation:

x	O	1	2
y	1	3	5

When x = O,
$y = 2x + 1$
$= (2 \times O) + 1 = 1$

When x = 2,
$y = 2x + 1$
$= (2 \times 2) + 1 = 5$

Plotting the Points and Drawing the Graph

EXAMPLE: **...continued from above.**

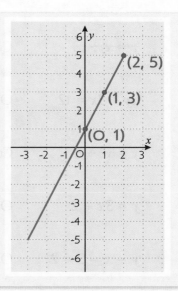

3) Plot each pair of x- and y-values from your table.

The table gives the coordinates:
(O, 1), (1, 3) and (2, 5).

4) Now draw a straight line through your points — remember to extend the line through all the x-values given in the question.

> If one point looks a bit wacky, check 2 things:
> • the y-value you worked out in the table,
> • that you've plotted it properly.

EXAM TIP

Plot three coordinates then draw a straight line through them...

If a question asks you to draw a graph for certain values of x, don't forget to extend the line — if you just join up the three points you've chosen to plot, you won't get all the marks.

Warm-Up and Practice Questions

Now that you've had a quick introduction to the world of graphs, it's time for some practice questions. But first, let's get you started with a few quick warm-up questions.

Warm-Up Questions

1) a) Draw a grid with the x-axis going from -4 to 4 and the y-axis going from -4 to 4.
   b) Plot these points on the grid you've drawn: a) $(0, 4)$ b) $(-2, -4)$

2) a) Draw a grid with the x-axis going from -6 to 6 and the y-axis going from -6 to 6.
   b) Plot these three lines on the grid you've drawn: (i) $y = 2$ (ii) $x = 1$ (iii) $-y = x$

3) Decide which of these equations are straight line equations:

   a) $-y = 2x$ b) $y + 3x = 0$ c) $xy + x = 5$ d) $y = \dfrac{1}{x} + 5$ e) $y + 2x = x$

4) Draw the graph of $y = x - 3$ for values of x from 0 to 6.

5) Draw the graph of $y = -2x + 4$ for values of x from -2 to 2.

Practice Questions

Now that you're all warmed up it's time for some practice questions — I've shown you how to do the first one, but you're on your own for the whole of the next page.

1 The points A, B and C are three of the vertices of a rectangle ABCD.

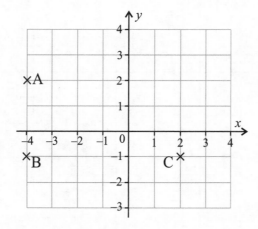

a) Write down the coordinates of A, B and C.

   A = ...(–4, 2)......   B = ...(–4, –1)......   C = ...(2, –1)......

   [3 marks]

b) Write down the coordinates of D, the fourth vertex of the rectangle.

   To get from B to A, you go 3 up —
   so do the same from C to find vertex D.   ......(2, 2)......

   [1 mark]

c) What is the equation of the line BC?

   A horizontal line through –1. $y = -1$
   ....

   [1 mark]

Practice Questions

2   Look at the rectangle in the diagram below. Give the equations of the lines:

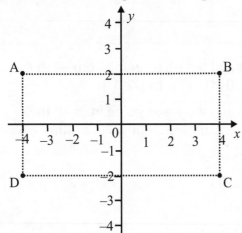

a)   AB

....

[1 mark]

b)   BC

....

[1 mark]

c)   CD

....

[1 mark]

d)   DA

....

[1 mark]

3   The graph of $y = 8 - x$ is a straight line.

a)   Complete the table of values for the equation $y = 8 - x$.

x	0	3	6
y			

[1 mark]

b)   Plot the graph of $y = 8 - x$ on the axes below.

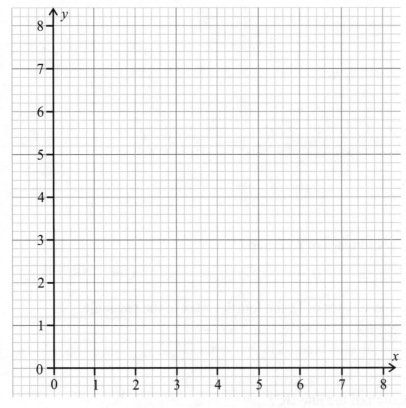

[1 mark]

c)   Write down the coordinates of the point where the line $y = 8 - x$ crosses the x-axis.

....

[1 mark]

Reading Off Graphs

Here's a page for you on reading graphs. It doesn't matter what type of graph you're reading off, you just use the same method every time.

Getting Answers from a Graph

> **FOR A SINGLE CURVE OR LINE**, you **ALWAYS** get the answer by:
> 1) **drawing a straight line to the graph from one axis,**
> 2) and then **down or across to the other axis.**

EXAMPLE:

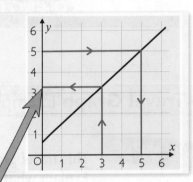

a) Find the value of x when $y = 5$.

Draw a line across from 5 on the y-axis to the graph, then down to the x-axis. Read off the x-value.

$x = 5$

b) Find the value of y when $x = 3$.

Draw a line up from 3 on the x-axis to the graph and then across to the y-axis. Read off the y-value.

$y \approx 3.2$

Sometimes the answer won't be a whole number and you'll have to estimate — $\approx$ means 'is approximately equal to'.

Graphs might have a Real-Life Context

EXAMPLE:

The graph shows the height of a ball as it is thrown up in the air.

Use the graph to find the approximate times when the ball is 3 m above the ground.

① Draw a line straight across from 3 on the 'height of ball' axis on the graph. Careful — this line crosses the graph twice.

② Draw straight lines down to the 'time' axis at each of these points. Read off the values.

    0.4 seconds and 1.2 seconds

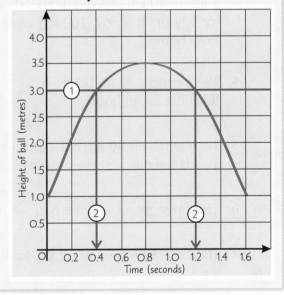

Always draw the lines to make sure you've got it right...

Reading graphs is easy once you know how — you just use the same method for every graph.

Travel Graphs

Here's another type of graph for you — this time it's back to <u>straight lines</u>. The axes mean something different here, but you use the same method as on the last page for reading off values.

Know What **Travel Graphs** Show

1) A <u>TRAVEL GRAPH</u> is always <u>DISTANCE</u> (↑) against <u>TIME</u> (→)
2) <u>FLAT SECTIONS</u> are where it's <u>STOPPED</u>.
3) The <u>STEEPER</u> the graph the <u>FASTER</u> it's going.
4) The graph <u>GOING UP</u> means it's travelling <u>AWAY</u>.
5) The graph <u>COMING DOWN</u> means it's <u>COMING BACK AGAIN</u>.

Travel Graph Example

EXAMPLE:

This travel graph shows a car journey.
Explain what is happening at each stage of the car journey.

① The car travels for <u>60 km</u> at a <u>steady speed</u> for <u>1 hour</u>.

② The car <u>stops</u> for <u>30 minutes</u> (flat sections mean 'stopped').

③ The car travels away from home for another <u>40 km</u> at a <u>steady speed</u> for <u>1 hour</u>. It is now <u>100 km</u> away from home.

④ The car <u>stops</u> again but this time for <u>an hour</u>.

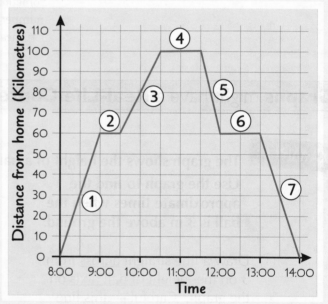

⑤ The car travels <u>40 km</u> back towards home at a <u>steady speed</u> for <u>30 minutes</u>. This is the <u>quickest</u> the car travels as it's the <u>steepest part</u> of the graph.

⑥ The car <u>stops</u> for another <u>hour</u> — 60 km away from home.

⑦ The car travels the last <u>60 km</u> back home at a <u>steady speed</u> for an <u>hour</u>.

The slope of a travel graph shows the speed...

Make sure you know what each different feature of a travel graph is telling you and what it means. You can read off values from travel graphs like you did on the previous page.

Conversion Graphs

Conversion graphs help you switch between different units, e.g. from £ to dollars.

Reading off Conversion Graphs

Reading off conversion graphs is the same as reading off any other graph.
You use the same method as you saw on page 59. Here's a reminder of how it's done:

> 1) Draw a straight line from the value you know on one axis to the graph.
> 2) Change direction and draw a line straight to the other axis. Then read off the value.

Conversion Graph Examples

EXAMPLE: The conversion graph below can be used to convert between pounds and euros.

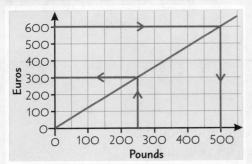

a) **Convert 250 pounds into euros.**

Draw a line up from 250 on the pounds axis to the graph. Then draw a line straight across to the euros axis.

300 euros

b) **Convert 600 euros into pounds.**

Draw a line across from 600 on the euros axis to the graph. Then draw a line straight down to the pounds axis.

500 pounds

EXAMPLE: The conversion graph below can be used to convert between miles and kilometres.

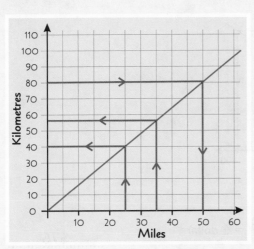

a) **Convert 25 miles into kilometres.**

Draw a line up from 25 on the miles axis till it hits the line, then go across to the km axis.

40 km

b) **Convert 80 kilometres into miles.**

Draw a line across from 80 on the km axis till it hits the line, then go down to the miles axis.

50 miles

c) **Estimate how many kilometres are equal to 35 miles.**

Sometimes you won't be able to find an exact answer and you'll have to estimate.

56 km

Conversion graphs allow you to switch between units...

With conversion graphs, it's a simple matter of reading values from a graph — nothing too tricky.

Warm-Up and Practice Questions

Once you can read off one type of graph you can read them all — so these questions shouldn't surprise you. It's just a matter of working out what the numbers actually mean.

Warm-Up Questions

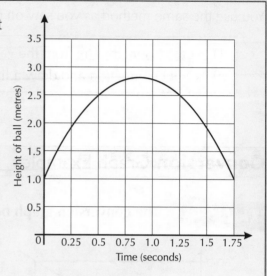

1) The graph on the right shows the height of a ball as it is thrown up in the air. Use it to:

   a) find the height of the ball after 0.5 seconds.

   b) find the approximate times when the ball is 1.5 metres above the ground.

2) What does the flat section of a travel graph tell you?

3) What does the steepness of a travel graph tell you?

4) What is always plotted up the vertical axis of a travel graph?

5) Using the miles to kilometres conversion graph on the previous page, estimate how many miles are equal to 70 km.

Practice Questions

As promised, there will be no surprises for you in these questions. You should be used to the drill by now — first, I get to answer a question, then it's your turn.

1   This graph can be used to convert pounds (£) into US dollars ($).
Use the graph to answer the following questions.

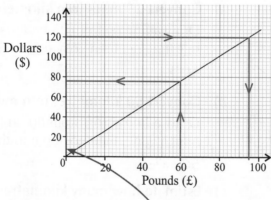

   a)   Estimate how much £60 is in dollars.

On the y-axis each square represents $\frac{20}{5}$ = 4 dollars.

..............$76..............

[1 mark]

   b)   Estimate how much $120 is in pounds.

..............£95..............

[1 mark]

Practice Questions

2   Kara and Kerry did a sponsored walk.
- They set off at noon and jogged for the first quarter of an hour.
- Then they walked for the next hour.
- After a rest, they set off to walk back.
- Kerry's mother drove to meet them and, as it started to rain, gave them a lift back.

The travel graph on the right shows their journey.

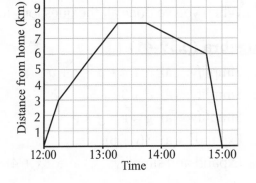

a)   For how many kilometres did they jog?

.... km
[1 mark]

b)   How many minutes did they have for the break?

.... mins
[1 mark]

c)   At what time did Kerry's mother pick them up?

....
[1 mark]

d)   How far did they jog and walk altogether?

.... km
[1 mark]

3   This graph can be used to convert litres into gallons.

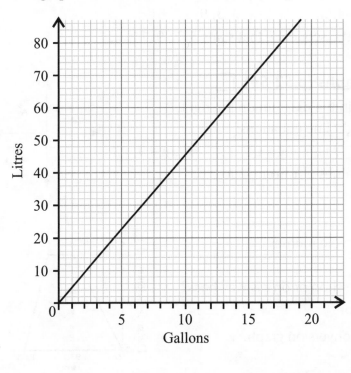

a)   The petrol tank in Arjun's car can hold 50 litres of petrol. Estimate how many gallons it can hold.

.... gallons
[1 mark]

b)   Arjun already has 7.5 gallons of petrol in his car. How many litres of petrol does he need to buy to fill up the rest of the petrol tank?

.... litres
[2 marks]

Revision Summary

Well, that wraps up <u>Section Two</u> — time to test yourself and find out <u>how much you really know</u>.

* Try these questions and <u>tick off each one</u> when you <u>get it right</u>.
* When you've done <u>all the questions</u> for a topic and are <u>completely happy</u> with it, tick off the topic.

Algebra (p.39-41) ☑

1. Simplify: a) $a + a + a + a + a$ b) $3b + 8b - 2b$
2. Simplify: a) $d + 3e + 5d - 2e$ b) $9f + 2 - 11f + 7$
3. Simplify: a) $g \times g \times g \times g$ b) $m \times n \times 9$
4. Expand: a) $3(v + 8)$ b) $-7(2w + 5)$
5. Expand and simplify: a) $x(3x + 4) + 6x$ b) $y(7y + 5) + 3(y - 5)$

Formulas (p.42-43) ☑

6. Use the formula $P = 3Q + 8$ to find P when: a) $Q = 7$ b) $Q = -3$

7. The formula for converting from Celsius (C) to Fahrenheit (F) is $F = \frac{9}{5}C + 32$.
   Use the formula to convert $-20\,°C$ into Fahrenheit.

8. Lucian is organising a camping trip and buys s sleeping bags and t tents.
   Sleeping bags cost £8 each and tents cost £15 each. He spends £P in total.
   Write a formula for P in terms of s and t.

Solving Equations (p.44-45) ☑

9. Solve: a) $x + 12 = 19$ b) $x - 6 = 16$ c) $3x = 36$ d) $\frac{x}{4} = 20$
10. Solve: a) $3x + 5 = 14$ b) $9x - 11 = 25$ c) $9x - 6 = x + 10$

Number Patterns and Sequences (p.48-49) ☑

11. For each of the following sequences, find the next term and write down the rule you used.
    a) 2, 8, 14, 20, ...   b) 5, 2, –1, –4, ...   c) 3, 9, 27, 81, ...
12. Find an expression for the nth term of the sequence that starts 5, 7, 9, 11, ...

Coordinates and Straight Line Graphs (p.52-56) ☑

13. Give the coordinates of points A to D in the diagram on the right.
14. Say which of these equations are straight line equations:
    a) $y = -2x^2$ b) $y = -3x$ c) $-y + x = 0$ d) $xy + 9 = 3$
15. Draw the graph of $y = 2x + 2$ for the values of x from –2 to 2.

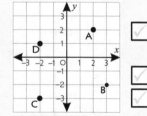

Reading Off Graphs (p.59-61) ☑

16. The graph on the right shows Bob's bicycle journey
    to the shop and back.
    a) Did he ride faster on his way to the shop or on his way back?
    b) How long did he spend in the shop?

17. Explain how to convert units using a conversion graph.

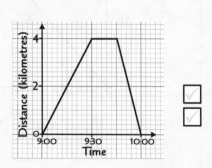

Ratios

I can tell you're going to love this section. Let's start off with a few ratios.

Reducing **Ratios** to Their **Simplest Form**

To <u>reduce</u> a ratio to a simpler form, <u>divide all the numbers</u> in the ratio
by the <u>same thing</u> (like cancelling down fractions on p.25).
It's in the <u>simplest form</u> when there's nothing left you can divide by.

> **EXAMPLE:** **Write the ratio 10 : 15 in its simplest form.**
>
> Both numbers have a <u>factor of 5</u>, so <u>divide</u> them by <u>5</u>.
> You can't reduce this any further. So this is the <u>simplest form</u>.
>
> $\div 5 \left(\dfrac{10:15}{2:3} \right) \div 5$
> $=$

Scaling Up **Ratios**

If you know the <u>ratio between parts</u> and the actual size of <u>one part</u>,
you can <u>scale the ratio up</u> to find the other parts.

> **EXAMPLE:** **Purple paint is made from red paint and blue paint in the ratio 5 : 4.**
> **If 20 pots of red paint are used, how much blue paint is needed?**
>
> You need to <u>multiply by 4</u> to go from 5 to 20 on
> the left-hand side (LHS) — so do that to <u>both sides</u>:
> So 16 pots of blue paint are needed.
>
> red paint : blue paint
> $= \times 4 \left(\dfrac{5:4}{20:16} \right) \times 4$

Proportional **Division**

In a <u>proportional division</u> question, a <u>TOTAL AMOUNT</u> is split into parts <u>in a certain ratio</u>.
The key word here is <u>PARTS</u> — concentrate on 'parts' and it all becomes quite painless.

> **EXAMPLE:** **Kim and Chris share £200 in the ratio 3 : 7. How much does Chris get?**
>
> 1) <u>ADD UP THE PARTS</u>:
>   The ratio 3 : 7 means there will be a total of 10 <u>parts</u>:   3 + 7 = 10 parts
>
> 2) <u>DIVIDE TO FIND ONE "PART"</u>:
>   Just divide the <u>total amount</u> by the number of <u>parts</u>:   £200 ÷ 10 = £20 (= 1 part)
>
> 3) <u>MULTIPLY TO FIND THE AMOUNTS</u>:
>   We want to know <u>Chris's share</u>, which is <u>7 parts</u>:   7 parts = 7 × £20 = £140

Learn these simple methods for questions involving ratios...

Don't be put off by complicated terms like "proportional division" — the methods are quite simple.
Make sure you know how to scale up ratios, and the three steps for proportional division.

Proportion Problems

Proportion problems all involve amounts that <u>increase</u> or <u>decrease together</u>.

The **Golden Rule** for **Proportion** Questions

You can solve lots of different proportion questions using the same method.
All you have to do is remember this <u>golden rule</u>:

> ### DIVIDE FOR ONE, THEN TIMES FOR ALL

EXAMPLE:

3 painters can paint 9 rooms per day.
How many rooms per day could 7 painters paint?

Start by <u>dividing by 3</u> to find how many
rooms <u>1 painter</u> could paint per day.   *9 ÷ 3 = 3 rooms per day*

Then <u>multiply by 7</u> to find how many
rooms <u>7 painters</u> could paint per day.   *3 × 7 = 21 rooms per day*

Scaling **Recipes** Up or Down

Scaling recipes is a useful <u>real-life skill</u> — have a look at this example of how it's done.

EXAMPLE:

**Rizwana is making some white bread using
the recipe shown on the right. She wants to
make enough to serve 30 people. How much
of each ingredient will Rizwana need?**

> **White Bread (serves 4)**
> 320 g bread flour
> 40 g soft butter
> 16 g yeast
> 200 ml water

Use the <u>GOLDEN RULE</u> again: | DIVIDE FOR ONE, THEN TIMES FOR ALL

which means: <u>Divide each amount by 4</u> to find how much <u>FOR ONE PERSON</u>,
then <u>multiply by 30</u> to find how much <u>FOR 30 PEOPLE</u>.

So for 1 person you need: *And for 30 people you need:*

320 g ÷ 4 = 80 g bread flour   ⇒   *30 × 80 g = 2400 g bread flour*
40 g ÷ 4 = 10 g soft butter   ⇒   *30 × 10 g = 300 g soft butter*
16 g ÷ 4 = 4 g yeast   ⇒   *30 × 4 g = 120 g yeast*
200 ml ÷ 4 = 50 ml water   ⇒   *30 × 50 ml = 1500 ml water*

Sometimes you can <u>just multiply</u> — e.g. in the example above, if you wanted to know the
ingredients for <u>16 servings</u> of bread, you could just times everything in the recipe by 4.

If you're a bit unsure of what to do, just remember — the GOLDEN RULE <u>always works</u>...

Proportion problems — divide for one, then times for all...

Always check your answer at the end to make sure it makes sense, e.g. if there are more
people doing an activity in the same amount of time, then they should get more of it done.

Proportion Problems

These questions are all about working out which product is the best <u>value for money</u>.

Best Buy Questions — Find the **Amount per Penny**...

These are similar to the <u>proportion questions</u> you saw on p.66, but here you're comparing the '<u>value for money</u>' of 2 or 3 similar items. For these, follow this <u>GOLDEN RULE</u>...

DIVIDE BY THE PRICE <u>IN PENCE</u> (TO GET THE AMOUNT <u>PER PENNY</u>)

**EXAMPLE:** **Ralph's Red Hot Chilli Relish comes in three different sizes, as shown below. Which of these represents the best value for money?**

100 g at £2.50   200 g at £3.20   400 g at £8

The <u>GOLDEN RULE</u> says:

DIVIDE BY THE PRICE <u>IN PENCE</u> TO GET THE AMOUNT <u>PER PENNY</u>

In the 100 g jar you get   100 g ÷ 250p = 0.4 g per penny
In the 200 g jar you get   200 g ÷ 320p = 0.625 g per penny
In the 400 g jar you get   400 g ÷ 800p = 0.5 g per penny

The 200 g jar is the best value for money because you get more relish per penny.

With any question comparing 'value for money', <u>DIVIDE BY THE PRICE</u> (in pence) and it will always be the <u>BIGGEST ANSWER</u> that is the <u>BEST VALUE FOR MONEY</u>.

...or Find the **Price per Unit**

For some questions, the numbers mean it's easier to <u>divide by the amount</u> to get the <u>cost per unit</u> (e.g. per gram, per litre, etc.). In that case, the <u>best buy</u> is the <u>smallest answer</u> — the <u>lowest cost</u> per unit. Doing the example above in this way, you'd get:

The relish in the 100 g jar costs   250p ÷ 100 g = 2.5p per gram
The relish in the 200 g jar costs   320p ÷ 200 g = 1.6p per gram
The relish in the 400 g jar costs   800p ÷ 400 g = 2p per gram

The 200 g jar is the best value for money because it's the cheapest per gram.

Find the amount per penny or find the price per unit...

All you need to know is that the best buy is the biggest amount per penny or the lowest cost per unit.

Percentage Increase and Decrease

There are two different ways of finding the new amount after a percentage increase or decrease:

Method 1 — Find the % then Add or Subtract

EXAMPLE: **A dress has increased in price by 30%. It originally cost £40. What is the new price of the dress?**

1) Divide by 100 to turn the percentage into a decimal.   30% = 30 ÷ 100 = 0.3

2) Multiply the original amount by the decimal.   0.3 × £40 = £12 ← This is 30% of £40.

3) Add this onto (or subtract from) the original value.   £40 + £12 = £52

It's an increase so add it on.

Method 2 — The Multiplier Method

Find the multiplier — the decimal that represents the percentage change.
E.g. 5% increase is 1.05 (= 1 + 0.05) and 5% decrease is 0.95 (= 1 – 0.05).

EXAMPLE: **A hat is reduced in price by 20% in the sales. It originally cost £12. What is the new price of the hat?**

1) Find the multiplier.   20% decrease = 1 – 0.20 = 0.8 ←

2) Multiply the original amount by the multiplier.   £12 × 0.8 = £9.60

A % decrease has a multiplier less than 1.

Simple Interest

Simple interest means a certain percentage of the original amount is paid at regular intervals (usually once a year). The amount of interest is the same every time it's paid.

EXAMPLE: **Elsa invests £1000 in an account which pays 2% simple interest each year. How much interest will she earn in 5 years?**

1) Work out the amount of interest earned in one year: 2% = 2 ÷ 100 = 0.02
2% of £1000 = 0.02 × £1000 = £20

2) Multiply by 5 to get the total interest for 5 years: 5 × £20 = £100

Learn both methods — then you can pick your favourite...

The multiplier method might be quicker than finding the percentage then adding or subtracting it, but you should use whichever method you're most comfortable with.

Warm-Up and Practice Questions

That's ratio and proportion done and dusted. Check out how much sank in by having a go at these warm-up questions. If you get any wrong, have a look back over the last few pages, then try again.

Warm-Up Questions

1) Give the following ratios in their simplest form: a) 7 : 21   b) 12 : 10   c) 8 : 28

2) 35 litres of fruit punch is made from orange juice and apple juice in the ratio 4 : 3.
   a) How much orange juice is used?   b) How much apple juice is used?

3) 4 lumberjacks chop 12 trees in a day.
   How many trees could 13 lumberjacks chop in a day?

4) 240 g of flour is needed to make enough dough balls for 6 people.
   How much flour do you need to serve 15 people?

5) Which is the better buy: 400 ml of juice for £1.60, or 1 litre of the same juice for £3?

6) An antique clock costing £4000 is reduced by 15% in a sale. What is its new price?

7) An account pays 5% simple interest each year.
   In 4 years, how much interest would £80 make?

Practice Questions

By now you should be nicely warmed up — I'd hate for you to pull a mathematical muscle doing these strenuous practice questions. Have a look at this worked question before you sprint on to the others.

1   To build a new house, 8 windows and 2 doors are needed.

a)   Write the ratio of windows to doors in its simplest form.

Write the numbers as a ratio: ÷2 ⟮ **8:2** ⟯ ÷2
Divide both sides by 2:   **4:1**

....................4:1....................
[1 mark]

b)   The builders ordered 36 windows for some new houses.
How many doors do they need to complete the houses?

Use the ratio from part a).   **4:1**
You need to multiply by 9 to get from   ×9 ⟮   ⟯ ×9
4 to 36 — so do that to both sides.   **36:9**

....................9....................
[1 mark]

c)   For any house, the cost of the windows and doors is split in the ratio 2 : 3. If the builders spend £2500 on new windows and doors, how much do they spend in total on windows?

Add up the parts of the ratio: **2 + 3 = 5 parts**

Divide the total cost by the number of parts: **£2500 ÷ 5 = £500**

Multiply the cost of one part by
the 'windows share' to find the cost: **£500 × 2 = £1000**

....................£1000....................
[2 marks]

Practice Questions

2 Alice bought 14 calculators for £28. How much would 22 calculators cost?

£ ....
[2 marks]

3 Shaun and David share 35 DVDs in the ratio 5 : 2. How many DVDs does Shaun get?

....
[3 marks]

4 The cost of a mobile phone fell by 15% when the new model came out.
The phone originally cost £120. How much does it cost now?

£ ....
[2 marks]

5 Washing up liquid comes in bottles of three different sizes: 500 ml for £2.50,
700 ml for £4.20 or 1.2 litres for £5.40. Which bottle is the best value for money?

....
[2 marks]

6 The Wisemoney Bank pays 1.5% simple interest each year. Raul invests £2000.
How much money will he have in total after 10 years?

£ ....
[3 marks]

Metric and Imperial Units

There's nothing too bad on this page — just some facts to learn, but plenty of them.
Take a breath, steel yourself, then dive in and see how you get on.

Metric Units

1) Length   mm, cm, m, km
2) Area   mm², cm², m², km²,
3) Volume   mm³, cm³, m³, ml, litres
4) Mass   g, kg, tonnes
5) Speed   km/h, m/s

'Weight' is often used instead of 'mass' in everyday language.

MEMORISE THESE KEY FACTS:

1 cm = 10 mm	1 tonne = 1000 kg
1 m = 100 cm	1 litre = 1000 ml
1 km = 1000 m	1 litre = 1000 cm³
1 kg = 1000 g	1 cm³ = 1 ml

Imperial Units

1) Length   inches, feet, yards, miles
2) Area   square inches, square feet, square miles
3) Volume   cubic inches, cubic feet, gallons, pints
4) Mass   ounces, pounds, stones, tons
5) Speed   mph (miles per hour)

IMPERIAL UNIT CONVERSIONS

1 foot = 12 inches
1 yard = 3 feet
1 gallon = 8 pints
1 stone = 14 pounds (lb)
1 pound = 16 ounces (oz)

Metric-Imperial Conversions

Learn these approximate conversions to help you change from metric units to imperial units:

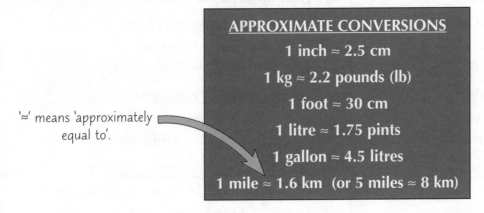

APPROXIMATE CONVERSIONS

1 inch ≈ 2.5 cm

1 kg ≈ 2.2 pounds (lb)

1 foot ≈ 30 cm

1 litre ≈ 1.75 pints

1 gallon ≈ 4.5 litres

1 mile ≈ 1.6 km   (or 5 miles ≈ 8 km)

'≈' means 'approximately equal to'.

REVISION TASK

Learn these metric and imperial conversions...

Cover up the page and scribble down all the different metric units. Then write down as many of the imperial units and approximate metric-imperial conversions as you can remember. If you missed any, cover up the page again and have another go until you're happy with it.

Conversion Factors

A <u>conversion factor</u> is a number that tells you <u>how many times bigger or smaller</u> one thing is compared to another. You can use them to <u>change</u> between different units.
E.g. a kilogram (kg) is 1000 times bigger than a gram (g), so the conversion factor is 1000.

3-Step **Method** for Converting

1) Find the <u>conversion factor</u> (always easy).
2) <u>Multiply AND divide</u> by it
3) <u>Choose the common-sense answer</u>.

Examples of Converting

EXAMPLE: **A zoo has a lemur which weighs 3000 g. What is the lemur's weight in kg?**

1) Find the <u>conversion factor</u>

1 kg = 1000 g
Conversion factor = 1000

2) <u>Multiply AND divide</u> by it

3000 × 1000 = 3 000 000 kg — ridiculous
3000 ÷ 1000 = 3 kg — makes sense

3) Choose the <u>sensible answer</u>

3000 g = 3 kg

EXAMPLE: **Nicholas is in a golf competition and has a 30 foot putt to win the match.**

a) How far is this in yards?

1) Find the <u>conversion factor</u>

1 yard = 3 feet
Conversion factor = 3

2) <u>Multiply AND divide</u> by it

30 × 3 = 90 yards
30 ÷ 3 = 10 yards

3) Choose the <u>sensible answer</u> — there should be fewer yards than feet

30 feet = 10 yards

b) How far is this in inches?

1) Find the <u>conversion factor</u>

1 foot = 12 inches
Conversion factor = 12

2) <u>Multiply AND divide</u> by it

30 × 12 = 360 inches
30 ÷ 12 = 2.5 inches

3) Choose the <u>sensible answer</u> — there should be more inches than feet

30 feet = 360 inches

The conversion factor is the number in the conversion that isn't 1...

Once you've got the facts on the previous page straight in your head, you'll need to know how to use the 3-step method for converting. Make sure you understand all these examples before moving on.

Section Three — Ratio, Proportion and Rates of Change

Conversion Factors

Here are some trickier examples of conversion factors. Don't fret, just use the same method as you saw on the previous page and you'll sail straight to the answer.

Converting Between **Metric** and **Imperial**

Converting from metric units to imperial units looks worse than it is.
If you need a reminder about conversion factors, have another quick look at the last page.

EXAMPLE: **Mrs Wu has made 36 litres of orange squash for the school sports day.**

a) How many gallons of orange squash has she made?

1) Find the conversion factor

1 gallon ≈ 4.5 litres
Conversion factor = 4.5

2) Multiply AND divide by it

36 × 4.5 = 162 gallons
36 ÷ 4.5 = 8 gallons

3) Choose the sensible answer — there should be fewer gallons than litres

36 litres = 8 gallons

b) If she poured the squash into pint glasses, how many glasses could she fill?

1) Find the conversion factor

1 litre ≈ 1.75 pints
Conversion factor = 1.75

2) Multiply AND divide by it

36 × 1.75 = 63 pints
36 ÷ 1.75 = 20.571... pints

3) Choose the sensible answer — there should be more pints than litres

36 litres will fill 63 pint glasses

EXAMPLE: **Write the following measurements in order of size from smallest to largest:**
8500 cm³, 6.5 litres, 14 pints

1) First, write all three measurements in the same unit — I'm going to choose litres

1 litre = 1000 cm³
Conversion factor = 1000

1 litre ≈ 1.75 pints
Conversion factor = 1.75

8500 × 1000 = 8500000 litres ✗
8500 ÷ 1000 = 8.5 litres ✓

14 × 1.75 = 24.5 litres ✗
14 ÷ 1.75 = 8 litres ✓

2) Write them out in order

6.5 litres, 8 litres, 8.5 litres

3) Convert back to the original units

6.5 litres, 14 pints, 8500 cm³

Learn the method for converting — it's the same every time...

The method for converting between metric and imperial units never changes — only the conversion factor does. Always remember to check your answer looks sensible.

Reading Timetables

I'm sure you're a dab hand at reading clocks, but here's a quick reminder...

am means morning.
pm means afternoon or evening.

12 am (00:00) means midnight.
12 pm (12:00) means noon.

12-hour clock	24-hour clock
12.00 am	00:00
1.12 am	01:12
12.15 pm	12:15
1.47 pm	13:47
11.32 pm	23:32

The hours on 12- and 24-hour clocks are different after 1 pm. To go from 12-hour to 24-hour add 12 hours, and subtract 12 go the other way.

$$3.24 \text{ pm} \underset{- \, 12 \text{ h}}{\overset{+ \, 12 \text{ h}}{\rightleftarrows}} 15:24$$

Do **Time** Calculations in **Stages**

 **EXAMPLE:** **How many minutes are there between 7.20 pm and 10.05 pm?**

1) Split the time between 7.20 pm and 10.05 pm into simple stages.

7.20 pm   9.20 pm   10.00 pm   10.05 pm
      + 2 hours   + 40 minutes   + 5 minutes

2) Convert the hours to minutes.   2 hours = 2 × 60 = 120 minutes

3) Add to get the total minutes.   120 + 40 + 5 = 165 minutes

Avoid calculators — the decimal answers they give are confusing, e.g. 2.5 hours = 2 hours 30 mins, NOT 2 hours 50 mins.

Using **Timetables**

If you've ever been to a bus or train station you'll have seen lots of timetables. Reading a timetable to find what bus or train to catch is a pretty important skill.

EXAMPLE: **Look at the timetable below. What is the time of the latest train leaving Cramford that would get you to Cloudy Lane before 3.00 pm?**

1) Work out the time you need to be at Cloudy Lane using the 24-hour clock.

3:00 + 12:00 = 15:00 (or 1500)

2) Look across the row for the Cloudy Lane times and find the latest train that arrives before 1500.

1415, 1432, 1449 and 1506

Train Timetable				
Ashingtown	1315	1332	1349	1406
Cramford	1330	1347	1404	1421
Newpeth	1345	1402	1419	1436
Bedcastle	1400	1417	1434	1451
Cloudy Lane	1415	1432	1449	1506

3) Look up that column until you get to the Cramford row, and read off the time that train leaves Cramford. Change your answer back into the 12-hour clock.

1404 (or 14:04), so in the 12-hour clock: 14:04 − 12:00 = 2.04 pm

 Check whether the question is in the 12- or 24-hour clock...
If you find time calculations confusing, draw a timeline for the information in the question.

Warm-Up and Practice Questions

For conversions, just find the conversion factor, then multiply and divide by it and think about which answer makes more sense. When you're ready, try these warm-up questions for practice.

Warm-Up Questions

1) Convert: a) 1 metre into centimetres   b) 1 foot into inches   c) 1 pound into ounces

2) Convert the following: a) 5600 cm³ into litres   b) 7 stone into pounds

3) A goat eats 80 ounces of food in a day.
How many pounds of food does the goat eat in a day?

4) An elephant statue weighs 660 pounds. Roughly how much does it weigh in kilograms?

5) Write the following measurements in increasing order of size: 2 metres, 7 feet, 180 cm

6) Write 13:32 using the 12-hour clock.

7) A film lasts 145 minutes. a) How long is this in hours and minutes?
b) If you start watching at 8:15 pm, what time will you finish?

Practice Questions

Have a look at this worked practice question — then try the questions on the next page for yourself. Once you've done them, you'll have been converted into a conversions expert.

1   Mr Roe is struggling with the metric system.

a) He knows his car will hold 12 gallons of petrol. Approximately how many litres is this?

First, find the conversion factor: **1 gallon ≈ 4.5 litres, so conversion factor = 4.5**
Then multiply and divide: **12 × 4.5 = 54 litres,   12 ÷ 4.5 = 2.66... litres**
Choose the sensible answer — there
should be more litres than gallons.

...........54........ litres
[2 marks]

b) In a recent medical test, he weighed 198 lb. Roughly what was his weight in kilograms?

1 kg ≈ 2.2 pounds, so conversion factor = 2.2
198 × 2.2 = 435.6 kg,   198 ÷ 2.2 = 90 kg

You'd expect fewer kg than pounds,
so choose the smaller answer.

...........90........ kg
[2 marks]

c) Mr Roe's height was also measured. It was found to be 1.80 m.
Calculate his approximate height in feet.

1.80 m = 180 cm   **1 foot ≈ 30 cm, so conversion factor = 30**
180 × 30 = 5400 feet,   180 ÷ 30 = 6 feet

You'd expect
fewer feet than
cm, so this is
the answer.

...........6........ feet
[2 marks]

Section Three — Ratio, Proportion and Rates of Change

Practice Questions

2   Justine is buying lemonade for a party.
    Each cup holds 220 ml and she has 300 cups to fill.

    a)   Calculate how much lemonade she needs to buy in millilitres.

    .... ml
    [1 mark]

    b)   Use your answer to part a) to find how much lemonade she needs to buy in litres.

    .... litres
    [1 mark]

3   Eric is looking at the timetable for his new school. Each lesson is 50 minutes long.

    a)   The last lesson finishes at 15:35. What time is this in the 12-hour clock?

    ....
    [1 mark]

    b)   On Friday mornings, his Maths lesson lasts twice as long as a normal lesson.
         If his Maths lesson starts at 9.05 am, what time will it finish?

    ....
    [2 marks]

4   Use the bus timetable given to
    answer the following questions.

Penny Lane	0715	0730	...	1715	1800
Tuppence Street	0725	0742	...	1733	1812
Shilling Drive	0756	0821	...	1805	1859
Thrifty Avenue	0813	0838	...	1833	1925
Bus Station	0820	0850	...	1845	1955

    a)   If Mandeep catches the 7.25 am
         bus from Tuppence Street,
         what time will he get to the bus station? Give your answer in the 12-hour clock.

    ....
    [1 mark]

    b)   One morning he doesn't arrive at the bus stop on Tuppence Street until 7.30 am.
         How long does he have to wait until the next bus?

    .... minutes
    [1 mark]

    c)   His mum works on Thrifty Avenue. She needs to get to the bus station
         to meet Mandeep before 7.15 pm. What time is the latest bus she can catch?
         Give your answer in the 12-hour clock.

    ....
    [1 mark]

Section Three — Ratio, Proportion and Rates of Change

Maps

Scales tell you what a distance on a map or drawing represents in real life. They can be written in different ways, but they all say something like "1 cm represents 5 km".

Map Scales

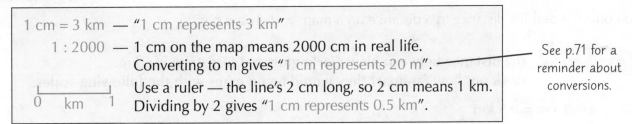

1 cm = 3 km — "1 cm represents 3 km"

1 : 2000 — 1 cm on the map means 2000 cm in real life.
Converting to m gives "1 cm represents 20 m".

Use a ruler — the line's 2 cm long, so 2 cm means 1 km.
Dividing by 2 gives "1 cm represents 0.5 km".

|——————|
0   km   1

See p.71 for a reminder about conversions.

To convert between maps and real life, learn these rules:

- Make sure your scale is of the form "1 cm = ..."
- To find **REAL-LIFE** distances, **MULTIPLY** by the **SCALE**.
- To find **MAP** distances, **DIVIDE** by the **SCALE**.
- Always check your answer looks sensible.

Converting From **Map Distances** to **Real-Life Distances**

To convert a distance on a map to a real-life distance you always multiply.

EXAMPLE: **This map shows three places in the UK.**

a) **Work out the distance from Grimsby to Scunthorpe in km.**

1) Measure with a ruler:
   Distance on map = 3 cm

2) Read off the scale:
   Scale is 1 cm = 10 km

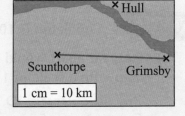

× Hull

× Scunthorpe   × Grimsby

| 1 cm = 10 km |

3) For real life, multiply:
   Real distance is: 3 × 10 = 30 km   This looks sensible. ✓

b) **Work out the distance from Scunthorpe to Hull in miles.**

1) Measure with a ruler:
   Distance on map = 2 cm

2) Read off the scale:
   Scale is 1 cm = 10 km

3) For real life, multiply:
   Real distance is: 2 × 10 = 20 km

4) Convert to miles (see p.72-73):
   1 mile ≈ 1.6 km, so conversion factor = 1.6

   20 × 1.6 = 32,   20 ÷ 1.6 = 12.5

   Choose the sensible answer. There should be fewer miles than kilometres.

   So the real distance is approximately 12.5 miles

REVISION TASK

Always pay close attention to the scale on the map...

Only one set of rules to learn here, and they work for both maps and scale drawings (p.79), so there are no excuses for not knowing them. Cover the page and jot them down.

Maps

If you've mastered the previous page, this one should be a doddle — it's the same rules with a few directions thrown in for good measure.

Converting From **Real-Life Distances** to **Map Distances**

To convert a real-life distance to a distance on a map, you always divide.

EXAMPLE: **The distance between New Garlington and Jordstone is 6 km.**
Work out how far apart they would be on maps with the following scales:

a) 1 cm = 0.5 km

Divide the real-life distance by the scale to find the map distance.

Real-life distance = <u>6 km</u>

Scale is <u>1 cm = 0.5 km</u>

6 ÷ 0.5 = 12 cm

b) 1 : 100 000

Work out the scale in <u>cm : km</u>:

Divide the real-life distance by the scale:

1 cm : 100 000 cm = 1 cm : 1000 m
= <u>1 cm : 1 km</u>

6 ÷ 1 = 6 cm

Compass Directions

Compass points describe the direction of something. You'll have seen a compass before — make sure you know all 8 directions.

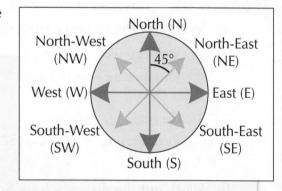

EXAMPLE: **Puddleton is 10 km east of Muddleton.**

a) How far apart would they be on a map with a scale of 1 cm = 5 km?

Real-life distance = 10 km
Scale is 1 cm = 5 km

 Divide for a <u>map distance</u>.

Distance on map = 10 ÷ 5 = 2 cm   This looks <u>sensible</u>. ✓

b) Mark Puddleton on the map on the right.

Measure 2 cm to the <u>east</u> (right) of Muddleton:

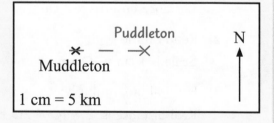

You need to know all 8 of the compass directions...

If you're struggling to learn the points of the compass use '<u>N</u>aughty <u>E</u>lephants <u>S</u>quirt <u>W</u>ater' to remember <u>N</u>orth <u>E</u>ast <u>S</u>outh <u>W</u>est. Don't forget to start at the top and work clockwise.

Scale Drawings

You get to do some <u>drawing</u> on this page, so prepare yourself for some serious amounts of fun.

You can go from the **Scale Drawing** to **Real Life**...

<u>Scale drawings</u> work just like <u>maps</u>. You'll have to use the rules on page 77 to convert between real life and scale drawings.

 **EXAMPLE:** **This is a scale drawing of Josephine's garden. 1 cm represents 2 m.**

a) **Find the real length and width of the patio in metres.**

1) Measure with a <u>ruler</u>.

Length on drawing = 3 cm
Width on drawing = 1.5 cm

2) <u>Multiply</u> to get real-life length.

Real length = 3 × 2 = 6 m
Real width = 1.5 × 2 = 3 m ⟵ Real-life units are in m.

Scale drawings will often (although not always) be shown on a grid.

...or from **Real Life** to a **Scale Drawing**

b) **Josephine's pond is 3 m long and 2 m wide. Draw the pond on the scale drawing.**

1) <u>Divide</u> to get the scale drawing length and width.

Length on drawing = 3 ÷ 2 = <u>1.5 cm</u>
Width on drawing = 2 ÷ 2 = <u>1 cm</u>

2) <u>Draw</u> the pond using a <u>ruler</u> in any sensible position and label it.

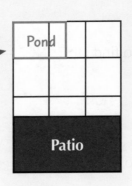

Make sure your scale drawings are always accurate...

There's no point doing all the calculations correctly if you get sloppy when it comes to measuring or drawing. Make sure you always use a ruler for drawing and don't forget to label what you've drawn.

Speed

Learn the formula triangle on this page and it'll give you three formulas for the price of one...

Speed = Distance ÷ Time

Speed is the distance travelled per unit time — e.g. the number of km per hour or metres per second. This is the basic formula for calculating speed from distance and time:

$$\text{SPEED} = \frac{\text{DISTANCE}}{\text{TIME}}$$

You also need to be able to find distance from speed and time, and time from speed and distance. Luckily there's no need for any algebra — it all becomes simple if you use the formula triangle below.

Using the **Formula Triangle**

A formula triangle is a handy tool for remembering formulas.

Here's the formula triangle for speed — use the words SaD Times to help you remember the order of the letters (S ^{D} T).

So if it's a question on speed, distance and time, just say SAD TIMES.

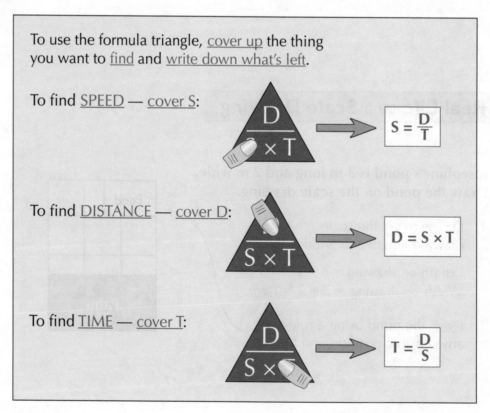

To use the formula triangle, cover up the thing you want to find and write down what's left.

To find SPEED — cover S:

$$S = \frac{D}{T}$$

To find DISTANCE — cover D:

$$D = S \times T$$

To find TIME — cover T:

$$T = \frac{D}{S}$$

Cover up what you want to find on the formula triangle...

REVISION TASK The best way to remember this formula triangle is to cover the page and scribble it down. Then try using the formula triangle to write down the formulas for speed, distance and time.

Speed

Make sure you're happy with previous page before you tackle this one. Once you've learnt the formula triangle, you can use it to solve any <u>speed</u>, <u>distance</u> or <u>time</u> problem.

Speed is **Measured** in "Distance per Time"

EXAMPLE:

a) A sled travelled 800 m in 40 seconds. What was the average speed of the sled?

1) Write down the <u>formula triangle</u>.

2) You want speed, so <u>covering S</u> gives: $S = \dfrac{D}{T}$

3) <u>Put in</u> the numbers. $S = \dfrac{800 \text{ metres}}{40 \text{ seconds}}$

4) Don't forget the <u>units</u>. $= 20$ m/s

b) A snowmobile travelled 35 miles in 1 hour and 15 minutes. Find the average speed of the snowmobile in miles per hour.

1) Convert the units.
15 minutes = 0.25 hours,
so 1 hour and 15 minutes = 1.25 hours

2) Write down the <u>formula triangle</u>.

3) You want speed, so <u>covering S</u> gives: $S = \dfrac{D}{T}$

4) <u>Put in</u> the numbers. $S = \dfrac{35 \text{ miles}}{1.25 \text{ hours}}$

5) Don't forget the <u>units</u>. $= 28$ mph

Use the Speed to Find **Distance** or **Time**

EXAMPLE:

A bike travels at 21 miles per hour for 2 hours. How far has it travelled?

1) Write down the <u>formula triangle</u>.

2) You want distance, so <u>covering D</u> gives: $D = S \times T$

3) <u>Put in</u> the numbers. $D = 21 \times 2$

4) Give the <u>units</u>. $= 42$ miles

EXAMPLE:

A car travels 30 km at 60 km per hour. How long does this take?

1) Write down the <u>formula triangle</u>.

2) You want time, so <u>covering T</u> gives: $T = \dfrac{D}{S}$

3) <u>Put in</u> the numbers. $T = \dfrac{30 \text{ km}}{60 \text{ km/h}}$

4) Give the <u>units</u>. $= 0.5$ hours
$= 30$ minutes

Don't forget to include the units in your answer...

To write the units for speed, put the units for the distance, then a /, then the units for time. The slash means 'per', e.g. km/h means 'km per hour'. The exception is 'miles per hour' — just write 'mph'.

Warm-Up and Practice Questions

This is the last set of questions for this section — whizz through these warm-up questions, practice questions and revision questions, then you can have a well-earned cup of tea.

Warm-Up Questions

1) On a map with a scale of 1 cm = 10 km, Cambridge and Peterborough are 5 cm apart. Work out the real-life distance from Cambridge to Peterborough.

2) Piel and Tusk are 21 km apart. How far apart would they be on a map with scale 1 cm = 3 km?

3) Amani makes a scale drawing of the town park, where 1 cm represents 2 m. A rectangular fountain measures 2 m by 6 m. What would it measure on the scale drawing?

4) A cannonball travelled at an average speed of 20 m/s for 10 seconds. How far did it travel?

5) Sian runs 6 km in 36 minutes. What is her speed in km/h?

Practice Questions

Here are some worked practice questions to guide you through the perilous page ahead. Remember to take your time and write down each step of your working so you don't make any silly mistakes.

1   A company makes model trains on a scale of 1 : 64.

    a)   How many centimetres long would a train be in real life if the model measured 37.5 cm?

        1 cm on the model = 64 cm in real life   This is 24 m, which is a

        To find the real-life length,   **37.5 × 64 = 2400 cm** ⟵ sensible length for a train.
multiply by the scale:

        ....2400........................ cm
[1 mark]

    b)   What is the length of the model of a train measuring 20 m long in real life? Give your answer in cm.

        64 m in real life = 1 m on the model

        To find the model length,   **20 ÷ 64 = 0.3125 m**
divide by the scale:

        Multiply by 100 to convert   **0.3125 m × 100 = 31.25 cm**
your answer to cm:

        ....31.25........................ cm
[2 marks]

2   A rocket travels at 4.8 miles per second when it leaves Earth. How long would it take for the rocket to travel 30 miles?

        Write down the formula, $\text{Time} = \dfrac{\text{Distance}}{\text{Speed}}$
then put in the numbers.

        $= \dfrac{30}{4.8} = 6.25 \text{ seconds}$

        ....6.25........................ seconds
[2 marks]

Practice Questions

3   The map shows the location of 4 towns.

   a)   What is the real-life distance between
      Beachby and Cressford?
      Give your answer in kilometres.

                          .... km
                             [2 marks]

           Magton
             •
                                   •
                                  Cressford
                                 N
         Loppham •   ↑
     1 cm = 5 km   • Beachby

   b)   The town of Topshot is 20 km from Magton.
      How many centimetres apart would they be on the map?

                                          .... cm
                                          [1 mark]

   c)   Topshot is east of Magton. Mark the location of Topshot on the map.

                                          [1 mark]

4   a)   An elephant swam 6 km in 4 hours. How fast did it swim?

                                        .... km/h
                                          [1 mark]

   b)   When the elephant reached land it began walking at an average speed of 3 km/h.
      Calculate how far it had travelled after walking for 5 hours.

                                        .... km
                                          [1 mark]

5   Juliet is making a scale drawing of her bedroom
   where 1 cm represents 0.5 m.

   a)   Find the real length and width of the drawers.

                         .... m by .... m
                                  [2 marks]

Drawers

Bed

Door

   b)   The bookcase is between the bed and the door. The bookcase measures 1 m by 0.25 m.
      Add the bookcase to the scale drawing.

                                           [2 marks]

Revision Summary

Just as you thought you were done with Section Three, some sneaky revision questions appeared.

- Try these questions and tick off each one when you get it right.
- When you've done all the questions for a topic and are completely happy with it, tick off the topic.

Ratios and Proportion (p.65-67) ☑

1. Reduce these ratios to their simplest form: a) 2:10   b) 14:16   c) 27:18 ☑
2. A tub contains screws and nails in the ratio 3:7.
   If there are 9 screws, how many nails are there? ☑
3. Isla and Emily split a 400 g cake in the ratio 5:3. How much cake does Isla get? ☑
4. 4 boys can wash 20 cars in a day. How many cars could 6 boys wash in a day? ☑
5. 20 sweets cost £1.40. How much would 12 sweets cost? ☑
6. A recipe for 4 people requires 20 olives. How many olives are needed for 18 people? ☑
7. A shop sells three different sizes of cheese: 300 g for £1.50, 450 g for £2
   and 750 g for £3. Which is the best buy? ☑

Percentage Increase and Decrease (p.68) ☑

8. A shop increases its prices by 15%. How much does a £6 mug cost after the increase? ☑
9. The price of a £1200 bike has decreased by 35%. How much is it worth now? ☑
10. Kamil invests £150 in an account that pays 1% simple interest each year.
    How much will there be in the account after 4 years? ☑

Units, Conversions and Time (p.71-74) ☑

11. From memory, write down all the metric unit conversions and all the imperial unit
    conversions from page 71. Now do the same for the metric-imperial conversions. ☑
12. Convert 6000 mm into cm. ☑
13. Convert 360 inches into yards. ☑
14. A large watermelon weighs 10 kg. Approximately what is this in pounds? ☑
15. Convert the following: a) 80 km to miles   b) 2.5 feet to cm ☑
16. A film starts at 6.40 pm and finishes at 8.20 pm. How long is the film in minutes? ☑

Maps and Scale Drawings (p.77-79) ☑

17. The distance between two towns is 20 miles.
    How far apart would they be on a map with a scale of 1 cm:5 miles? ☑
18. On a scale drawing, the dimensions of a car park are 5 cm by 2.5 cm.
    The scale is 1 cm = 10 m. What are the real-life dimensions of the car park? ☑
19. Phillip starts at his home and walks 2 km south to the bus station. He then takes the bus
    4 km west to the cinema. Make a scale drawing of his journey with scale 1 cm = 2 km. ☑

Speed (p.80-81) ☑

20. A runner ran a 1500 m race in 4 minutes 10 seconds. What was her average speed in m/s? ☑
21. Ramin cycles for 3 hours at a speed of 25 km/h. How far does he cycle? ☑

Symmetry

There are two types of <u>symmetry</u> you need to know — <u>line symmetry</u> and <u>rotational symmetry</u>.

Line Symmetry

This is where you draw one or more <u>MIRROR LINES</u> across a shape
and both sides will <u>fold exactly</u> together.

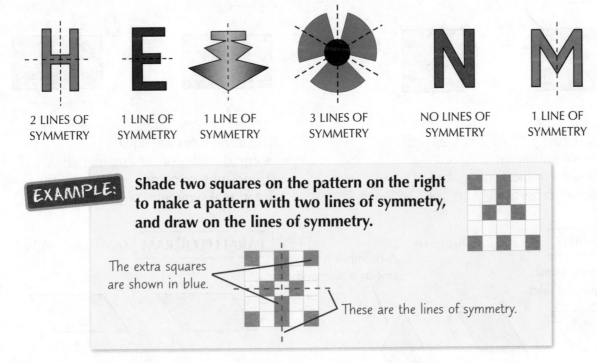

| 2 LINES OF SYMMETRY | 1 LINE OF SYMMETRY | 1 LINE OF SYMMETRY | 3 LINES OF SYMMETRY | NO LINES OF SYMMETRY | 1 LINE OF SYMMETRY |

EXAMPLE: **Shade two squares on the pattern on the right
to make a pattern with two lines of symmetry,
and draw on the lines of symmetry.**

The extra squares
are shown in blue.

These are the lines of symmetry.

Rotational Symmetry

This is where you can <u>rotate</u> the shape into different positions that <u>look exactly the same</u>.

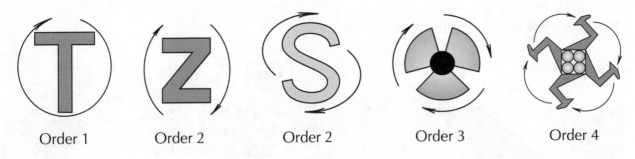

Order 1   Order 2   Order 2   Order 3   Order 4

The <u>ORDER OF ROTATIONAL SYMMETRY</u> is the posh way of saying:
'how many different positions look the same'.

- You should say the Z-shape above has '<u>rotational symmetry of order 2</u>'.
- When a shape has <u>only 1 position</u> (like the T above) you can <u>either</u> say that it has
'rotational symmetry of <u>order 1</u>' or that it has '<u>NO rotational symmetry</u>'.

REVISION TIP

You can use a mirror to find lines of symmetry...

Try standing a mirror on the shapes at the top of the page — when the mirror is on a line of
symmetry, the image of the shape that you can see should look the same as the original shape.

Quadrilaterals

There are lots of <u>quadrilaterals</u> for you to learn on this page. You'll need to be able to draw them, spell their names correctly and learn all of their properties — so read on carefully.

Quadrilaterals (Four-Sided Shapes)

SQUARE   The little square means it's a right angle.

 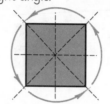

<u>4 equal sides</u>
<u>4 equal angles</u> of <u>90°</u> (<u>right angles</u>).
<u>4 lines</u> of symmetry,
rotational symmetry of <u>order 4</u>.
Diagonals cross at <u>right angles</u>.

RECTANGLE

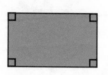 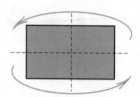

<u>2 pairs</u> of <u>equal sides</u>
(opposite sides are equal).
<u>4 equal angles</u> of <u>90°</u> (<u>right angles</u>).
<u>2 lines</u> of symmetry,
rotational symmetry of <u>order 2</u>.

RHOMBUS   (A square pushed over)

Matching arrows show parallel sides.

A rhombus is the same as a diamond.

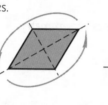 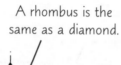

<u>4 equal sides</u> (opposite sides are <u>parallel</u>).
<u>2 pairs</u> of <u>equal angles</u>.
<u>2 lines</u> of symmetry,
rotational symmetry of <u>order 2</u>.
Diagonals cross at <u>right angles</u>.

PARALLELOGRAM   (A rectangle pushed over)

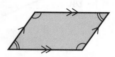 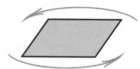

<u>2 pairs</u> of <u>equal sides</u> (each pair are <u>parallel</u>).
<u>2 pairs</u> of <u>equal angles</u>.
<u>NO lines</u> of symmetry,
rotational symmetry of <u>order 2</u>.

TRAPEZIUM

 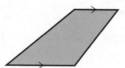

<u>1 pair</u> of <u>parallel sides</u>.
<u>NO lines</u> of symmetry*.
No rotational symmetry.

KITE

<u>2 pairs</u> of <u>equal sides</u>.
<u>1 pair</u> of <u>equal angles</u>.
<u>1 line</u> of symmetry.
No rotational symmetry.
Diagonals cross at <u>right angles</u>.

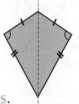

*except for an <u>isosceles trapezium</u> (a trapezium where the non-parallel sides are the <u>same length</u>), which has <u>1 line</u> of symmetry.

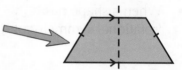

 REVISION TASK

Trapeziums either have one or no lines of symmetry...

Learn the names of all the shapes and make sure you know how to spell them (parallelogram is a tricky one). Then learn the properties of each shape, and have a go at drawing them all.

Triangles and Regular Polygons

There are some more 2D shapes coming up on this page — let's start off with all the different types of triangles, then build up to shapes with lots of sides.

Triangles (Three-Sided Shapes)

EQUILATERAL Triangles

3 equal sides and
3 equal angles of 60°.
3 lines of symmetry,
rotational symmetry of order 3.

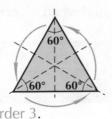

SCALENE Triangles

All three sides different.
All three angles different.
No symmetry (pretty obviously).

ISOSCELES Triangles

2 sides the same.
2 angles the same.
1 line of symmetry.
No rotational symmetry.

These dashes mean that the two sides are the same length.

RIGHT-ANGLED Triangles

1 right angle (90°).
No lines of symmetry*.

*except for a right-angled isosceles triangle, which has 1 line of symmetry.

Regular Polygons

A polygon is a many-sided shape. A regular polygon is one where all the sides and angles are the same. The regular polygons are a never-ending series of shapes with some fancy features.

EQUILATERAL TRIANGLE
3 sides
3 lines of symmetry
Rotational symmetry of order 3

SQUARE
4 sides
4 lines of symmetry
Rotational symmetry of order 4

REGULAR PENTAGON
5 sides
5 lines of symmetry
Rotational symmetry of order 5

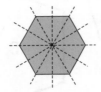

REGULAR HEXAGON
6 sides
6 lines of symmetry
Rotational symmetry of order 6

REGULAR HEPTAGON
7 sides
7 lines of symmetry
Rotational symmetry of order 7
(A 50p piece is like a heptagon.)

REGULAR OCTAGON
8 sides
8 lines of symmetry
Rotational symmetry of order 8

Regular polygons have equal sides and angles...

There's nothing too tricky on this page. Remember, once you know the number of sides of a regular polygon, you also know the number of lines of symmetry and its order of rotational symmetry.

Congruence

Here's a special word that's handy to know when you're describing shapes — <u>congruence</u>.
You need to be able to spot when two shapes are <u>congruent</u>, so best get your head around it now.

Congruent — Same Shape, Same Size

<u>Congruence</u> is a maths word which sounds really complicated when it's not.

> If two shapes are <u>**CONGRUENT**</u>, they are <u>**EXACTLY THE SAME**</u>
> — the <u>**SAME SIZE**</u> and the <u>**SAME SHAPE**</u>.

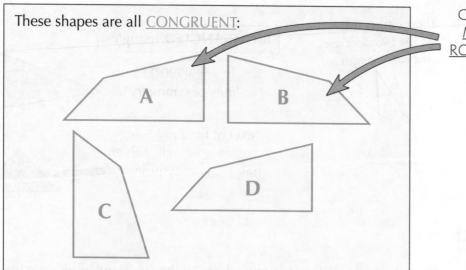

These shapes are all <u>CONGRUENT</u>:

Congruent shapes can be
<u>MIRROR IMAGES</u> or
<u>ROTATIONS</u> of each other.

EXAMPLE: **Two of the shapes below are congruent.**
Write down the letters of the congruent shapes.

Just pick out the two shapes that are <u>exactly the same</u> —
remember that the shape might have been <u>rotated</u> or <u>reflected</u>.

By eye, you can see that the congruent shapes are A and C.

When thinking about congruence, take a look in the mirror...

EXAM TIP If you're trying to work out if two shapes are congruent, only focus on their shape and size,
not which way they're facing — congruent shapes can be rotations or mirror images.

Similarity

There are already lots of important words in this section, but here's one more for you — similarity. Just make sure you don't get it mixed up with congruence...

Similar — Same Shape, Different Size

Similar has a special meaning in maths, but nothing complicated:

> If two shapes are **SIMILAR**, they are exactly the **SAME SHAPE** but **DIFFERENT SIZES**.

When you have similar shapes, the angles are always the same and one shape is an enlargement of the other (see p.116). So all circles are similar — so are equilateral triangles, squares, regular pentagons...

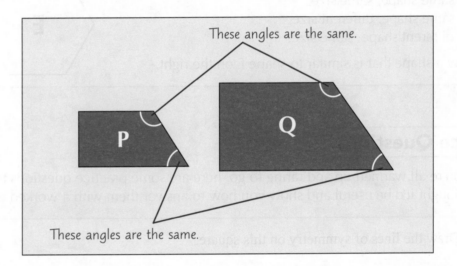

These angles are the same.

P   Q

These angles are the same.

EXAMPLE: **Two of the shapes below are similar.**
Write down the letters of the similar shapes.

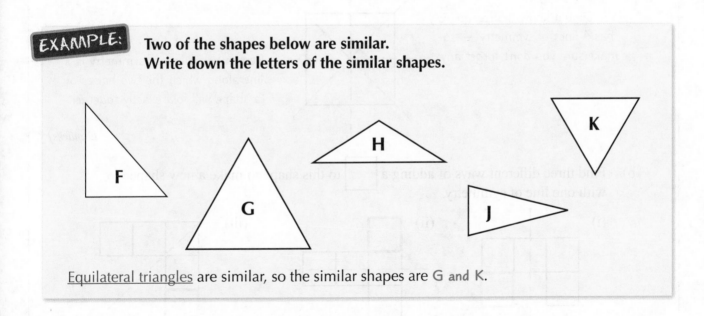

F   G   H   K   J

Equilateral triangles are similar, so the similar shapes are G and K.

Don't mix up congruence and similarity...

To help remember the difference between similarity and congruence, think 'similar siblings, congruent clones' — siblings are alike but not exactly the same, clones are identical.

Warm-Up and Practice Questions

Once you're happy with these pages, run through these warm-up questions so your mental muscles are eager and ready for the practice questions below. On your marks, get set, go...

Warm-Up Questions

1) How many lines of symmetry does a 'T' shape have?

2) What is the order of rotational symmetry of an 'H' shape?

3) I am thinking of a shape with four sides. It has 2 pairs of equal sides and its diagonals cross at right angles. It has no rotational symmetry. What is the name of the shape I'm thinking of?

4) A regular polygon has 20 sides. How many lines of symmetry does it have? What is its order of rotational symmetry?

5) Which of these describes congruent shapes?
   A: same shape, same size,
   B: same shape, different size,
   C: different shape, same size.

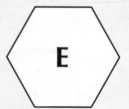

6) Draw a shape that is similar to shape E on the right.

Practice Questions

Now that you're all warmed up and raring to go, here are some practice questions to get stuck into. But first, I thought it'd be useful and show you how to answer them with a worked example.

1 a) Draw the lines of symmetry on this square.

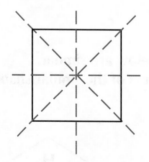

You should know that a square has 4 lines of symmetry — so make sure you don't forget any.

Remember, a line of symmetry is a line along which the two halves of a shape will fold exactly together.

[2 marks]

   b) Find three different ways of adding a ☐ to this shape to make a new shape with one line of symmetry.

(i)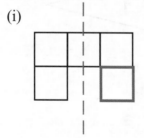

(ii)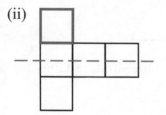

(iii)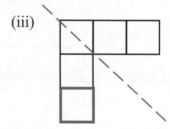

Check what you've done by adding the line of symmetry. You should be able to see whether your new shape will fold exactly together along it.

[3 marks]

Section Four — Geometry and Measures

Practice Questions

2   Fill in the missing numbers.

    a)   A parallelogram has .... pairs of equal sides (which are parallel).

        It has .... line(s) of symmetry and rotational symmetry of order ....

[3 marks]

    b)   An equilateral triangle has .... equal sides and .... line(s) of symmetry.

[2 marks]

    c)   A regular hexagon has .... equal sides and rotational symmetry of order ....

[2 marks]

3   Look at the following shapes.

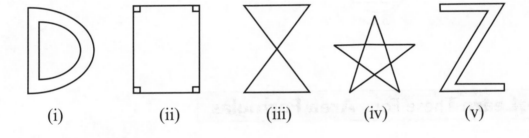

       (i)   (ii)   (iii)   (iv)   (v)

    a)   Draw all the lines of symmetry on each of the shapes.

[3 marks]

    b)   What is the order of rotational symmetry for each shape?

       (i) ....   (ii) ....   (iii) ....   (iv) ....   (v) ....

[3 marks]

4   Look at these four shapes and
    complete the sentences:

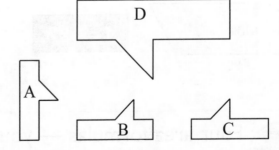

    a)   Shapes ...... and ...... are congruent.

[1 mark]

    b)   Shapes ...... , ... and ...... are similar.

[1 mark]

Perimeter and Area

Perimeter is the <u>distance</u> all the way around the <u>outside</u> of a <u>2D shape</u>.

Perimeter — **Distance** Around the **Edge** of a Shape

To find a <u>perimeter</u>, you <u>add up</u> the <u>lengths</u> of all the sides — here's the best way to do it:

> 1) Put a <u>big blob</u> at one corner and then <u>go around</u> the shape.
> 2) <u>Write</u> down the <u>length</u> of <u>every side</u> as you go along.
>   (Even sides that seem to have <u>no length</u> given — you must <u>work them out</u>.)
> 4) Keep going until you <u>get back</u> to the big blob.
> 5) <u>Add up</u> all the lengths you've written down.

EXAMPLE: **Find the perimeter of the shape drawn on the grid below. Each grid square represents 1 cm².**

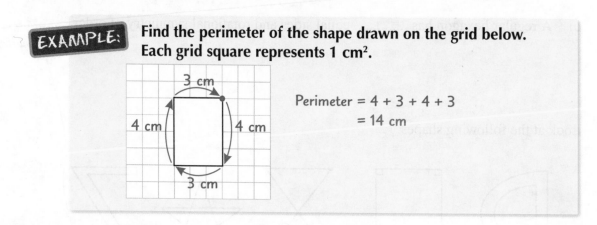

Perimeter = 4 + 3 + 4 + 3
= 14 cm

You Must **Learn** These Four **Area Formulas**

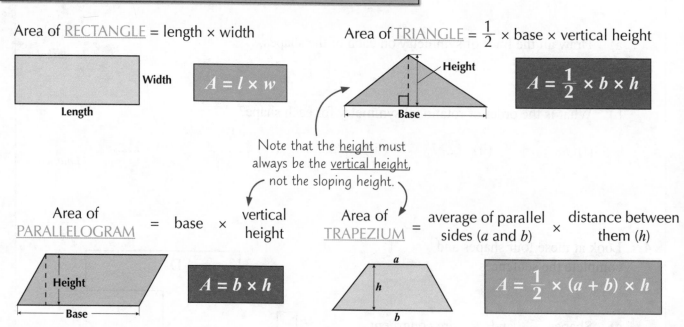

Area of <u>RECTANGLE</u> = length × width

$A = l \times w$

Area of <u>TRIANGLE</u> = $\frac{1}{2}$ × base × vertical height

$A = \frac{1}{2} \times b \times h$

Note that the <u>height</u> must always be the <u>vertical height</u>, not the sloping height.

Area of <u>PARALLELOGRAM</u> = base × vertical height

$A = b \times h$

Area of <u>TRAPEZIUM</u> = average of parallel sides (a and b) × distance between them (h)

$A = \frac{1}{2} \times (a + b) \times h$

REVISION TIP

Four area formulas — you'll have to learn them all...

These four area formulas are really important, so make sure you've memorised them all before moving on. (Actually, they might even turn out to be useful on the next page too...)

Areas

You've seen the area formulas — now you can see how to use them in questions.

Using the Area Formulas

Rectangle

EXAMPLE: **Find the area of the rectangle on the right.**

5 cm

2 cm

Just put the numbers into the formula:

area of rectangle = length × width

= 2 × 5

= 10 cm^2

Area is measured in square units (i.e. cm^2, m^2 etc.).

Triangle

EXAMPLE: **Find the area of the triangle below.**

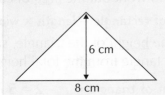

6 cm

8 cm

Just put the numbers into the formula:

area of triangle = $\frac{1}{2}$ × base × vertical height

= $\frac{1}{2}$ × 8 × 6

= 24 cm^2

Parallelogram

EXAMPLE: **Find the area of the parallelogram below.**

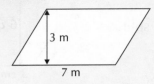

3 m

7 m

Use the formula for area:

area of parallelogram = base × vertical height

= 7 × 3

= 21 m^2

Trapezium

EXAMPLE: **Find the area of the trapezium below.**

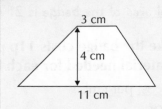

3 cm

4 cm

11 cm

Use the formula for area:

area of trapezium = $\frac{1}{2}$(a + b) × height

= $\frac{1}{2}$(3 + 11) × 4

= 7 × 4

= 28 cm^2

Square your units when working out areas...

The answer should be in square units of whatever units were used in the question. So a shape measured in mm will have an area in mm^2, and a shape measured in cm will have an area in cm^2.

Area of Compound Shapes

Make sure you know the <u>area formulas</u> from p.92 — you need them again here.

Areas of **More Complicated** Shapes

You sometimes have to find the area of <u>strange-looking</u> shapes. What you always find with these questions is that you can break the shape up into <u>simpler ones</u> that you can deal with.

> 1) <u>SPLIT THEM UP</u> into the basic shapes:
> <u>RECTANGLES</u>, <u>TRIANGLES</u>, etc.
> 2) Work out the area of each bit <u>SEPARATELY</u>.
> 3) Then <u>ADD THEM ALL TOGETHER</u>.

Basic Rectangle

Basic Triangle

EXAMPLE: **Find the area of the shape below.**

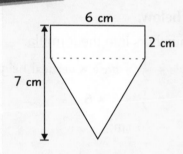

1) Split the shape into a <u>rectangle</u> and <u>triangle</u> as shown and work out the <u>area</u> of each shape:

Area of rectangle = length × width = 6 × 2 = <u>12 cm²</u>

2) To find the <u>height</u> of the triangle, subtract the height of the rectangle from the total height of the shape.

Height of triangle = 7 − 2 = 5 cm

Area of triangle = $\frac{1}{2}$ × base × height = $\frac{1}{2}$ × 6 × 5 = <u>15 cm²</u>

So the <u>total area</u> of shape = 12 + 15 = 27 cm²

EXAMPLE: **The shape of a school badge is shown on the right.**
a) Find the area of the badge.

You need to work out the <u>area</u> of the badge — so split it into two shapes (a <u>rectangle</u> and a <u>trapezium</u>):

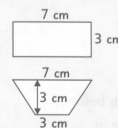

Area of the rectangle = l × w
= 7 × 3 = <u>21 cm²</u>

Area of the trapezium = $\frac{1}{2}$(a + b) × h
= $\frac{1}{2}$(7 + 3) × 3 = <u>15 cm²</u>

So the <u>total area</u> of the badge is 21 + 15 = 36 cm²

b) The material needed to make the badge costs 11p per cm².
Work out the cost of the material needed for each badge.

Just multiply the <u>area</u> by the <u>cost</u> per cm²:

Cost = 36 × 11 = 396p = £3.96

Add up the separate areas at the end...

As long as you know the area formulas, there's nothing on this page to trip you up — it's just a case of splitting up complicated shapes into basic shapes and working out the area of each bit separately.

Circles

Another page, another formula (or two) to learn. This time, it's all about <u>circles</u>...

Radius and Diameter

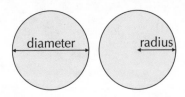

diameter

radius

The <u>DIAMETER</u> goes <u>right across</u> the circle, passing through the <u>centre</u>.
The <u>RADIUS</u> goes from the <u>centre</u> of the circle to any point on the <u>edge</u>.

The <u>DIAMETER IS EXACTLY DOUBLE THE RADIUS</u>

So if the <u>radius</u> is 4 cm, the <u>diameter</u> is 8 cm,
and if the <u>diameter</u> is 24 m, the <u>radius</u> is 12 m.

Area, Circumference and π

There are two more important formulas for you to <u>learn</u> — <u>circumference</u> and <u>area</u> of a circle.
The circumference is the <u>distance round the outside</u> of the circle (its <u>perimeter</u>).

1) <u>CIRCUMFERENCE</u> $= \pi \times$ diameter
$= \pi \times$ radius $\times 2$

$$C = \pi \times D \text{ or } C = 2 \times \pi \times r$$

$\pi = 3.141592.... = \underline{3.142}$ (approximately)
The <u>big thing</u> to remember is that π (<u>called "pi"</u>) is just an ordinary
number (3.14159...) which is often <u>rounded off</u> to <u>3.142</u>. You can
just <u>use the π button</u> on your <u>calculator</u> (which is <u>more accurate</u>).

2) <u>AREA</u> $= \pi \times$ (radius)^2

$$A = \pi \times r^2$$

EXAMPLE: **a) Find the circumference of the circle below. Give your answer to 1 d.p.**

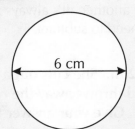

6 cm

You're given the diameter, so use $C = \pi \times D$:
Circumference $= \pi \times$ diameter
$= \pi \times 6$
$= 18.849... = 18.8$ cm (1 d.p.)

b) Find the area of the circle. Give your answer to 1 d.p.

Here, you need the <u>radius</u> to find the area — so <u>divide</u> the <u>diameter</u> by 2:
Radius = diameter ÷ 2 = 6 ÷ 2 = 3 cm
Now put the numbers into the <u>formula</u> for <u>area</u>:
Area $= \pi \times$ (radius)^2
$= \pi \times 3^2$
$= 28.274... = 28.3$ cm^2 (1 d.p.)

REVISION TASK

Don't mix up the formulas for area and circumference...

Make sure you learn the formulas properly. Scribble them down and re-write them until
you can write them again without looking. It's the best way of making sure they sink in.

Circle Questions

ALWAYS check that you're using the right value in circle formulas — don't get the radius and diameter muddled up. If you need the one you haven't been given, multiply or divide by 2.

Circumference Problems with Circles

There's a whole range of circle questions you could be asked — but if you learn the circle formulas you should be fine. Make sure you read the questions carefully to find out what you're being asked to do.

EXAMPLE: **Muna is planning a fun run in a park around a circular lake with radius 50 m. If the run needs to be at least 5 km long, what is the smallest number of laps of the lake needed to cover this distance?**

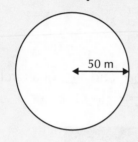

First find the diameter of the lake:

Diameter = radius × 2 = 50 × 2 = <u>100 m</u>

Now find the circumference of the lake:

Circumference = π × diameter = π × 100 = <u>314.159... m</u>

Convert the run distance to m (see p.72):

5 km = <u>5000 m</u>

Now divide the run distance by the circumference to see how many laps will be needed:

5000 ÷ 314.159... = 15.915...

So **16 laps** are needed to cover at least 5 km.

You need to round up as 15 laps wouldn't be far enough (it'd be less than 5 km).

Area Problems with Circles

With area questions, you'll sometimes have to subtract one area from another. It's always a good idea to draw a diagram — that way you can see which bit you need to subtract.

EXAMPLE: **Molly has a circular tablecloth with diameter 2 m. She cuts out a square with side length 1.4 m from the tablecloth, and throws away the rest of the cloth. How much cloth does she throw away? Give your answer to 2 d.p.**

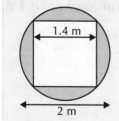

You need to find the shaded area by taking the area of the square away from the area of the circle:

The radius of the circle is 2 ÷ 2 = 1 m

Area of circle = π × r^2 = π × 1^2 = π × 1 = <u>3.141... m^2</u>

Area of square = 1.4 × 1.4 = <u>1.96 m^2</u>

Area thrown away = area of circle − area of square

= 3.141... − 1.96 = 1.181... = <u>1.18 m^2</u> (2 d.p.)

Draw a diagram when asked about circles...

Once you can find the circumference and area of a circle, you can tackle pretty much any circle question. Always draw a diagram to help you picture what the question is asking you to do.

Warm-Up and Practice Questions

Learn the stuff on the last few pages then have a go at the questions below
to check you've got it all nicely stored in your head. See? Easy as pi.

Warm-Up Questions

1) Find the perimeter of a square with sides of length 5 cm.

2) Find the perimeter of an equilateral triangle with sides of length 6 cm.

3) Find the area of a parallelogram with a base of 8 cm and a height of 5 cm.

4) The parallel sides of a trapezium measure 2 m and 6 m and the distance
between them is 7 m. Find the area of the trapezium.

5) Find the area of the shape on the right.

6) A circle has a radius of 13 cm. What is its diameter?

7) Find the circumference and area of a circle with
a diameter of 20 mm, both to 1 d.p.

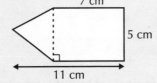

8) Arun has a circular lawn of radius 20 m with a circular fountain of radius 1 m
in the middle of it. Find the area of the lawn, giving your answer to 2 d.p.

Practice Questions

Now here are some lovely practice questions to help you learn this topic inside out.
I've started you off with a worked example so you know what sort of thing to do.

1   Here is a trapezium.

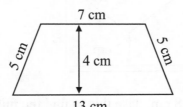

a)   Find the perimeter of the trapezium.

You need to add up the
lengths of all the sides   ⟍   7 + 5 + 13 + 5 = 30

.........30......... cm

[1 mark]

b)   Find the area of the trapezium.

$A = \frac{1}{2} \times (a + b) \times h$ ⟵——— This is the formula for the area
of a trapezium from p.92.

$= \frac{1}{2} \times (7 + 13) \times 4$

$= 40$

.........40......... cm²

[2 marks]

Practice Questions

2   Toby is designing a new circular pond for his garden.

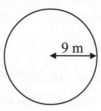

9 m

a)   What is the area of the pond? Give your answer to 2 d.p.

.... m²
[2 marks]

b)   He decides to put a fence around the outside of the pond. How many metres of fence
does he need to buy? Give your answer to 2 d.p.

.... m
[2 marks]

3   This shape is made up of a rectangle with a triangle cut out of it. The shape is symmetrical.

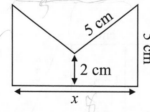

5 cm

5 cm

2 cm

x

a)   The perimeter of the shape is 28 cm. Use this to find the missing length, *x*.

.... cm
[2 marks]

b)   Find the area of the shape.

.... cm²
[3 marks]

3D Shapes

Here are some 3D shapes. You'll definitely have come across some of these before (like cubes and spheres). Others might be less familiar, like regular tetrahedrons — you need to know all of them.

Eight **Solids** to Learn

3D shapes are solid shapes. These are the ones you need to know:

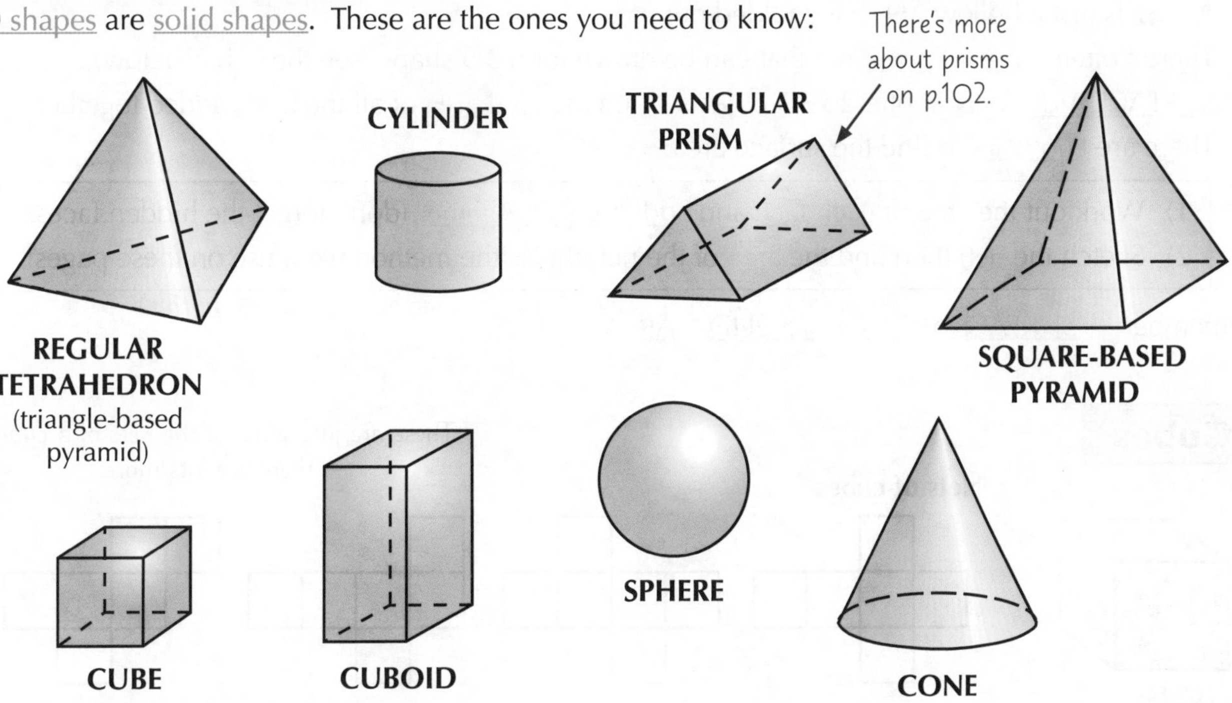

There's more about prisms on p.102.

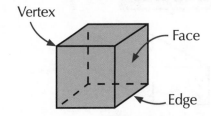

CYLINDER

TRIANGULAR PRISM

REGULAR TETRAHEDRON
(triangle-based pyramid)

SQUARE-BASED PYRAMID

CUBE

CUBOID

SPHERE

CONE

Different Parts of Solids

There are different parts of 3D shapes you need to be able to spot. These are vertices (corners), faces (the flat bits) and edges. You might be asked to find the number of vertices, faces and edges — just count them up, and don't forget the hidden ones.

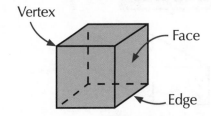

Vertex — Face — Edge

 **EXAMPLE:** **For the cuboid on the right, write down the number of faces, the number of edges and the number of vertices.**

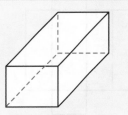

A cuboid has 6 faces (there's one on the bottom and two at the back that you can't see).

It has 12 edges (again, there are some hidden ones — the dotted lines in the diagram).

It has 8 vertices (one is hidden).

It's one vertex but two vertices...

If you're asked to count the number of faces, edges and vertices of a 3D shape it can be helpful to do a quick sketch of the shape — you'll be less likely to miss out a vertex or count the same edge twice.

Nets and Surface Area

Pencils and rulers at the ready — you might get to do some drawing over the next two pages.
It's mainly limited to squares, rectangles and triangles, but you might get the odd circle to draw.

Nets and Surface Area

1) A NET is just a hollow 3D shape folded out flat.

2) There's often more than one net that can be drawn for a 3D shape (see the cubes below).

3) SURFACE AREA only applies to 3D objects — it's the total area of all the faces added together.

4) There are two ways to find the surface area:

> 1) Work out the area of each face and add them all together (don't forget the hidden faces).
>
> 2) Sketch the net, then find the area of the net (this is the method we'll use on these pages).

Remember — SURFACE AREA OF A SOLID = AREA OF NET.

Cubes

These are just some of the nets of a cube
— there are lots more.

Nets of cubes

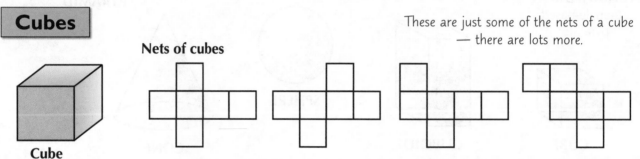

Cube

A cube has 6 square faces, so its surface area is just 6 × (area of square face).

Cuboids

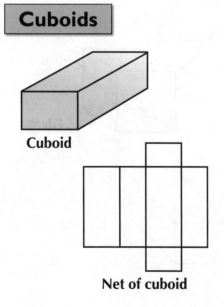

Cuboid

Net of cuboid

The net of a cuboid is made
up of 3 different rectangles
— there are 2 of each size.

EXAMPLE: Find the surface area of this cuboid:

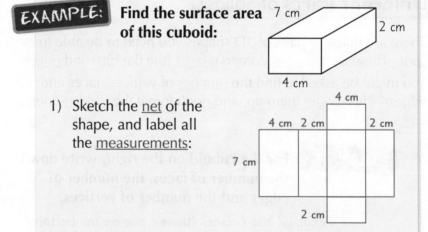

7 cm   2 cm
4 cm

1) Sketch the net of the shape, and label all the measurements:

4 cm   4 cm   2 cm   2 cm
7 cm
2 cm

2) Then work out the area of each face and add them up — there are 2 each of 3 different rectangles.

Surface area = 2(2 × 7) + 2(4 × 7) + 2(4 × 2)
= 28 + 56 + 16 = 100 cm²

EXAM TIP

To make sure the net is right, imagine folding it back up...

Even if you're not asked to draw the net of a shape, it's a good idea to do a quick sketch and
label it — it's really helpful for finding the surface area and means you won't miss any bits out.

Nets and Surface Area

Another page on <u>nets</u> and <u>surface area</u> — and now things get really exciting.

Triangular Prisms

 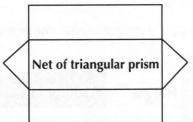

Triangular Prism

Net of triangular prism

EXAMPLE: **Find the surface area of the triangular prism above.** Have a look back at p.92 for more on areas.

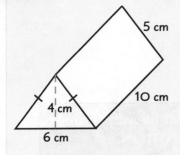

You can see from the <u>net</u> above that a triangular prism has <u>3 rectangular faces</u> and <u>2 triangular faces</u>. It's an <u>isosceles triangle</u>, so the rectangular faces will be of <u>two different sizes</u>.

Area of bottom rectangular face = 10 × 6 = 60 cm²
Area of side rectangular face = 10 × 5 = 50 cm²
Area of triangular face = ½ × 6 × 4 = 12 cm²
Total surface area = 60 + (2 × 50) + (2 × 12)

There are two faces of each of these sizes.

= 60 + 100 + 24 = 184 cm²

Pyramids

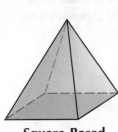 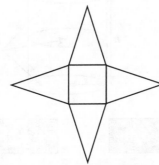

Square-Based Pyramid | **Net of square-based pyramid**

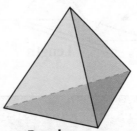 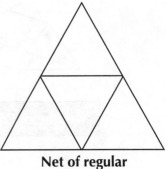

Regular Tetrahedron | **Net of regular tetrahedron**

EXAMPLE: **Find the surface area of the square-based pyramid below.**

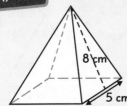

You can see from the <u>net</u> above that a square-based pyramid has <u>1 square face</u> and <u>4 triangular faces</u>.

Area of square face = 5 × 5 = 25 cm²
Area of triangular face = ½ × 5 × 8 = 20 cm²
Total surface area = 25 + (4 × 20) = 25 + 80 = 105 cm²

Find the area of the faces and add them up...

You have to be a bit careful when finding the surface area of a triangular prism — the rectangles will be different sizes (unless the triangle is equilateral), so don't get caught out.

Volume

Now it's time to work out the <u>volumes</u> of 3D shapes. Here are some formulas to help you do this.

Volumes of Cuboids

A <u>cuboid</u> is a <u>rectangular block</u>. Finding its volume is really easy:

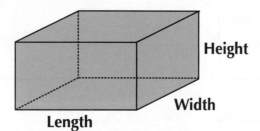

Height

Width

Length

> **Volume of Cuboid = length × width × height**
>
> $V = L \times W \times H$

Volumes of Prisms

> <u>A PRISM</u> is a solid (3D) object which is the same shape all the way through
> — i.e. it has a <u>CONSTANT AREA OF CROSS-SECTION</u>.

<u>Triangular Prism</u>

Constant area of cross-section

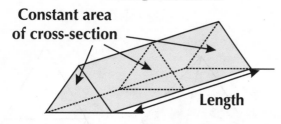

Length

<u>Cylinder</u>
(circular prism)

Constant area of cross-section

h

r

> **Volume of Prism = area of cross-section × length**
>
> $V = A \times L$

EXAMPLE: **Find the volume of the triangular prism on the right.**

First find the <u>area</u> of the <u>cross-section</u> (using the formula for the area of a triangle from p.92):

Area of triangle = $\frac{1}{2}$ × base × height = $\frac{1}{2}$ × 8 × 7 = 28 cm²

Then put the numbers into the <u>formula</u> for <u>volume</u>:

V = A × L = 28 × 15 = 420 cm³

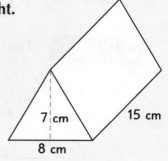

7 cm

15 cm

8 cm

Remember, find the cross-sectional area and multiply by the length...

Two more formulas to learn on this page, but they're not too bad really. The prism formula works on any prism, no matter what the shape of the cross-section — even if it's something really weird.

Warm-Up and Practice Questions

Use these warm-up questions to test your knowledge on 3D shapes. Once you feel pretty confident about them, go on to the practice questions below to make sure you're OK with it all.

Warm-Up Questions

1) a) Write down the name of the shape on the right.
   b) How many faces, edges and vertices does this shape have?

2) Draw the net of a cuboid with length 6 cm, width 3 cm and height 2 cm.

3) Find the surface area of a cube with side length 4 cm.

4) Find the surface area of a square-based pyramid with base sides measuring 2 cm and triangular faces with vertical height 5 cm.

5) The cross-sectional area of an octagonal prism is 28 cm². The length of the prism is 6 cm. Find the volume of the prism.

Practice Questions

And now the practice questions. Like always, here's a worked example so you know what sort of thing to aim for. Read through it, then have a go at the questions on the next page.

1 This is a triangular prism.

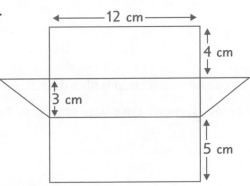

a) Draw a net of the prism.

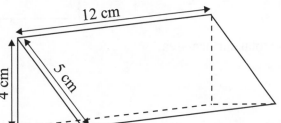

Mentally unfold the prism to get the net

The prism has two triangular faces and three rectangular faces.

[2 marks]

b) Find the surface area of the prism.

Total surface area = area of each rectangle + 2 × area of the triangle

$$= (12 \times 4) + (12 \times 3) + (12 \times 5) + 2 \times \left(\frac{1}{2} \times 3 \times 4\right)$$
$$= 48 + 36 + 60 + 2 \times 6$$
$$= 144 + 12$$
$$= 156 \text{ cm}^2$$

The area of a triangle is $\frac{1}{2}$ × base × height.

.................156............. cm²

[3 marks]

Practice Questions

2   The diagram below shows a pentagonal-based pyramid. State the number of:

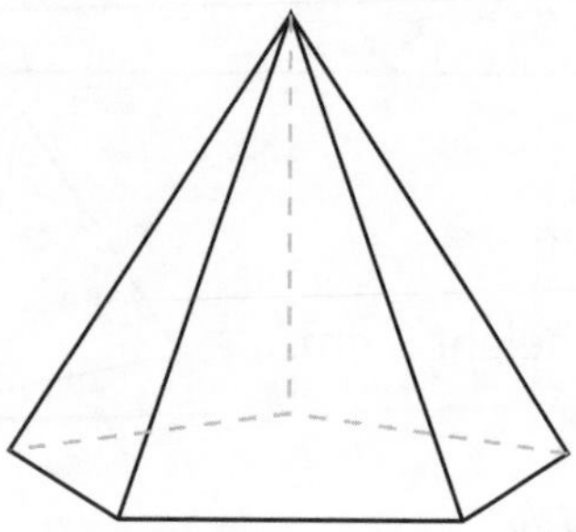

a)   vertices   ....

[1 mark]

b)   faces   ....

[1 mark]

c)   edges   ....

[1 mark]

3   Look at the cuboid and net below.

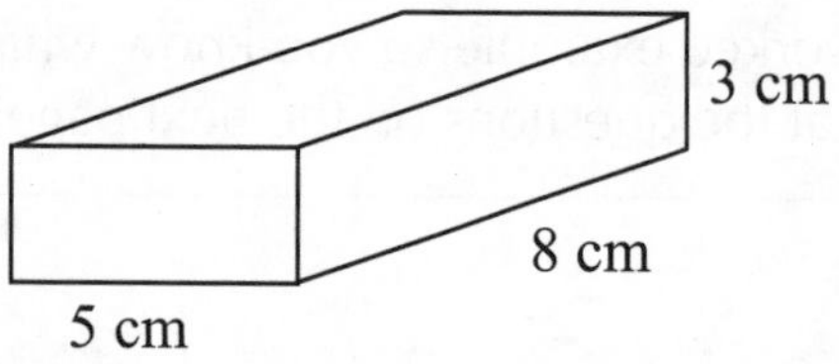

3 cm

8 cm

5 cm

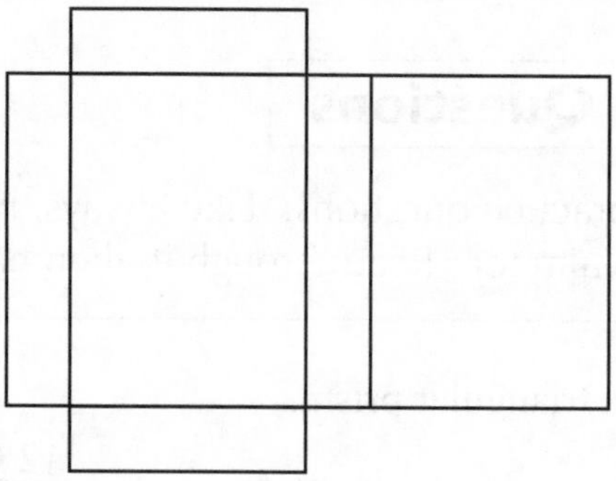

Use the net to find the total surface area.

.... cm²

[3 marks]

4   A tube of sweets has a circular cross-section with a diameter of 6.2 cm.

a)   Find the area of the cross-section. Give your answer to 2 d.p.

.... cm²

[2 marks]

b)   The tube is 10 cm long. Find the volume of the tube to 1 d.p.

.... cm³

[2 marks]

Lines and Angles

There's nothing too scary on this page — just some special angles and some fancy notation.

Four Special Angles

There are 360° in a full turn, and it can be divided into 4 special angles:

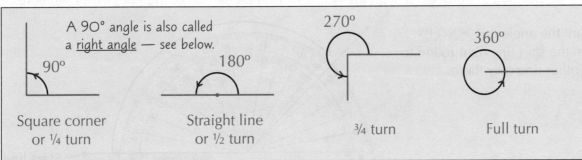

A 90° angle is also called a right angle — see below.

90° — Square corner or ¼ turn

180° — Straight line or ½ turn

270° — ¾ turn

360° — Full turn

When two lines meet at 90° they are said to be PERPENDICULAR to each other.

Fancy Angle Names

Some angles have special names which you need to know.

ACUTE angles
Sharp pointy ones (less than 90°)

OBTUSE angles
Flatter ones (between 90° and 180°)

RIGHT angles
Square corners (exactly 90°)

REFLEX angles
Ones that bend back on themselves (more than 180°)

Three-Letter Angle Notation

The best way to say which angle you're talking about in a diagram is by using THREE letters.
For example in the diagram, angle BAC = 35°.

1) The middle letter is where the angle is.
2) The other two letters tell you which two lines enclose the angle.

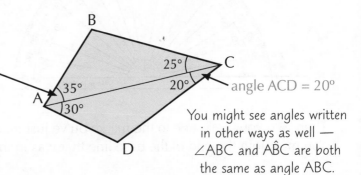

angle ACD = 20°

You might see angles written in other ways as well — ∠ABC and AB̂C are both the same as angle ABC.

Cover this page and write down everything you remember...

There's no way around it — you need to know what the different types of angles are called and what they look like. Scribble them down, cover the page and scribble them down again until you've got it.

Measuring Angles

Being able to <u>measure</u> and <u>draw angles</u> is a really important skill.
Make sure you know how to use a <u>protractor</u> properly.

Measuring Angles with a **Protractor**

1) <u>ALWAYS</u> position the protractor with the <u>base line</u> of it along one of the lines as shown here:

2) Count the angle in <u>10° STEPS</u> from the <u>start line</u> right round to the other line over there.

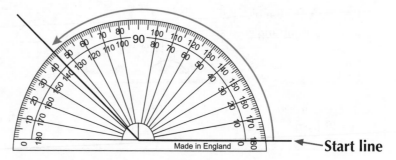

← **Start line**

> <u>DON'T JUST READ A NUMBER OFF THE SCALE</u> — chances are it'll be the wrong one because there are <u>TWO scales</u> to choose from.
>
> The answer here is 135° (NOT 45°) which you will only get right if you start counting 10°, 20°, 30°, 40° etc. from the <u>start line</u> until you reach the <u>other line</u>.

There are <u>two big mistakes</u> that people make with protractors:

> 1) Not putting the <u>0° line</u> at the <u>start</u> position.
> 2) Reading from the <u>WRONG SCALE</u>.

Drawing Angles with a **Protractor**

Draw a <u>straight horizontal line</u> to be your <u>base line</u>. Put the <u>protractor</u> on the line so that the <u>middle</u> of the protractor is on one <u>end</u> of the line as shown:

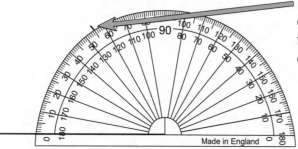

Draw a <u>little line</u> or <u>dot</u> next to the angle you're drawing (count up in tens from 0° to make sure you follow the <u>right scale</u>). Here, I'm drawing an angle of 55°, so I'm using the <u>outside</u> scale.

Be careful — reading from the wrong scale is a very very common error!

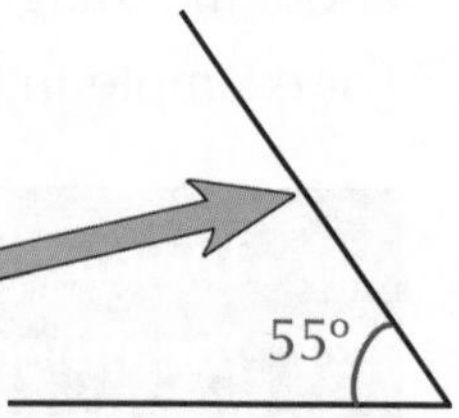

Then <u>join</u> your <u>base line</u> to the <u>mark</u> you've just made with a <u>straight line</u>. You must join the end of the base line that was in the <u>middle</u> of the protractor.

55°

REVISION TASK

Always count from the base line when measuring angles...

The best way to make sure you know all of the stuff on this page is to try it yourself — get out your protractor, ruler and pencil and have a go at drawing an angle of 72°.

Five Angle Rules

The <u>angle rules</u> on this page are really important — they pop up all over the place, so make sure you <u>learn</u> them all. Then learn them <u>again</u>, just to make sure.

5 Simple Rules — That's All

1) Angles in a <u>triangle</u> add up to 180°.

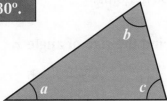

$$a + b + c = 180°$$

2) Angles on a <u>straight line</u> add up to 180°.

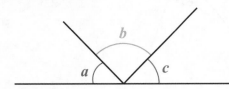

$$a + b + c = 180°$$

3) Angles in a <u>quadrilateral</u> add up to 360°.

Remember that a quadrilateral is a <u>4-sided</u> shape.

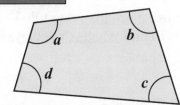

$$a + b + c + d = 360°$$

4) Angles <u>round a point</u> add up to 360°.

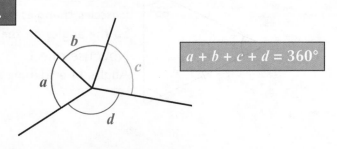

$$a + b + c + d = 360°$$

5) <u>Isosceles triangles</u> have <u>2 sides</u> the same and <u>2 angles</u> the same.

These dashes indicate two sides the same length.

These angles are the same.

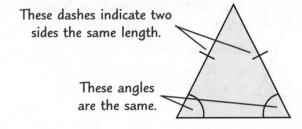

In an isosceles triangle, you only need to know <u>one angle</u> to be able to find the other two.

No excuses for not learning these five simple rules...

None of the rules here are too tough, but make sure you don't get them mixed up. On the next page, there are some examples showing how you can use these rules to answer questions, so keep reading...

Five Angle Rules

It's time to see all the angle rules from the previous page in action.

Using **One Rule**

It's a good idea to write down the rules you're using when finding missing angles
— it helps you keep track of what you're doing.

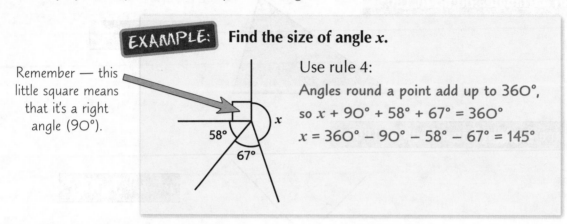

Remember — this little square means that it's a right angle (90°).

EXAMPLE: **Find the size of angle x.**

Use rule 4:

Angles round a point add up to 360°,
so $x + 90° + 58° + 67° = 360°$

$x = 360° - 90° - 58° - 67° = 145°$

58°

67°

x

Using **More Than One Rule**

It's a bit trickier when you have to use more than one rule — but writing down the rules is a
big help again. The best method is to find whatever angles you can until you can work out
the ones you're looking for.

EXAMPLE: **Find the size of angle x.**

The dashes mean it's an isosceles triangle, so use rule 5:
Isosceles triangles have 2 sides and 2 angles the same.
So the angles on the right of the triangle are both 65°

Now use rule 1:

Angles in a triangle add up to 180°, so $65° + 65° + x = 180°$

$x = 180° - 130°$

$x = 50°$

65°

x

EXAMPLE: **Find the size of angle x.**

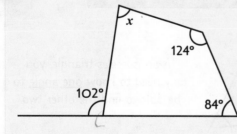

First use rule 2 to find the unknown
angle at the bottom of the quadrilateral:

$180° - 102° = 78°$

Then use rule 3:

$x + 78° + 124° + 84° = 360°$

$x = 360° - 78° - 124° - 84°$

$x = 74°$

x

124°

102°

84°

Write down the rules you're using to get started...

If you're really stuck, fill in any angles you can find and see where it gets you.

Parallel Lines

Parallel lines point in the same direction. They're always the same distance apart and never meet.

Angles Around **Parallel Lines**

When a line crosses two parallel lines...

> 1) The two bunches of angles are the same.
> 2) There are only two different angles: a smaller one and a bigger one.
> 3) These ALWAYS ADD UP TO 180°. E.g. 30° and 150° below.

The two lines with the arrows on are parallel:

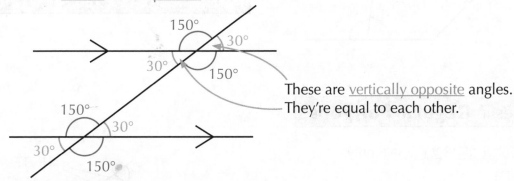

These are vertically opposite angles.
They're equal to each other.

Alternate and **Corresponding** Angles

Watch out for these 'Z' and 'F' shapes popping up.
They're a dead giveaway that you've got a pair of parallel lines.

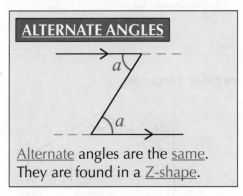

ALTERNATE ANGLES

Alternate angles are the same.
They are found in a Z-shape.

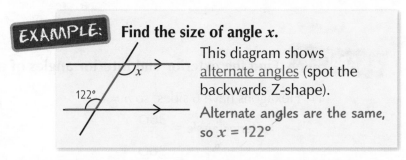

EXAMPLE: Find the size of angle x.

This diagram shows alternate angles (spot the backwards Z-shape).

Alternate angles are the same, so x = 122°

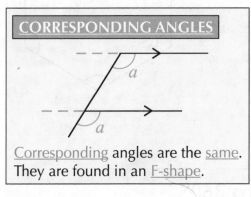

CORRESPONDING ANGLES

Corresponding angles are the same.
They are found in an F-shape.

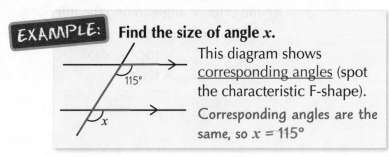

EXAMPLE: Find the size of angle x.

This diagram shows corresponding angles (spot the characteristic F-shape).

Corresponding angles are the same, so x = 115°

Lines with arrows on are parallel...

It's OK to use Z and F to help you identify the angles. Just make sure you know the proper names too.

Interior and Exterior Angles

These pages are all about finding angles in <u>polygons</u>. Here are three simple <u>formulas</u> you need to know.

Interior and Exterior Angles

You need to know <u>what</u> interior and exterior angles are and <u>how to find them</u>.
For <u>ANY POLYGON</u> (regular or irregular):

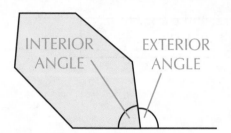

INTERIOR
ANGLE

EXTERIOR
ANGLE

SUM OF EXTERIOR ANGLES = 360°

INTERIOR ANGLE = 180° – EXTERIOR ANGLE

Angles in Regular Polygons

For <u>REGULAR POLYGONS</u> only:

$$\text{EXTERIOR ANGLE OF} \atop \underline{\text{REGULAR}} \text{ POLYGON} = \frac{360°}{n}$$

(n is the number of sides)

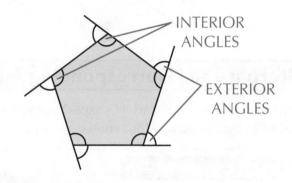

INTERIOR
ANGLES

EXTERIOR
ANGLES

EXAMPLE: **Find the exterior and interior angles of a regular hexagon.**

1) Hexagons have 6 sides, so $n = 6$:

$$\text{exterior angle} = \frac{360°}{n}$$
$$= \frac{360°}{6}$$
$$= 60°$$

2) Use the exterior angle to find the interior angle:

interior angle = 180° – exterior angle
= 180° – 60°
= 120°

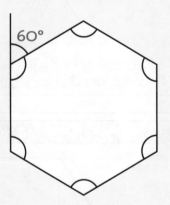

60°

Exterior angles will always add up to 360°...

A common mistake is to think exterior angle = 360° – interior angle. Remember that when you extend the sides of the polygon, the interior and exterior angles lie on a straight line. Have a go at working out the size of an exterior and an interior angle of a regular octagon.

(Ans, Exterior = 45°, Interior = 135°)

Interior and Exterior Angles

Here's another handy formula — this time, it's about the <u>sum</u> of the interior angles...

The Tricky One — **Sum** of **Interior** Angles

This formula for the <u>sum of the interior angles</u> works for <u>ALL</u> polygons, even irregular ones.

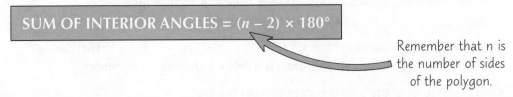

> SUM OF INTERIOR ANGLES = $(n - 2) \times 180°$

Remember that n is the number of sides of the polygon.

EXAMPLE: **Find the sum of the interior angles of the polygon below.**

1) The polygon is a <u>pentagon</u>, so $n = 5$.

2) Use the formula above to find the <u>sum</u> of interior angles

Sum of interior angles = (n − 2) × 180°

                   = (5 − 2) × 180°

                   = 3 × 180°

                   = 540°

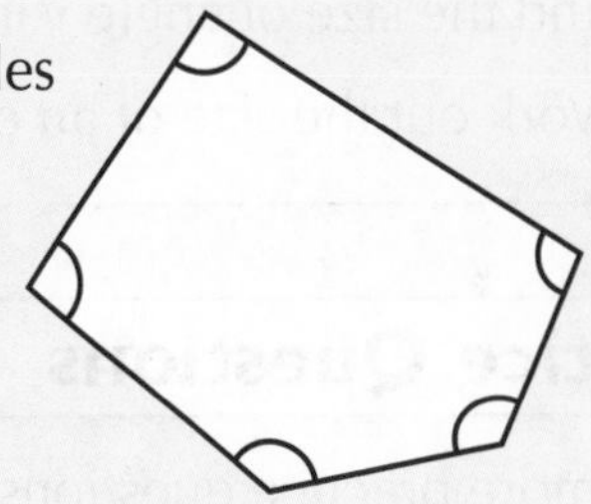

Use the **Sum** to find **Missing Angles**

You can use this rule along with the other <u>angle rules</u> you learned on p.107. If you know what the <u>sum</u> of the <u>interior angles</u> in a shape is, you can use it to <u>find</u> the value of <u>missing angles</u>.

EXAMPLE: **Find the missing angle in the diagram below.**

1) Find the <u>sum</u> of the interior angles of the 7-sided shape:

Sum of interior angles = (n − 2) × 180°

                   = (7 − 2) × 180°

                   = 5 × 180°

                   = 900°

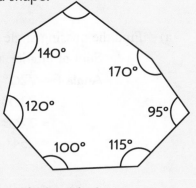

2) Subtract from 900° to find the missing angle:

900° − 170° − 95° − 115° − 100° − 120° − 140° = 160°

 EXAM TIP

Learn the formula for the sum of the interior angles...

If you've got a complicated shape, put a little mark on each edge as you count them to make sure you haven't missed any. Then you can just stick *n* in the formula, and you're flying.

Warm-Up and Practice Questions

Here are some warm-up questions to see how you're getting on.
If there's anything you're unsure about, go back and check — then test yourself below.

Warm-Up Questions

1) Are the following angles acute, obtuse, reflex or right angles?
   a) 98° b) 234° c) 11°

2) Draw an angle measuring: a) 45° b) 70° c) 150°.
   Measure the angles you've just drawn to check that they're correct.

3) Find the size of angle *x* in the diagram on the right.

4) A quadrilateral has angles measuring 74°, 86° and 146°.
   Find the size of the other angle.

5) Find the size of angle *y* in the diagram on the right.

6) Work out the size of an exterior angle and an interior angle of a regular pentagon.

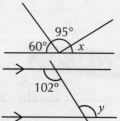

Practice Questions

Time for more practice questions. Like usual, there's a worked example to ease you into it.
Remember — sometimes you need to work out one angle before you can find another.

1 The shape below is an irregular hexagon.

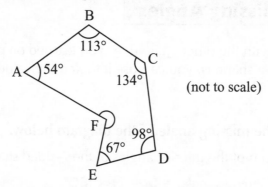

(not to scale)

a) Find the missing angle at F.

   Sum of interior angles = (6 − 2) × 180° = 4 × 180° = 720°

   Angle F = 720° − sum of the other angles
   = 720° − (54° + 113° + 134° + 98° + 67°)
   = 720° − 466°
   = 254°

   ....254°............
   [3 marks]

b) The interior angle at B is 113°. What is the exterior angle at B?

   Exterior angle = 180° − interior angle
   = 180° − 113°
   = 67°

   ....67°............
   [1 mark]

Section Four — Geometry and Measures

Practice Questions

2 Angles *a* and *b* are shown in the diagram below.

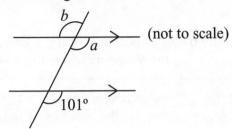

(not to scale)

101°

a) Find angle *a*.

a = ...°
[1 mark]

b) Find angle *b*.

b = ...°
[1 mark]

3 Angles *p*, *q* and *r* are shown in the diagram below.

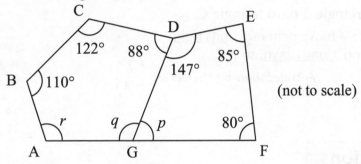

C   D   E
122° 88°   85°
147°
B 110°
(not to scale)
r   q   p   80°
A   G   F

a) Find angle *p*.

p = ...°
[2 marks]

b) Find angle *q*.

q = ...°
[1 mark]

c) Find angle *r*.

r = ...°
[2 marks]

4 Find angle *x* in the diagram below.

C
(not to scale)   75°
115°
x   65
A   B

x = ...°
[2 marks]

Transformations

A transformation just means 'a way of moving a shape about, or changing its size, on a coordinate grid'.

1) Translations

A translation is just a SLIDE around the page. When describing a translation,
you must say how far along and how far up the shape moves using a vector.

> Vectors describing translations look like this.
> x is the number of spaces right, y is the number of spaces up. $\begin{pmatrix} x \\ y \end{pmatrix}$

If the shape moves left x will be negative, and if it moves down y will be negative.

EXAMPLE: **Describe the transformation that maps:**

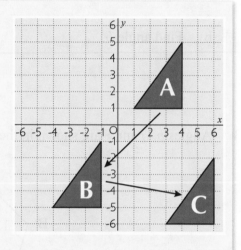

a) **triangle A onto triangle B.**

To get from triangle A to triangle B you need
to move 5 units left and 6 units down, so it's:

A translation by the vector $\begin{pmatrix} -5 \\ -6 \end{pmatrix}$

b) **triangle B onto triangle C.**

It's a movement of 7 units right
and 1 unit down, so it's:

A translation by the vector $\begin{pmatrix} 7 \\ -1 \end{pmatrix}$

2) Reflections

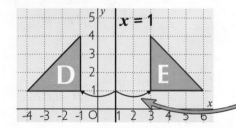

Triangle D is mapped onto triangle E
by a reflection in the line $x = 1$. ← See p.53 for more on straight lines.

Notice, the matching corners are equal distances from the mirror line.

To describe a reflection, you must give the equation of the mirror line.

EXAMPLE: **Describe the transformation that maps:**

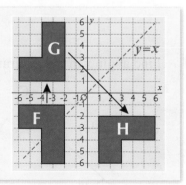

a) **shape F onto shape G.**

A reflection in the x-axis

b) **shape G onto shape H.**

A reflection in the line $y = x$

The only thing a translation changes is the shape's position...

To describe translations, give a vector. To describe reflections, give the equation of the mirror line.

Transformations

3) Rotations

To describe a rotation, you need 3 details:

1) The angle of rotation (usually 90° or 180°)
2) The direction of rotation (clockwise or anticlockwise)
3) The centre of rotation

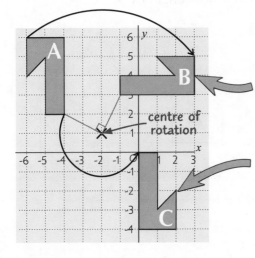

centre of rotation

Shape A is mapped onto Shape B by a rotation of 90° clockwise about point (–2, 1).

Shape A is mapped onto Shape C by a rotation of 180° about point (–2, 1).

For a rotation of 180°, it doesn't matter whether you go clockwise or anticlockwise.

EXAMPLE: **Rotate Triangle D 90° clockwise about (0, 0).**

The best way to tackle this is with tracing paper:

1) Trace the shape and mark the centre of rotation at (0, 0).

2) Put your pencil point on the centre of rotation and rotate the tracing paper 90° clockwise. You'll know when you've gone far enough — the horizontal side will be vertical, and vice versa.

3) Mark the corners of the shape in their new positions on the grid, then draw the shape.

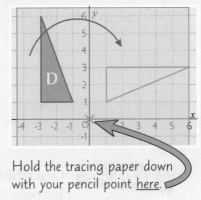

Hold the tracing paper down with your pencil point here.

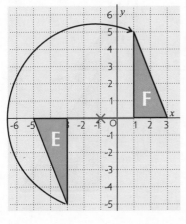

EXAMPLE: **Describe the transformation that maps Triangle E onto Triangle F.**

A rotation of 180° about (–1, 0).

You can use tracing paper to help you find the centre of rotation. Trace the original shape and then try putting your pencil on different points until the traced shape rotates onto the image. When this happens your pencil must be on the centre of rotation.

REVISION TASK

Use tracing paper to help you see transformations...

Trace shape G (on the last page), hold the paper in place with your pencil at (0, 0), and turn the paper 90° clockwise. Mark where the corners of the new shape are and join them up.

Enlargements

You've made it to the fourth and final transformation now. Get ready for... enlargements.

4) Enlargements

The scale factor for an enlargement tells you how long the sides of the new shape are compared to the old shape. E.g. a scale factor of 3 means you multiply each side length by 3.

EXAMPLE: **Enlarge shape X by a scale factor of 2.**

1) Make each side twice as long as the matching side on shape X. Start with the horizontal and vertical sides.

2) Take care with the sloping sides — they're much trickier.

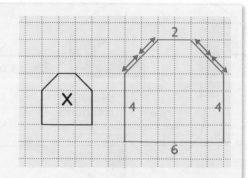

Describing an Enlargement

For an enlargement, you must specify:

> 1) The scale factor.
> 2) The centre of enlargement.

There's a formula for the scale factor:

$$\text{scale factor} = \frac{\text{new length}}{\text{old length}}$$

EXAMPLE: **Describe the transformation that maps Triangle A onto Triangle B.**

1) Use the formula to find the scale factor. (Just do this for one pair of sides.)

Old length of triangle base = 2 units
New length of triangle base = 4 units

$$\text{scale factor} = \frac{\text{new length}}{\text{old length}} = \frac{4}{2} = 2$$

2) To find the centre of enlargement, draw lines that go through matching corners of both shapes and see where they cross.

So the transformation is
an enlargement of scale factor 2, centre (0, 6).

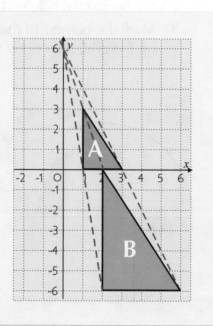

If the shape changes in size then it's an enlargement...

Here, you need to give the scale factor and the centre of enlargement to describe the transformation.

Warm-Up and Practice Questions

This topic is all about moving and changing shapes on a grid. Remember the four different types of transformations and how to describe them. Once you're confident with them, have a go at these:

Warm-Up Questions

1) Describe the transformation that maps rectangle A onto rectangle B in the diagram on the right.

2) Triangle F has corners (1, 0), (3, 0) and (1, 5) and triangle G has corners (–3, 2), (–3, 4) and (–8, 2). Draw the triangles F and G on a grid and describe the rotation that maps triangle F onto triangle G.

3) Draw the triangles X (1, 2), (–1, 3), (–1, 5) and Y (7, –4), (1, –1), (1, 5) on a grid and describe the enlargement that maps triangle X onto triangle Y.

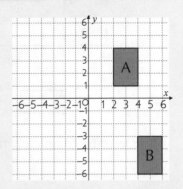

Practice Questions

I expect you can't wait to get going on these practice questions. In that case, I won't delay you any longer. Here's a worked example to start you off.

1 Shape B is an enlargement of shape A.

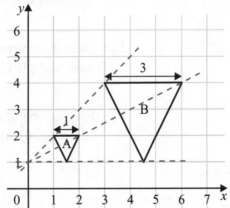

a) Find the scale factor of the enlargement.

$$\text{Scale factor} = \frac{\text{new length}}{\text{old length}} = \frac{3}{1} = 3$$

Choose a side from shape A to compare to the corresponding side from shape B.

....................3....................
[2 marks]

b) Find the coordinates of the centre of the enlargement.

Draw lines through matching corners of both shapes (see diagram) — the lines cross at (0, 1).

....................(0, 1)....................
[2 marks]

Section Four — Geometry and Measures

Practice Questions

2   Here is a coordinate grid with three rectangles.

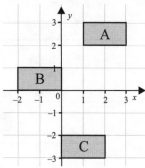

a)   Find the translation vector that maps:

(i)   A onto B   ....

[1 mark]

(ii)   A onto C   ....

[1 mark]

b)   Describe completely the rotation that maps rectangle B onto rectangle C.

....

[2 marks]

3   Triangle A is shown on a grid below.

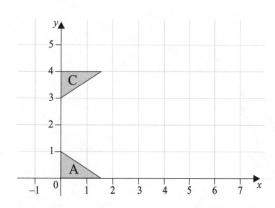

a)   Translate triangle A by the vector $\begin{pmatrix} 4 \\ 3 \end{pmatrix}$ and label it B.

[2 marks]

b)   Draw the mirror line that reflects triangle A onto triangle C onto the grid on the left.

[1 mark]

c)   Enlarge triangle A by scale factor 2, centre (0, 0) and label it D.

[2 marks]

4   Triangle ABC is shown on the grid to the right.

a)   Reflect triangle ABC in the line $x = 1$ and label it DEF.

[2 marks]

b)   Rotate the triangle DEF 90° anti-clockwise around the point (5, 1).

[2 marks]

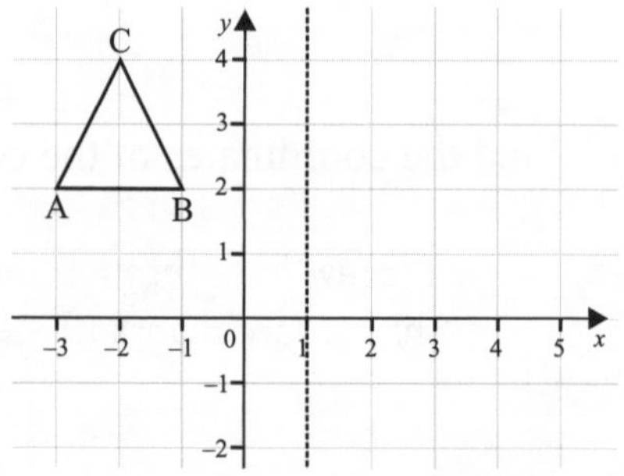

Triangle Construction

How you construct a triangle depends on what information you're given about the triangle...

Three Sides — use a Ruler and Compasses

Here's how you construct a triangle when you're given the lengths of three sides.
For the triangle ABC below, AB = 5 cm, BC = 3 cm, AC = 4 cm.

1) First, sketch and label a triangle so you know roughly what's needed. It doesn't matter which line you make the base line.

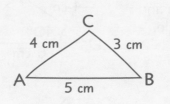

2) Draw the base line. Label the ends A and B.

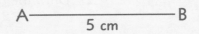

3) For AC, set the compasses to 4 cm, put the point at A and draw an arc.

4) For BC, set the compasses to 3 cm, put the point at B and draw an arc.

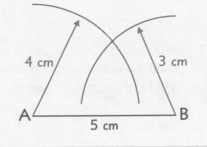

5) Where the arcs cross is point C. Now you can finish your triangle.

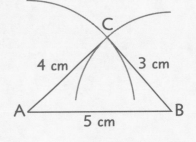

Pencils are your new best friend...

Always do your constructions in pencil — that way, if it goes a bit wrong, you can always rub it out and have another go. Once you've finished, grab your ruler and measure each line to check it's the length it's supposed to be — then you'll know your drawing is correct.

Triangle Construction

Sides and Angles — use a Ruler and Protractor

Now, here's how you construct a triangle when you're given an angle and the length of two sides. For the triangle DEF below, DE = 6 cm, DF = 4 cm, angle EDF = 40°.

1) Roughly sketch and label the triangle.

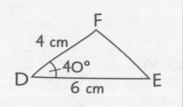

2) Draw the base line.

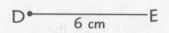

3) Draw angle EDF (the angle at D) — place the centre of the protractor over D, measure 40° and put a dot.

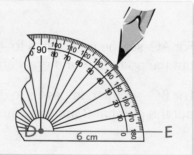

4) Measure 4 cm towards the dot and label it F. Join up D and F. Now you've drawn the two sides and the angle. Just join up F and E to complete the triangle.

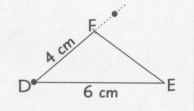

Compass for sides, protractor for angles...

Don't get mixed up with how to do each of the triangle constructions on the last two pages. Look at the information you're given and you can work out what tools you need for the job straight away.

Constructions

The best way to learn how to do these <u>constructions</u> is to have a go.

Two More **Constructions**

When you're doing these constructions, make sure you:

1) Keep the compass setting <u>THE SAME</u> while you make <u>all the marks</u>.
2) <u>Leave</u> your compass marks <u>showing</u>.

1) The **Perpendicular Bisector** of a **Line**

The perpendicular bisector of line segment AB is a line at <u>right angles</u> to AB, passing through the <u>midpoint</u> of AB. This is the method to use if you're asked to draw it.

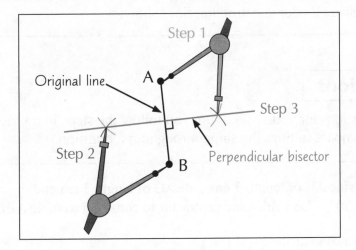

2) The **Bisector** of an **Angle**

The bisector of an angle divides an angle exactly in <u>half</u> — so you get <u>two equal angles</u>.

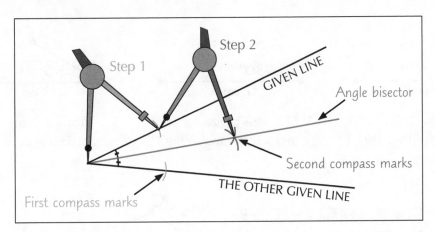

Don't change your compass settings when constructing...

It'll make you draw your construction wrong. Also, don't rub out your compass lines when doing constructions — you have to leave all your working showing to get all the marks.

Warm-Up and Practice Questions

Constructions can be pretty fun once you know what you're doing. Look back over the pages, then test yourself on each type by having a go at the warm-up questions below.

Warm-Up Questions

1) Construct a triangle with sides 3 cm, 4 cm and 4 cm.
   Leave your construction marks showing.

2) Construct triangle ABC where AB is 5 cm, AC is 4 cm and angle BAC is 50°.
   Make sure you leave all your construction lines showing.

3) Draw a straight line, then construct its perpendicular bisector.
   Make sure you leave all your construction lines showing.

4) Draw two straight lines to create an acute angle, then construct the bisector of this angle.
   Make sure you leave all your construction lines showing.

Practice Questions

Some more practice questions for you. Make sure you follow the steps in the right order and always keep your compass settings the same throughout a question.

1   Triangle ABC has side AB of length 7 cm, side AC of length 3 cm and angle CAB of size 30°. Use a ruler and protractor to construct triangle ABC.

Firstly, sketch what the triangle will look like so you've got the dimensions in the right places

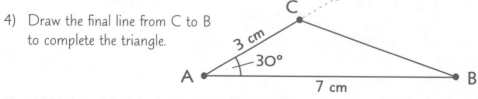

1) Draw the base line. Here we've used the side of length 7 cm.

2) Use your protractor to measure an angle of 30°.

3) Measure 3 cm towards the dot and draw in this line.

4) Draw the final line from C to B to complete the triangle.

[3 marks]

Practice Questions

2 OM and ON are two straight lines.
   Use a pair of compasses to draw the bisector of angle MON below.

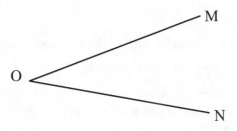

[2 marks]

3 Side BC of the equilateral triangle ABC has been accurately drawn below.

B ———————————— C

a) Use a ruler and compasses to complete the accurate drawing of triangle ABC.

[2 marks]

b) Construct the bisector of angle ACB of the triangle.
    You must show all your construction lines.

[2 marks]

4 DE is a straight line. Use a ruler and compasses to construct the
   perpendicular bisector of the line DE. Show all of your construction lines.

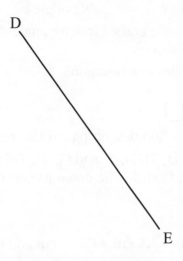

[2 marks]

Revision Summary

You've reached the end of the section — guess what you have to do now...
- Try these questions and tick off each one when you get it right.
- When you've done all the questions for a topic and are completely happy with it, tick off the topic.

2D Shapes (p.85-89) ☑

1. Write down the number of lines of symmetry and order of rotational symmetry for a rhombus. ☑
2. Name 2 quadrilaterals that have 2 pairs of equal angles. ☑
3. Name the 4 different types of triangle. ☑
4. A regular polygon has 7 sides. What is the name of this polygon? ☑
5. What are congruent and similar shapes? ☑

Perimeter and Area (p.92-96) ☑

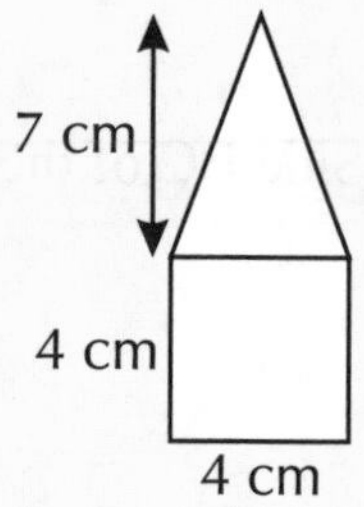

6. Find the perimeter and area of a rectangle that measures 11 cm by 5 cm. ☑
7. Find the area of a triangle with base 12 cm and vertical height 8 cm. ☑
8. Find the area of the shape on the right. ☑
9. Find the circumference and area of a circle with radius 8 cm to 1 d.p. ☑
10. How many complete rotations are needed for a wheel of diameter 10 cm to cover 1 m? ☑

7 cm
4 cm
4 cm

3D Shapes (p.99-102) ☑

11. Write down the number of faces, edges and vertices of a triangular prism. ☑
12. Find the surface area and volume of a cuboid measuring 2 cm by 3 cm by 5 cm. ☑
13. Sketch a net of a regular tetrahedron. ☑
14. Find the volume of a prism with cross-sectional area 40 cm² and length 10 cm. ☑

Angles (p.105-111) ☑

15. Give an example of: a) an acute angle, b) an obtuse angle, c) a reflex angle. ☑
16. Draw an angle that measures 35°. ☑
17. What are the five angle rules? ☑
18. What type of angles do you find in a Z-shape on parallel lines? ☑
19. For the diagram on the right, find the size of:
    a) angle x b) angle y c) angle z ☑ 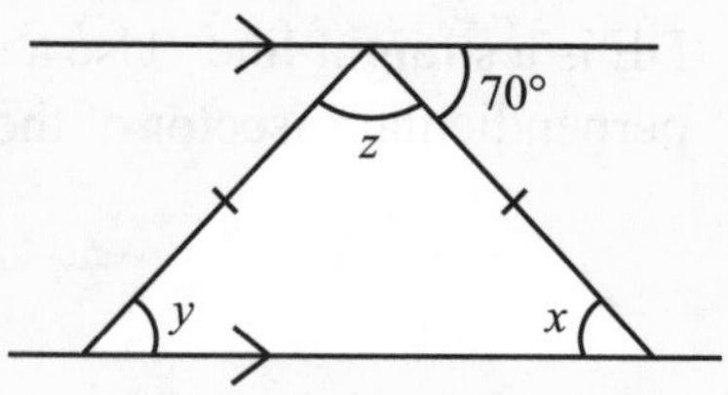
20. Work out the size of an exterior angle and an interior angle
    of a regular decagon (a ten-sided shape). ☑
21. What's the sum of the interior angles in a hexagon? ☑

70°
z
y
x

Transformations (p.114-116) ☑

22. What three details must you give when describing a rotation? ☑
23. Draw a triangle with coordinates (1, 1), (4, 1) and (3, 4). Enlarge the triangle by
    a scale factor of 3 and centre (–1, 0) and write down its coordinates after the enlargement. ☑

Constructions (p.119-121) ☑

24. Construct triangle ABC, where AB = 3.5 cm, AC = 3 cm and BAC = 50°. ☑
25. Draw an acute angle of any size, then bisect it, leaving your construction marks showing. ☑

Probability

Probability isn't as complicated as it looks — an '<u>event</u>' is just something that happens, and the <u>probability</u> of an event tells you <u>how likely</u> it is.

All Probabilities are **Between 0** and **1**

1) Probabilities can only have values <u>from 0 to 1</u> (including 0 and 1).

2) You should be able to put the probability of <u>any event</u> happening on this <u>scale of 0 to 1</u>.

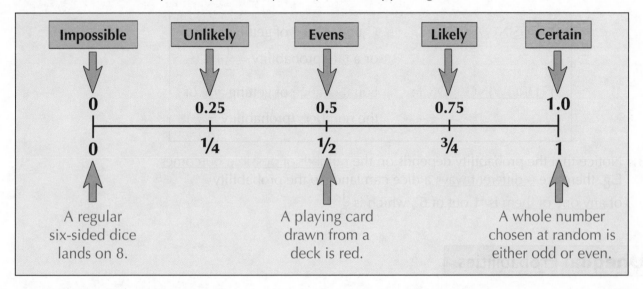

Impossible	Unlikely	Evens	Likely	Certain
0	0.25	0.5	0.75	1.0
0	¼	½	¾	1

A regular six-sided dice lands on 8.

A playing card drawn from a deck is red.

A whole number chosen at random is either odd or even.

3) You can give probabilities using <u>FRACTIONS</u>, <u>DECIMALS</u> or <u>PERCENTAGES</u>.
   E.g. a <u>probability</u> of $\frac{1}{2}$ can also be written as <u>0.5</u> or <u>50%</u>.

4) To <u>save on words</u>, you could write:
   'the <u>probability</u> of tossing a coin and getting a <u>head</u> is <u>0.5</u>' as: <u>P(H) = 0.5</u>.

   ⌐ P is for <u>probability</u>
   ∟ H is for <u>head</u>

The **Probability** of Something **Not** Happening = **1 – P**

1) If <u>only one</u> possible result can happen at a time,
   then the probabilities of <u>all</u> the results <u>add up to 1</u>.

   Probabilities always ADD UP to 1.

2) If the probability of something happening is <u>0.3</u>,
   then the chance of it <u>NOT HAPPENING</u> is <u>1 – 0.3</u> = <u>0.7</u>.

3) It's what's left when you <u>subtract it from 1</u> (or 100% for percentages).

 **EXAMPLE:** **The probability that a bus will be late is 0.75. Find the probability that the bus won't be late.**

P(not late) = 1 – P(late) = 1 – 0.75 = 0.25

 REVISION TIP

Probabilities are always between 0 and 1...

The closer a probability is to 1, the more likely the event is to happen — if it's closer to 0, it's less likely. Probabilities might be written as fractions, decimals or percentages, so it's important that you're happy with all three forms. Look back to p.24 if you need a reminder.

Equal and Unequal Probabilities

Now comes the fun part — how to actually find probabilities...

Equal Probabilities

1) When the different results or 'outcomes' of something happening all have the same chance of happening, then the probabilities will be EQUAL.

2) These are the two cases which usually come up:

> 1) TOSSING A COIN: Equal chance of getting a head or a tail (probability = $\frac{1}{2}$)
>
> 2) THROWING A DICE: Equal chance of getting any of the numbers (probability = $\frac{1}{6}$)

3) Notice that the probability depends on the number of possible outcomes. E.g. there are 6 different ways a dice can land, so the probability of any one of them is '1 out of 6', which is $\frac{1}{6}$.

Unequal Probabilities

In most cases, different outcomes have different probabilities — some are more likely than others.

 **A ball is picked at random from a bag containing 7 blue balls, 8 red balls and 5 green balls. Find P(blue).**

The chances of picking out the three colours are NOT EQUAL because there are different numbers of balls in each colour. The probability of picking a blue is:

$$P(\text{blue}) = \frac{\text{number of blues}}{\text{total number of balls}} = \frac{7}{20} \longleftarrow \text{(or 0.35 or 35\%)}$$

EXAMPLE: **What is the probability of winning £45 on this spinner?**

The pointer has the same chance of stopping on every sector. There are 2 out of 8 which say £45, so

$$P(\text{£45}) = \frac{2}{8} = \frac{1}{4} \longleftarrow \text{(or 0.25 or 25\%)}$$

The formula to use is: $$\text{Probability} = \frac{\text{Number of ways for something to happen}}{\text{Total number of possible outcomes}}$$

Always start by finding the total number of possible outcomes...

You'll often have to add things up to find the number to divide by — like in the 'balls in a bag' example.

Listing Outcomes

Listing outcomes is quite easy — all you have to do is write down all of the different things that could happen in the scenario you've been given.

Listing All Outcomes: Use a Sample Space

1) You might get asked to list all the possible outcomes for TWO THINGS HAPPENING TOGETHER. A simple question might be to list all the possible results from tossing two coins:

> The possible outcomes from TOSSING TWO COINS are:
> HH   HT   TH   TT

'TH' means tails on the first coin and heads on the second.

2) You can work out probabilities from your list.
   E.g. P(TT) = $\frac{1}{4}$, because there are 4 outcomes in total, and only 1 of these is TT.

3) For harder questions, you're better off listing all the possible results in a sample space diagram — a posh name for a table.

4) This sample space diagram shows the possible outcomes for the spinners below:

	Red	Blue	Green
1	1R	1B	1G
2	2R	2B	2G
3	3R	3B	3G

3 different outcomes on colour spinner.

3 different outcomes on number spinner.

5) Any number on the number spinner could come up with any colour on the colour spinner. Spinning them together gives 3 × 3 = 9 different combinations altogether. The sample space is a list of these 9 outcomes.

6) The probability of spinning e.g. a 2 and a GREEN (2G) is 1 out of 9, so $P(2G) = \frac{1}{9}$

7) If both spinners are number spinners, you can also fill in the sample space with the total of the two numbers:

EXAMPLE: Two spinners numbered 1-3 are spun and the scores added together. Fill in the sample space diagram, and use it to find the probability that the score is 5.

2nd spinner

	1	2	3
1	2	3	4
2	3	4	5
3	4	5	6

1st spinner

These are the totals of the two spinners, e.g. 3 + 3 = 6.

There are 2 different ways of scoring 5 out of 9 possible outcomes, so:

$$P(5) = \frac{2}{9}$$

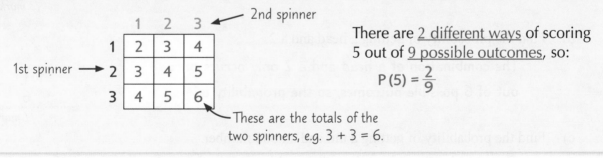

Sample space diagrams show all the outcomes...

Jotting down all the possible outcomes in a sample space diagram makes it much easier to understand what's going on — it's the best way to make sure you don't miss anything.

Warm-Up and Practice Questions

Your proficiency on probability problems will probably progress with practice.
So pick up a pen and perfect your performance with this pack of probability puzzlers.

Warm-Up Questions

1) Today is the 24th November. What is the probability of tomorrow being Christmas Day?

2) The probability of it raining today is 0.4. What is the probability that it won't rain?

3) On a fair 10-sided spinner numbered 1-10, what is the probability of spinning:
   a) a 7?   b) an odd number?   c) a number less than 5?

4) A box of chocolates contains 4 dark chocolates, 8 milk chocolates and 3 white chocolates. What is the probability of picking a milk chocolate?

5) There are 16 coloured balls in a bag. The probability of picking a red ball is P(red) = $\frac{1}{2}$. How many red balls are there in the bag?

6) A dice is rolled and a coin is tossed.
   Draw a sample space diagram showing the possible outcomes.

Practice Questions

The probability of you getting a question on probability in a maths test is pretty close to 1, so have a go and see how you get on. The first one has been done for you.

1 Layla tosses a coin and then spins the fair spinner shown below.

a) Draw a diagram to show all the possible outcomes.

The 2 possible outcomes for tossing the coin. →

	1	2	3
Heads	H1	H2	H3
Tails	T1	T2	T3

← The 3 possible outcomes for the spinner.

[3 marks]

b) Find the probability of getting a head and a 2.

The combination of a head and a 2 only occurs once, out of 6 possible outcomes, so the probability is $\frac{1}{6}$.

$\frac{1}{6}$
....
[1 mark]

c) Find the probability of getting a tail and an odd number.

The combination of a tail and an odd number occurs twice (T1 and T3) out of 6 possible outcomes,

so the probability is $\frac{2}{6} = \frac{1}{3}$. ← Simplify fractions where possible.

$\frac{1}{3}$
....
[1 mark]

Practice Questions

2 Shade the spinner so that the probability
of landing on a shaded section is 25%.

[1 mark]

3 When rolling a fair six-sided dice, you have an equal chance of getting each number.

a) What is the probability of rolling the dice and getting a 5?

....
[1 mark]

b) Mark the probability of getting a 5 on the probability scale below.

0　　　　　　　　　　　1

[1 mark]

4 The letters that spell the word MATHEMATICS are placed in a bag.
A letter is picked at random. Find:

a) the probability of picking out a vowel.

....
[1 mark]

b) the probability of picking out an 'X'.

....
[1 mark]

5 The probability that a train is not on time is 0.22.
What is the probability that the train is on time?

....
[1 mark]

6 There are 8 balls in a bag. The bag contains blue, red and green balls.
The probability of picking a blue ball is $\frac{1}{8}$ and the probability of picking a red ball is $\frac{1}{4}$.
How many green balls are there in the bag?

....
[2 marks]

Venn Diagrams

Venn diagrams are a way of displaying data in intersecting circles — they're very useful.

A **Set** is a **Collection of Objects**

1) Sets are just collections of things (e.g. numbers).

2) A pair of curly brackets {} tell you it's a set.

3) The things in the set are called elements.

Here are some examples of sets:

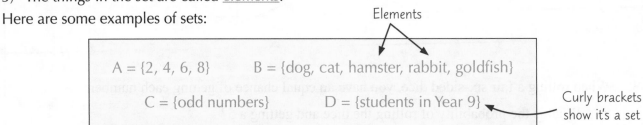

Elements

A = {2, 4, 6, 8}   B = {dog, cat, hamster, rabbit, goldfish}

C = {odd numbers}   D = {students in Year 9}

Curly brackets show it's a set

4) n(A) just means 'the number of elements in set A'. So here, n(A) = 4 and n(B) = 5.

Show **Sets** on **Venn Diagrams**

1) On a Venn diagram, each set is represented by a circle.

2) Elements of a set go inside its circle. Elements that don't belong to the set go outside the circle.

3) If some elements are in both sets, the circles overlap and these elements go in the overlap (this is called the intersection).

4) So if set P was {fruits} and set Q was {things that are yellow}, the Venn diagram would look something like this:

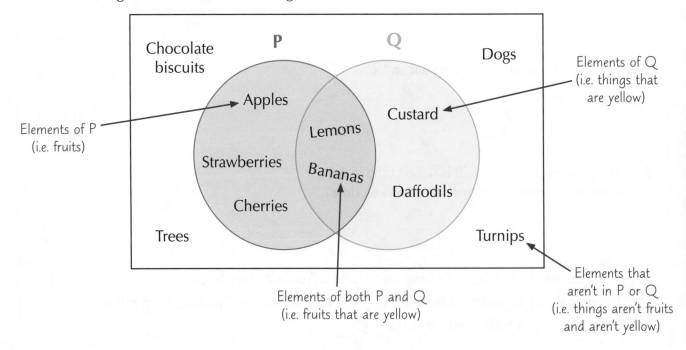

Elements of P (i.e. fruits)

Elements of Q (i.e. things that are yellow)

Elements of both P and Q (i.e. fruits that are yellow)

Elements that aren't in P or Q (i.e. things aren't fruits and aren't yellow)

Things in both sets go in the overlap of the two circles...

REVISION TASK Think of two sets. List the elements of each set inside curly brackets, then draw yourself a Venn diagram to show them. Add some things that aren't in either set outside the circles.

Venn Diagrams

Another page on Venn diagrams now — and things get a little trickier here.

The **Universal Set** is the Set of **Everything**

1) The <u>universal set</u> can be a bit confusing. It's the <u>group of things</u> that the elements of a set are selected <u>from</u> — so if A = {even numbers}, the universal set might be {numbers from 1-20}, which means that A is all the even numbers from 1-20.
2) The universal set is shown by this funny symbol: ξ.
3) On a <u>Venn diagram</u>, the universal set is a rectangle that goes round the <u>outside</u> of the circles.

EXAMPLE: ξ = {numbers from 1 to 10}, A = {factors of 10} and B = {prime numbers}.
   a) Find A and B.

Just <u>write out</u> the elements of each set:
ξ = {1, 2, 3, 4, 5, 6, 7, 8, 9, 10}
A = {1, 2, 5, 10} and B = {2, 3, 5, 7}

It's a good idea to write out the universal set (as long as it's not too big) so you can see which elements you have to choose from.

b) **Show sets A and B on a Venn diagram.**

Use the sets you've just found to put the numbers in the right places.

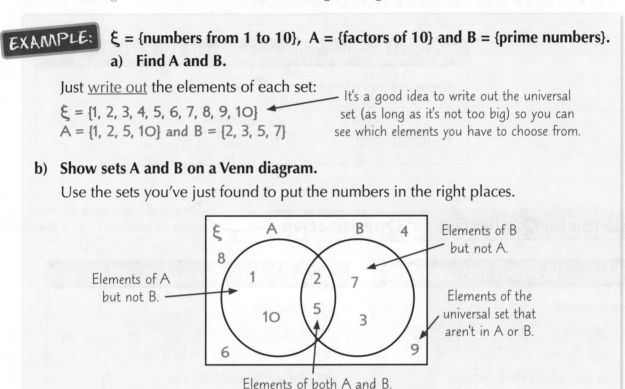

Elements of A but not B.
Elements of B but not A.
Elements of the universal set that aren't in A or B.
Elements of both A and B.

Show the **Number of Elements** on a Venn Diagram

You can also show the <u>number of elements</u> in each set on a Venn diagram — so for the example above, the Venn diagram would look like this:

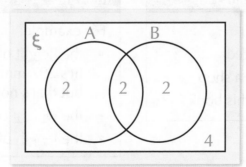

All the elements come from the universal set...

When you're given a universal set, all the elements should appear somewhere on the Venn diagram. Always check whether you have to put in the actual elements or just the number of elements.

Types of Data

Data is a fancy word for information. There are different types of data, which have fancy names...

Data can be **Primary** or **Secondary**

> ### PRIMARY data is data YOU'VE collected.
>
> There are two main ways you can get primary data:
>
> - A SURVEY, e.g. a questionnaire.
> - An EXPERIMENT (like you do in science lessons).

> ### SECONDARY data is collected by SOMEONE ELSE.
>
> There are lots of ways you can get secondary data, e.g. from:
>
> - newspapers
> - the internet
> - databases
> - historical records

Data can be **Qualitative** or **Quantitative**

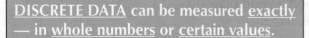

Think 'quantity means numbers' as a way to remember which is which.

> ### QUALITATIVE data is in WORD form.
>
> For example:
> - gender
> - eye colour
> - favourite football team

> ### QUANTITATIVE data is in NUMBER form.
>
> For example:
> - heights of people
> - the time taken to do a task
> - the weight of objects

Quantitative Data is **Discrete** or **Continuous**

> ### DISCRETE DATA can be measured exactly — in whole numbers or certain values.
>
> For example:
> - the number of goals scored
> - the number of people in a shop
> - the number of pages in this book

> ### CONTINUOUS DATA can take any value over a certain range.
>
> For example:
> - the height of this page (it's 297 mm to the nearest mm but that's not its exact height)
> - the weight of a pumpkin
> - the length of a carrot

Definitions can be dull but you're going to have to learn them...

Cover up this page and write down as many of the six definitions as you can remember. Check if you missed any, then think of five examples of each type of data.

Line Graphs and Pictograms

Data can be shown in different types of charts, tables and graphs.
Line graphs and pictograms make it easy to see what the data shows.

Line Graphs

1) A line graph is a set of points joined with straight lines.

2) They often have 'time' along the bottom to show how something changes over time.

3) You can draw two line graphs on the same diagram to compare two things, as shown below.

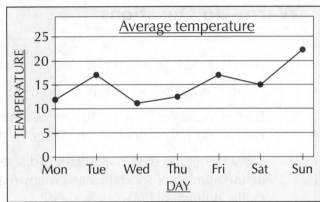

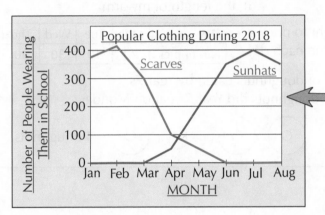

These graphs show clearly that as the year went on, fewer people wore scarves and more people wore sunhats.

Pictograms ← These use pictures instead of numbers.

Every pictogram has a key telling you what one symbol represents.

With pictograms, you MUST use the KEY.

EXAMPLE: This pictogram shows how many pizzas were sold by a pizzeria on different days.

a) **How many pizzas were sold on Tuesday?**
There's 1 whole circle (= 20 pizzas)...
... plus half a circle (= 10 pizzas). 30 pizzas

Key: ● represents 20 pizzas

b) **70 pizzas were sold on Friday.**
Use this information to complete the diagram.
You need 3 whole circles (= 60 pizzas),
plus another half a circle (= 10 pizzas).

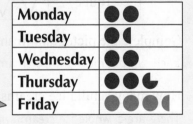

With pictograms, the key is key...

Make sure you know how much each symbol is worth before you start answering any questions —
look carefully at the key and watch out for part symbols when reading off the graph. If you're
asked to draw your own pictogram, do yourself a favour and choose a symbol that's easy to draw.

Warm-Up and Practice Questions

There's a few different ways of presenting data in these pages, so check you've got your head round them by having a go at these warm-up questions.

Warm-Up Questions

1) A = {1, 3, 5, 7, 9} and B = {2, 3, 5, 7, 11}. Draw a Venn diagram to show A and B.
2) For the sets on p.130, find n(P) and n(Q) (don't forget the element in the intersection).
3) Let ξ = {numbers from 1-20}, X = {odd numbers} and Y = {square numbers}. Find X and Y, then draw a Venn diagram showing the number of elements in each set.
4) Say whether this data is qualitative, discrete or continuous:
   a) the number of spectators at a rugby match
   b) the colours of pebbles on a beach
   c) the number of books on a shelf
   d) the length of my arm
5) Use the information in the table on the right to draw a line graph showing the number of pies eaten each day.

Day	Mon	Tue	Wed	Thu
No. of pies	20	10	30	40

6) Part of the pictogram showing the number of doughnuts eaten by Year 7s at break time is shown below. How many doughnuts did Year 7s eat on Monday?

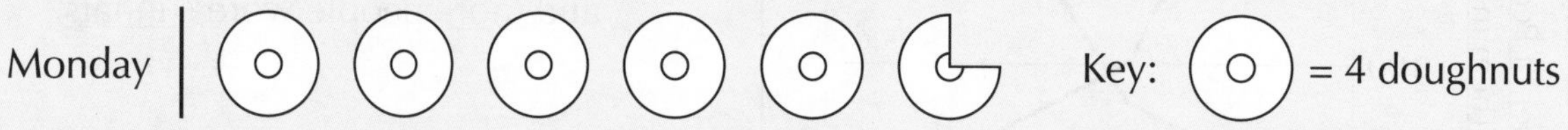

Practice Questions

Before you have a go at the trickier questions on the next page, read through this worked question — it'll show you how it's done.

1 The pictogram below shows the number of different flavours of ice cream eaten at Ellie's birthday party.

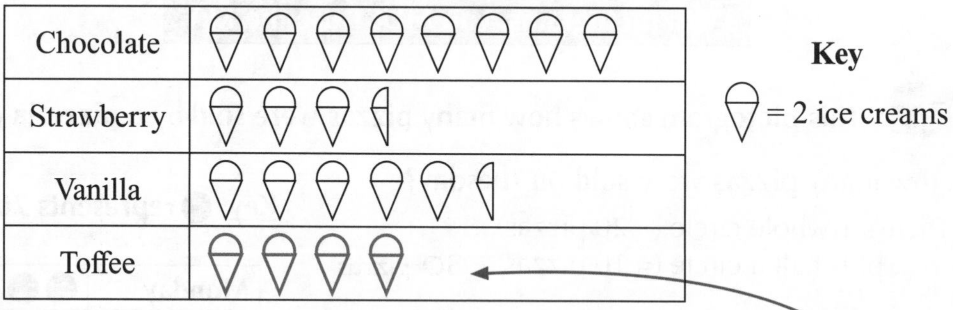

a) Complete the pictogram to show that 8 toffee ice creams were eaten.

Each symbol means 2 ice creams, so you need 4 ice cream symbols in the 'toffee' row.

[1 mark]

b) How many vanilla ice creams were eaten?

There are 5 whole ice cream symbols = 10 ice creams
plus 1 half ice cream symbol. = 1 ice cream
10 + 1 = 11 ice creams in total

11 ice creams

[1 mark]

c) How many more chocolate than strawberry ice creams were eaten?

Number of chocolate ice creams → 16 − 7 = 9 ← Number of strawberry ice creams

9 ice creams

[1 mark]

Practice Questions

2 The Jones family drew a graph of how many runs and swims
   they did during each month of 2018.

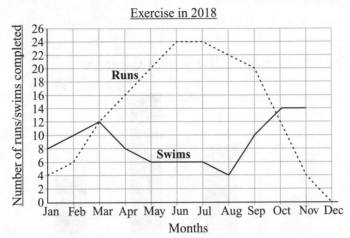

Exercise in 2018

a) In December, they went for 10 swims.
    Use this information to complete the graph above.

[1 mark]

b) In which month did the family go for the same number of runs and swims?

....
[1 mark]

c) How many more runs did they do in July than in September?

....
[1 mark]

d) How many more swims than runs did they do in November?

....
[1 mark]

3 There are 300 students in Year 9. 120 students study music, 110 study art
   and 30 study both music and art. 100 students study neither music nor art.

a) Show this information on this Venn
    diagram, where M = {music students}
    and A = {art students}.

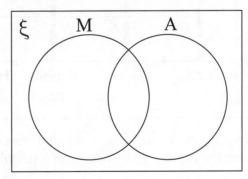

[3 marks]

b) How many students study at least one of music or art?

....
[1 mark]

Section Five — Probability and Statistics

Bar Charts

Here's the next exciting way of displaying data — <u>bar charts</u>.

Bar Charts Show Data as Bars

The <u>height</u> of each bar is the <u>frequency</u> (i.e. how many) for that group.

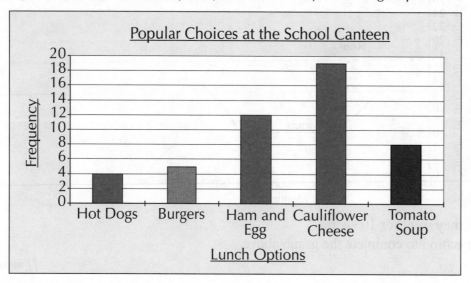

The bar chart above compares <u>separate items</u> (e.g. hot dogs, burgers) so the bars <u>don't touch</u>. You can see from the graph that <u>cauliflower cheese</u> was the most <u>popular</u> choice, and only <u>4</u> people chose <u>hot dogs</u>.

You can also show data on Bar-Line Graphs

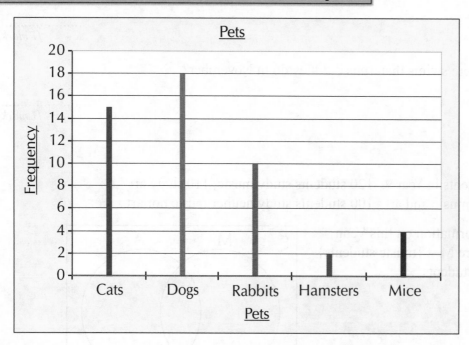

This is a <u>bar-line graph</u>. It's just like a bar chart, except it has <u>thin lines</u> instead of bars. Here, <u>dogs</u> were the most <u>popular</u> pets, and <u>2</u> people have <u>hamsters</u>.

Gaps in the data mean gaps between the bars...

If your data is qualitative (see p.132), you'll always have gaps between the bars because the categories don't merge into each other — your favourite colour might be blue or purple, but it can't be blurple.

Bar Charts

You're not quite done with bar charts yet — here are a couple of special types...

Bar Charts with **Touching Bars**

1) Sometimes the bars need to touch.

2) This is when you need to cover a range of numbers on the *x*-axis, rather than separate categories — so there should be no spaces between the bars (e.g. for measurements like height or length).

If your data is continuous (see p.132), the bars should touch.

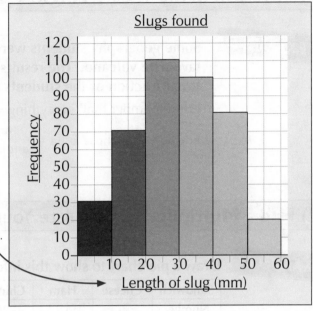

Dual Bar Charts

1) Dual bar charts show two sets of data together so you can compare them.

2) Each category has two bars — one for each set of data.

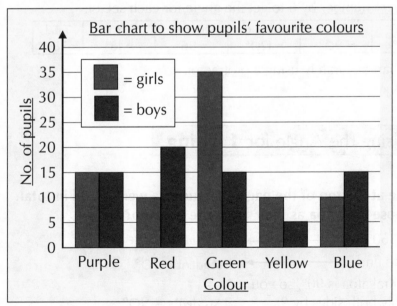

This is a dual bar chart. It's easy to see from the graph that more girls than boys liked green, and that the same number of girls and boys liked purple.

Dual bar charts compare two sets of data...

If you're drawing a bar chart in the exam, use a ruler to draw the bars as accurately as possible. Remember, all the bars should be the same width and the axes need to be labelled.

Pie Charts

You must learn the <u>Golden Rule</u> for pie charts: | The TOTAL of Everything = 360°

1) **Fraction** of the Total = **Angle ÷ 360°**

EXAMPLE: Some geography students were asked to name their
favourite volcano. The results are displayed in the pie chart.
What fraction of the students chose Etna?

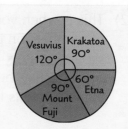

Just remember that 'everything = 360°'.

Fraction that chose Etna = $\dfrac{\text{angle of Etna}}{\text{angle of everything}} = \dfrac{60°}{360°} = \dfrac{1}{6}$

2) Find a **Multiplier** to Calculate Your **Angles**

EXAMPLE: Draw a pie chart to show this information:

Sandwich	Cheese	Ham	Chicken	Tuna	Egg
Number	6	15	20	16	3

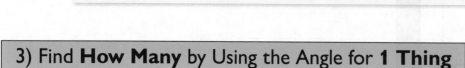

1) Find the <u>total</u> by <u>adding</u>.

   6 + 15 + 20 + 16 + 3 = 60

2) 'Everything = 360°' — so find the <u>multiplier</u> (or <u>divider</u>)
   that turns your total into 360°.

   Multiplier = 360 ÷ 60 = 6

3) Now <u>multiply every number</u> by 6 to get the <u>angle</u> for each sector.

Angle	6 × 6 = 36°	15 × 6 = 90°	20 × 6 = 120°	16 × 6 = 96°	3 × 6 = 18°	Total = 360°

4) Draw your pie chart accurately using a <u>protractor</u>.

3) Find **How Many** by Using the Angle for **1 Thing**

EXAMPLE: In the example at the top of the page, 36 students were asked in total.
How many chose Krakatoa as their favourite volcano?

1) 'Everything = 360°', so... ⟶ 36 students = 360°

2) <u>Divide by 36</u> to find... ⟶ 1 student = 10°

3) The <u>angle</u> for Krakatoa is 90°, so you
   need to <u>multiply both sides by 9</u>:　　9 students = 90°

   9 students chose Krakatoa

All the sectors in a pie chart add up to 360°...

Pie charts may look complicated, but take things one step at a time and remember the golden rule:
'everything = 360°'. Take your time and practise the three types of examples until you're confident.

Warm-Up and Practice Questions

Some of these graphs and charts look pretty similar at first glance, so make sure you know the big differences between them. Time to test your knowledge with a few warm-up questions...

Warm-Up Questions

1) The bar chart on the right shows the favourite slush drink colour of the students in Class 8C.
   a) Which is the most popular colour?
   b) How many students chose red?

Favourite Slush Drinks

2) Two bar charts are drawn. One bar chart has shoe size along the horizontal axis and the other has length of feet along the horizontal axis. Which bar chart has gaps between the bars? Explain why this is.

3) A pie chart is drawn, showing the favourite colours of 60 people.
   a) 10 people chose blue. Work out the angle for blue on the pie chart.
   b) The angle for green is 120°. How many people chose green?

Practice Questions

Practising lots of nice graph questions will help make sure you can cope with any that you come across. This first one has been done for you, so look over it before making a start on the next page.

1 An athletics team voted on the name for their new teddy bear mascot.
  The results are shown in the table below. Complete the bar chart to show this data.

Name	Bob	Fuzzy	Goldie	Ted	Winston
Frequency	5	8	6	2	10

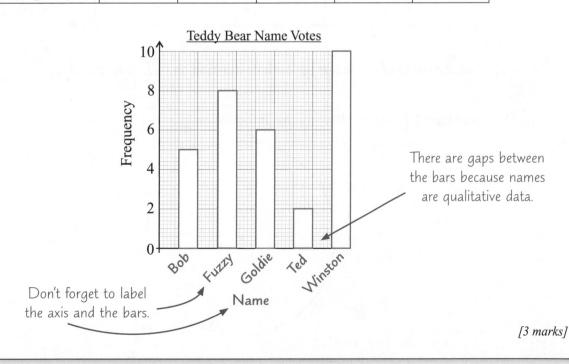

There are gaps between the bars because names are qualitative data.

Don't forget to label the axis and the bars.

[3 marks]

Section Five — Probability and Statistics

Practice Questions

2 A class of children were asked to choose their favourite flavour of crisps.

a) 6 girls and 2 boys chose Prawn Cocktail crisps as their favourite flavour.
Use this information to complete the dual bar chart below.

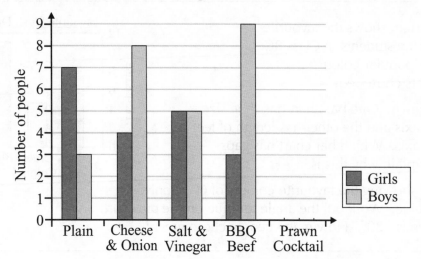

[1 mark]

b) How many more children chose BBQ Beef than Salt & Vinegar?

....
[2 marks]

3 45 pupils were asked where they went last year for their summer holiday.
Their responses were organised into this frequency table.

Destination	Frequency	Angle of sector
UK & Ireland	12	....
Europe	23	....
USA	7	....
Other	3	....

a) Calculate the angle of the sector for each destination and add it to the table.

[2 marks]

b) Draw and label a pie chart showing this information.

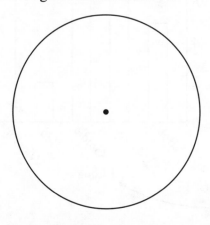

[2 marks]

Mean, Median, Mode and Range

Mean, median, mode and range pop up all the time — make sure you know what they are and how to find them. Learn the Golden Rule too — it's really important.

The **Four Definitions**

MODE = MOST common

MEDIAN = MIDDLE value (when values are in order of size)

MEAN = TOTAL of items ÷ NUMBER of items

RANGE = Difference between highest and lowest

> REMEMBER:
> Mode = most (emphasise the 'mo' when you say them)
> Median = mid (emphasise the m*d when you say them)
> Mean is the average, but it's mean because you have to work it out.

The **GOLDEN** Rule

There's one vital step for finding the median that lots of people forget:

Always REARRANGE the data in ASCENDING ORDER (and check you have the same number of entries)

You must do this when finding the median, but it's also really useful for working out the mode.

EXAMPLE: **For the numbers 6, 4, 7, 1, 2, 6, 3, 5, find:**

Check you have the same number of values after you've rearranged them.

a) **the median**

The MEDIAN is the middle value (when they're arranged in order of size) — so first, rearrange the numbers.

1, 2, 3, (4, 5) 6, 6, 7

When there are two middle numbers, the median is halfway between the two.

← 4 numbers this side | 4 numbers this side →

Median = 4.5

b) **the mode**

MODE (or modal value) is the most common value. Mode = 6

Some data sets have more than one mode, or no mode at all.

c) **the mean**

MEAN = $\dfrac{\text{total of items}}{\text{number of items}}$ $\quad \dfrac{1+2+3+4+5+6+6+7}{8} = \dfrac{34}{8} = 4.25$

d) **the range**

RANGE = difference between highest and lowest values, i.e. between 7 and 1. 7 − 1 = 6

Put the numbers in ascending order before finding the median...

Be sure to read the question carefully — you don't want to work out the wrong thing.

Frequency Tables

Frequency tables are like tally charts. The numbers can be arranged in either rows or columns. They're not too bad if you learn these key points:

> 1) The word **FREQUENCY** means **HOW MANY**.
> So a frequency table is just a '**How many in each group' table**.
> 2) The **FIRST ROW** (or column) gives the **CATEGORY**.
> 3) The **FREQUENCY ROW** (or column) tells you
> **HOW MANY THERE ARE** in that category.

Frequency tables show how many things there are in each category.

Category → | How many

Vehicle	Frequency
Car	5
Bus	20
Lorry	31

Grouped frequency tables group the data into classes.

Height (*h* cm)	Frequency
5-10	12
11-15	15
16-20	11

Filling in Frequency Tables

46 pupils in a school were asked how many sisters they had. The results were put into a frequency table as shown:

In Columns:

Category

In Rows:

No. of Sisters	0	1	2	3	4	5	6	Total:
Tally	ҬҤ‖	ҬҤ ҬҤ ҬҤ	ҬҤ ҬҤ ‖	ҬҤ ‖‖	‖‖	‖		
Frequency	7	15	12	8	3	1	0	46

The tally column is often left out.

The frequency is just a total of the tally for that group.

No. of Sisters	Frequency
0	7
1	15
2	12
3	8
4	3
5	1
6	0
Total:	**46**

You can use frequency tables to find averages — there's more on this on the next page.

Frequency means 'how many'...

Don't be put off by long words — frequency tables are really quite simple. They're just about counting how many of each category there are. Use the column or row headings to remind you what's what.

Averages from Frequency Tables

I hope you're happy with frequency tables, because there's one more thing to learn...

Find the **Mean** from a **Frequency Table**

To find the mean from a frequency table, you need to add an extra column to your table.

EXAMPLE: **Some people were asked how many posters they have on their bedroom walls. The table shows the results. Find the mean of the data.**

Number of posters	Frequency
0	1
1	10
2	12
3	9
4	6
5	2

1) If we had a list of the number of posters everyone had, it would look like this:

0, 1, 1, 1, 1, 1, 1, 1, 1, 1, 1, 2, 2, 2, 2, 2, 2, 2, 2, 2, 2, 2, 2, ...

One 0   10 lots of 1   12 lots of 2

2) There are 40 numbers in the list because 40 people were asked.

3) To find the mean, you'd add all these numbers and divide by 40.

4) It's exactly the same for the table — except we cheat by adding an extra column to the table:

To find the mode from a frequency table, just pick the category with the highest frequency.

Number of posters	Frequency	No. of posters × Frequency
0	1	0
1	10	10
2	12	24
3	9	27
4	6	24
5	2	10
Total	40	95

This is the same as adding 10 lots of 1.

This is the same as adding 6 lots of 4.

This is the total number of posters.

$$\underline{\text{MEAN}} = \frac{\text{3rd column total}}{\text{2nd column total}} = \frac{95}{40} = 2.375$$

total number of posters

total number of people asked

Always follow these steps:

1) Add up the TOTAL of the SECOND COLUMN.
2) Make a THIRD COLUMN by MULTIPLYING the FIRST COLUMN and SECOND COLUMN together.
3) Add up the TOTAL of the new THIRD COLUMN.
4) **MEAN = 3rd Column total ÷ 2nd Column Total**

Fill in the third column before finding the mean...

Cover the page and write down the four steps for finding the mean from a frequency table.

Scatter Graphs

Scatter graphs are really useful — they can show you if there's a link between two things.

Scatter Graphs Show **Correlation**

1) A scatter graph shows how closely two things are related. The fancy word for this is CORRELATION.
2) If the two things are related, then you should be able to draw a straight line (called a line of best fit) passing pretty close to most of the points on the scatter diagram.

STRONG correlation is when your points make a fairly straight line.

Ice cream sales
Temperature

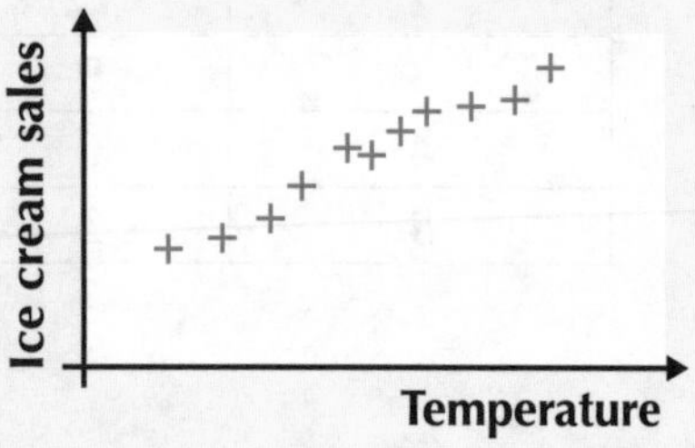

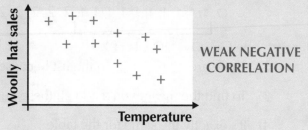

STRONG POSITIVE CORRELATION

If the points form a line sloping uphill from left to right, then there is POSITIVE correlation — both things increase or decrease together.

WEAK correlation means your points don't line up quite so nicely, but you can still draw a line of best fit through them.

Woolly hat sales
Temperature

WEAK NEGATIVE CORRELATION

If the points form a line sloping downhill from left to right, then there is NEGATIVE correlation — as one quantity increases, the other decreases.

3) If the two things are not related, you get a load of messy points. This scatter graph is a messy scatter — so there's no correlation between the two things.

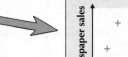

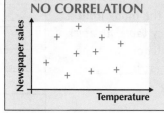

NO CORRELATION

Newspaper sales
Temperature

4) You can use a line of best fit to predict other values.

EXAMPLE: **This graph shows the value of a car (in £'000s) plotted against its age in years.**

a) Describe the strength and type of correlation shown by the graph.

Strong negative correlation

Value (£'000s)
0
1
2
3
4
5
6
7
8
Age of car (years)
0
1
2
3
4
5
6

b) Estimate the value of a 3 year old car.

1) Draw a line of best fit (shown in blue).
2) Draw a line up from 3 years to your line, and then across to the other axis.

A 3-year-old car is worth roughly £4500

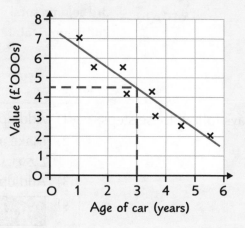

Correlation can be strong or weak, negative or positive...

REVISION TIP

Positive correlation is an uphill slope — say 'things are looking up' to help you remember.

Warm-Up and Practice Questions

You're almost at the end of the book, but don't start celebrating quite yet. Once you're happy with all the stuff on the last few pages, come and give these warm-up questions a try.

Warm-Up Questions

1) Find the median, mode, mean and range of these numbers: 10, 12, 8, 15, 9, 12, 11.

2) What is the median of the numbers 10, 20, 12, 21, 19, 9, 5 and 18?

3) 20 people were asked to name their favourite picnic food. The results are shown below. Put these results into a frequency table.
sausage rolls, crisps, pork pies, quiche, sandwiches, sausage rolls, pork pies, pork pies, crisps, quiche, crisps, sausage rolls, pork pies, sandwiches, sausage rolls, sandwiches, sandwiches, sausage rolls, quiche, pork pies

4) A class were asked how many cars their family had. The results are shown in the table below.

Number of cars	0	1	2	3	4
Frequency	3	15	12	5	0

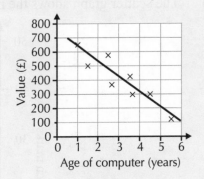

a) Find the mean for this data. Give your answer to 2 d.p.
b) Find the mode for this data.

5) What type of correlation would you expect to see between children's ages and heights?

6) Use the graph on the right to predict the age of a computer worth £450.

Practice Questions

Here's the final set of practice questions — and my last worked example.
I'm getting a bit emotional here... just give me a minute.

1 50 pupils in Year 9 were asked how many different vegetables they had with their dinner last night. The results are shown in the frequency table below.

Calculate the mean number of vegetables.

Number of vegetables	Frequency	No. of vegetables × Frequency
0	12	0
1	16	16
2	15	30
3	7	21
Total	50	67

Add a third column to the table.

Multiply the numbers in the first column by the numbers in the second column.

Calculate the totals for the second and third columns.

$$\text{Mean} = \frac{\text{3rd column total}}{\text{2nd column total}}$$

Total number of vegetables

Total number of people asked

$$= \frac{67}{50}$$

$$= 1.34$$

1.34
....
[3 marks]

Practice Questions

2   Matteo is a member of a pub quiz team. His team have played three games.
    In the first game they scored 42 points, in the second they scored 49 points
    and in the third they scored 44 points.

    Calculate the mean score for the three games.

    ....

    [2 marks]

3   The scatter graph shows the marks for ten pupils in their Maths and French examinations.

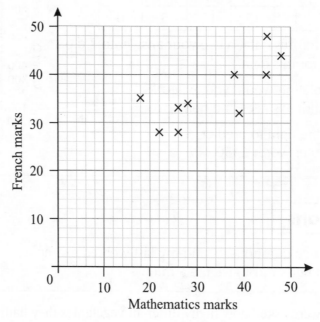

    a)   Draw a line of best fit on the graph.

    [1 mark]

    b)   Describe the type of correlation this data shows.

    ....

    [1 mark]

    c)   A pupil was absent for the French exam but scored 34 in the Maths exam.
         What mark would you expect him to have scored in French?

    ....

    [1 mark]

    d)   What is the range of the French marks?

    ....

    [1 mark]

Revision Summary

You know what's coming by now — here are some questions to check it's all sunk in.
- Try these questions and <u>tick off each one</u> when you <u>get it right</u>.
- When you've done <u>all the questions</u> for a topic and are <u>completely happy</u> with it, tick off the topic.

Probability (p.125-127) ☑

1. What does a probability of 1 mean?
2. In a game, you can either win or lose. If P(win) = 0.1, what is P(lose)?
3. In a bag of sweets, there are 5 cola bottles, 2 jelly snakes, 3 chocolate buttons and 2 chocolate mice. Find the probability of picking a cola bottle.
4. I have a spinner that is half black and half white. I spin it twice.
   a) Fill in this sample space diagram to show all the possible results.
   b) Find the probability of spinning a black and a white.

		Second spin	
		Black	White
First spin	Black		BW
	White		

Venn Diagrams (p.130-131) ☑

5. Let ξ = {integers from 1 to 12}, X = {prime numbers}, Y = {factors of 8}
   a) Find X and Y.
   b) Draw a Venn diagram showing sets X and Y.

Types of Data, Graphs and Charts (p.132-138) ☑

6. What is primary data? What is secondary data?
7. Is 'favourite flavours of ice cream' quantitative or qualitative data?
8. I measure the weight of some jacket potatoes. Is this data discrete or continuous?
9. Luke reads 4 books in January, 6 books in February, 5 books in March and 3 books in April. Draw a pictogram to show this information.
10. The table on the right shows how many camels a dealer sells each week. Draw a bar chart to show this information.

Week	1	2	3	4
Number of camels	4	8	18	22

11. Draw a pie chart to represent the data in the table on the right.

Colour of car	red	blue	black	silver
Number	15	5	10	30

12. On a pie chart, the angle representing 'not if you paid me £1 000 000' is 30°. If 120 people took part in the survey, how many gave this answer?

Averages and Frequency Tables (p.141-143) ☑

13. Find the mode, median, mean and range of this data: 2, 8, 7, 5, 11, 5, 4.
14. The frequency table below shows the number of TVs per house.
   a) How many houses had 3 TVs?
   b) Using the same frequency table, find the mode, mean and range for the number of TVs.

Number of TVs	0	1	2	3	4
Frequency	2	10	15	12	1

Scatter Graphs (p.144) ☑

15. Give an example of data that would show positive correlation on a scatter graph.

Mixed Practice Tests

OK, so you've done most of the hard work — but are you ready for the big Practice Exam?
To help you decide, here are some brilliant Mixed Practice Tests for you to have a go at.

- Scribble down your answers to the questions in a test. When you've answered them all, check your answers (see p.186-187). Tick the box next to each question you got right. Put a cross in the box if you got it wrong.
- If you're getting 7 or more out of 10 right on these tests, you should be ready for the Practice Exam on p.158-177.
- If you're getting less than that, go back and do some more revision. Have another go at the Revision Summaries — they're the best way to find out what you know and what you've forgotten.

Test 1

✓ / ✗

1. What is a prime number?

2. How many millilitres are in 20 litres?

    A   0.02
    B   200
    C   2000
    D   20 000

3. A reflex angle is...

    A   ...less than 90°.
    B   ...exactly 90°.
    C   ...between 90° and 180°.
    D   ...between 180° and 360°.

4. Give the coordinates of the point where the x- and y-axes cross.

5. What is the next number in this sequence: 1, 7, 13, 19, ... ?

    A   13
    B   22
    C   25
    D   29

6. What is discrete data?

7. K and L are related by the formula $K = 2L + 50$. Find K when $L = 15$.

8. What is $\frac{12}{20}$ as a percentage?

    A   12%
    B   60%
    C   80%
    D   0.6%

9. Work out the median of these numbers: 1 5 4 12 8

10. How many sides does a rhombus have?

Total (out of 10):

Mixed Practice Tests

Test 2

✓ / ✗

1. What is the probability of an impossible event happening?

☐

2. The mean of a set of data is...

   A ...the middle value.
   B ...the most common value.
   C ...the sum of all the values, divided by the number of values.
   D ...the difference between the largest and smallest value.

☐

3. What is the value of $\sqrt{64}$?

   A 4
   B 8
   C 6
   D 16

☐

4. What is the highest common factor of two numbers?

☐

5. How many significant figures is this number given to: 0.405?

   A One
   B Two
   C Three
   D Four

☐

6. How many pints are there in 3 gallons? (Hint: 1 gallon = 8 pints)

☐

7. What is the simplest form of the ratio 40:100?

   A 2:5
   B 4:10
   C 1:4
   D 20:50

☐

8. If two shapes are similar, they are...

   A ...exactly the same shape and the same size.
   B ...different shapes but the same size.
   C ...exactly the same shape but different sizes.
   D ...exactly the same size but have different angles.

☐

9. If $3x + 4 = 25$, what is the value of x?

☐

10. What is the formula for working out the sum of the interior angles
    for a polygon with n sides?

☐

Total (out of 10): ☐

Section Six — Exam Practice

Mixed Practice Tests

✓ / ✗

1. What are the coordinates of point A, shown on the grid below?

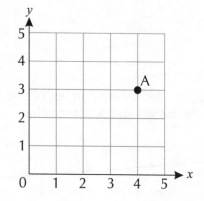

2. What is the range of these values: 1, 4, 5, 9?

3. A car travels at an average speed of 25 km/h for 2 hours.
   How far does the car travel in this time? Use the formula: speed = distance ÷ time.

   A 25 km
   B 50 km
   C 12.5 km
   D 100 km

4. Write down all the factors of 16.

5. The picture below is a scale drawing of a swimming pool.
   What is the length of the swimming pool?

   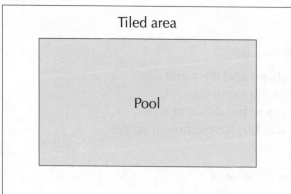

   A 6 m
   B 600 m
   C 12 m
   D 24 m

Mixed Practice Tests

6. Round 9.754 to one decimal place.

7. Write $\frac{2}{10}$ as a decimal.

8. What is the name of the shape on the right?

   A Regular tetrahedron
   B Triangular prism
   C Cuboid
   D Square-based pyramid

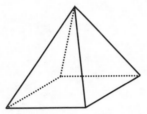

9. A pupil asks everyone in Year 7 to choose their favourite colour.
   Her results are shown in the bar chart below.
   How many more people chose red than green?

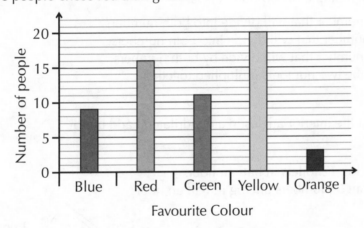

   A 16
   B 7
   C 5
   D 11

10. A sequence has the *n*th term $2n + 6$.
    What is the 8th term in this sequence?

    A 22
    B 8
    C 16
    D 28

Total (out of 10):

Mixed Practice Tests

Test 4

1. What is the formula used for calculating the area of a triangle?

2. Which of the following is an improper fraction?

    A   1

    B $\frac{2}{3}$

    C $\frac{3}{2}$

    D $1\frac{1}{3}$

3. What do the probabilities of all the possible results of an event add up to?

4. The lowest common multiple of two numbers is...

    A   ...the smallest number that will divide into both numbers.
    B   ...the biggest number that will divide into both numbers.
    C   ...the smallest number that will divide by both numbers.
    D   ...the value of the two numbers multiplied together.

5. What value do all of the interior angles in a quadrilateral add up to?

6. 4 plumbers can unclog 12 toilets in half an hour.
    How many toilets can 9 plumbers unclog in half an hour?

7. What is the perimeter of the rectangle on the right?

    A   7 cm
    B   14 cm
    C   10 cm
    D   25 cm

    5 cm   2 cm

    (Not to scale)

8. What direction is directly opposite south-east on a compass?

9. Expand this expression: $5(2x + 5)$.

10. A sandwich costs £1.20. The price of the sandwich is increased by 50%.
    What is the new price of the sandwich?

    A   £1.80
    B   £1.50
    C   60p
    D   £1.70

Total (out of 10):

Mixed Practice Tests

Test 5

1. What is next in the sequence 5, 10, 20, 40, ... ?

2. A = {1, 3, 5, 7, 9}
   What is the value of n(A)?

   A 25
   B 5
   C 9
   D 7

3. Simplify this expression: $3m + 5n + m + m - 2n$

4. What is the order of rotational symmetry of a regular pentagon?

5. There are 26 pupils in a classroom. 4 of the pupils have red hair.
   What fraction of the pupils have red hair?

   A $\frac{26}{4}$

   B $\frac{4}{13}$

   C $\frac{2}{13}$

   D $\frac{13}{2}$

6. Isosceles triangles...
   A ...have 2 sides of the same length and 2 angles the same.
   B ...always contain an angle of 90°.
   C ...have 3 lines of rotational symmetry.
   D ...have 3 sides of the same length.

7. A packet of pens contains blue pens and green pens in the ratio 3:2.
   There are 12 blue pens in the packet. How many green pens are there?

8. Obtuse angles are always...
   A ...less than 90°.
   B ...between 90° and 180°.
   C ...greater than 180°.
   D ...exactly 90°.

9. What is the mode of these numbers: 4 2 6 2 9?

10. What is $2^3 + 4^2$?

Total (out of 10):

Mixed Practice Tests

Test 6

1. Write down both square roots of 81.

2. How many lines of symmetry does this regular polygon have?

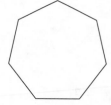

3. What is 0.42 as a percentage?

4. What is the value of angle *a* in the diagram below?

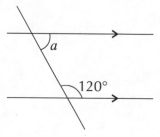

 A   60°
 B   120°
 C   180°
 D   240°

5. In a survey, some students were asked how often they go to the cinema.
    The pie chart below shows the results of the survey.
    What fraction of the students go to the cinema once a week?

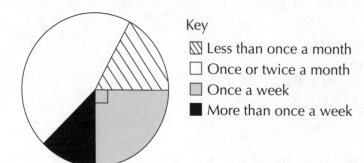

Key
╲ Less than once a month
□ Once or twice a month
▨ Once a week
■ More than once a week

 A $\frac{1}{4}$

 B $\frac{1}{8}$

 C $\frac{1}{10}$

 D $\frac{1}{12}$

Section Six — Exam Practice

Mixed Practice Tests

6. What is the formula for calculating the area of a circle?

   A Area = $2 \times \pi \times r$
   B Area = $\pi \times r^2$
   C Area = $2 \times \pi \times r^2$
   D Area = $2 \times r^2$

7. A straight line has been drawn on this set of axes.
   What is its equation?

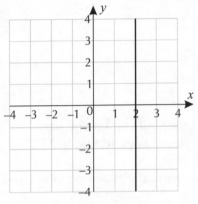

   A $x = 2y$
   B $y = 2x$
   C $x = 2$
   D $y = 2$

8. The pictogram on the right shows the number
   of houses built in a town in different months.
   How many houses were built in March?

   A 2
   B 18
   C 15
   D 12

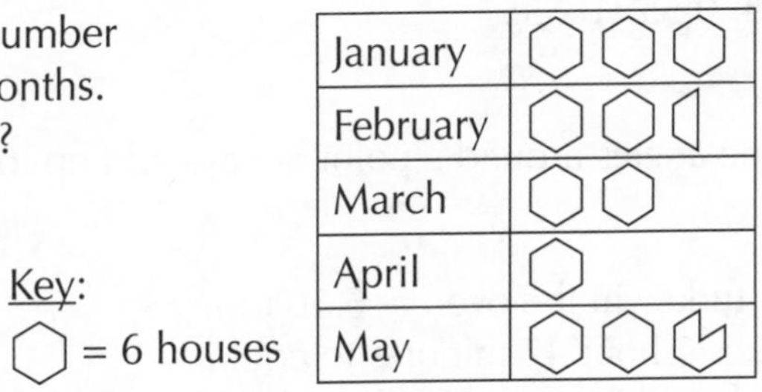

   Key:
   ⬡ = 6 houses

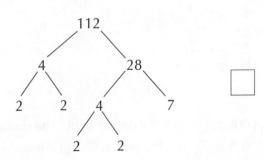

9. A man walks a distance of 30 metres in 20 seconds. Calculate the man's
   walking speed in metres per second using this formula: speed = distance ÷ time.

10. A completed factor tree for the
    number 112 is shown on the right.
    Write down the prime factorisation of 112.

    112
    4   28
    2 2   4   7
          2 2

    Total (out of 10):

Section Six — Exam Practice

Mixed Practice Tests

Test 7

1. A scalene triangle...

    A ...has three sides of equal length.
    B ...has two sides of equal length.
    C ...has three unequal sides.
    D ...has three equal interior angles.

2. Calculate $7 - 3 \times 2^2$

3. What is the surface area of a shape?

4. Congruent shapes are...

    A ...the same shape as each other but can be any size.
    B ...shapes whose interior angles always add up to 180°.
    C ...exactly the same as each other.
    D ...shapes in which all the interior angles are equally sized.

5. Which of these lists of numbers is in ascending order?

    A 0.1, 0.21, 0.088, 0.99
    B 0.009, 0.07, 0.2, 0.5
    C 0.04, 0.05, 0.7, 0.09
    D 0.5, 0.05 0.55, 0.555

6. What do all the angles around a point always add up to?

7. Jeremy puts a turkey in the oven at 6.50 pm.
   The turkey takes 1 hour 47 minutes to cook.
   At what time should Jeremy take the turkey out of the oven?

8. Estimate 102×3.1.

9. The triangle to the right is translated by the vector $\begin{pmatrix} 4 \\ 7 \end{pmatrix}$.
   What are the new coordinates of point A?

    A (4, 7)
    B (5, 8)
    C (−3, −6)
    D (7, 14)

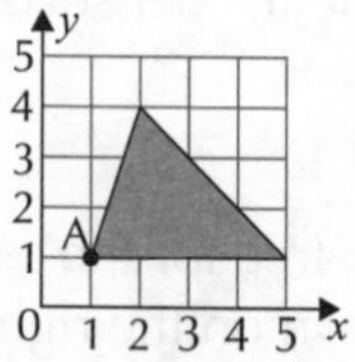

10. Look at the spinner on the right. The probability that it will land
    on A is $\frac{4}{10}$ and the probability that it will land on B is $\frac{3}{10}$.
    What is the probability that it will land on C?

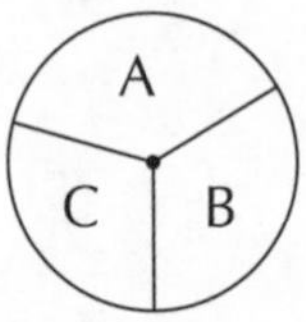

Total (out of 10):

Mixed Practice Tests

Test 8   ✓ / ✗

1. Round 827 682 to the nearest thousand.

2. What is continuous data?

3. Work out -4×-7.

4. The scatter graph on the right is showing...
    A   ...no correlation.
    B   ...strong negative correlation.
    C   ...weak positive correlation.
    D   ...strong positive correlation.

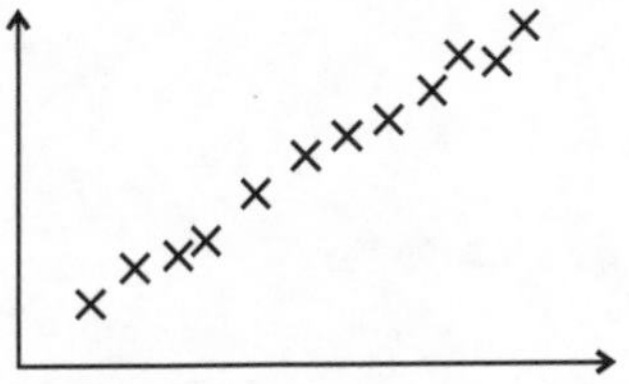

5. Part of a bus timetable is shown on the right. What is the time of the latest bus leaving Ashton that will arrive at Winderby before 1.50 pm?

Ashton	1305	1317	1329	1341
Rosebarrow	1312	1324	1336	1348
Beechley	1316	1328	1340	1352
Winderby	1321	1333	1345	1357
Newford	1325	1337	1349	1401

6. Which of the following is a prime number?
    A   22
    B   19
    C   33
    D   4

7. Amelia and Raj share 150 sweets in the ratio 6:9.
    How many sweets does each person get?
    A   Amelia gets 40 and Raj gets 70
    B   Amelia gets 60 and Raj gets 90
    C   Amelia gets 50 and Raj gets 100
    D   Amelia gets 90 and Raj gets 60

8. A circle has a radius of 6 cm. What is the diameter of the circle?

9. The bisector of an angle...
    A   ...divides the angle exactly in half.
    B   ...is constructed using a protractor.
    C   ...can only be found for acute angles.
    D   ...divides the angle into three.

10. $2 \times 2 \times 2$ can be written in the form 2^x.
    What is the value of x?

Total (out of 10):

Key Stage 3 Mathematics Foundation Level Practice Exam

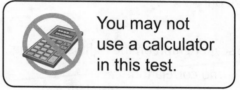

You may not use a calculator in this test.

Paper 1
Calculator NOT allowed

Instructions

- The test is one hour long.
- Make sure you have these things with you before you start:
  - pen
  - pencil
  - rubber
  - ruler
  - angle measurer or protractor
  - pair of compasses

  You may use tracing paper.
- The easier questions are at the start of the test.
- Try to answer all of the questions.
- Don't use any rough paper — write all your answers and working in this test paper.
- Check your work carefully before the end of the test.

Score: ☐ **out of 60**

1. Fill in the missing numbers in the following calculations.

(a) $\boxed{56} - \boxed{} = \boxed{47}$

(b) $\boxed{} \times \boxed{9} = \boxed{63}$

2. Look at the trapezium shown below.

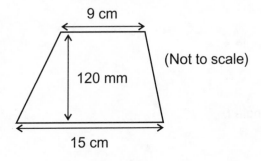

9 cm

(Not to scale)

120 mm

15 cm

(a) Convert 120 mm into cm.

.... cm

(b) Calculate the area of the trapezium. Give your answer in cm².

.... cm²

3. What is the name of the shape below?

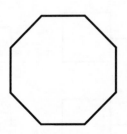

....

4. By rounding each number to one significant figure, estimate the value of $\dfrac{(6.2 \times 29)}{8.9}$.

....

2 marks

5. Look at the triangle below.

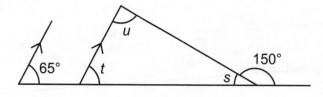

(a) Find the size of angle *s*.

s = ...°

1 mark

(b) Find the size of angle *t*.

t = ...°

1 mark

(c) Find the size of angle *u*.

u = ...°

1 mark

6. Write these numbers in order of size, starting with the smallest.

0.4 $\dfrac{1}{4}$ 0.15   0.05

....

2 marks

7. Fill in the next two numbers in each of the following sequences.

(a)

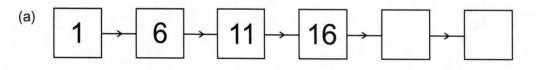

1 mark

(b)

1 mark

8.   Some pupils recorded the number of pets that each girl and boy in their class has.
     They plotted the information on the bar chart shown below.

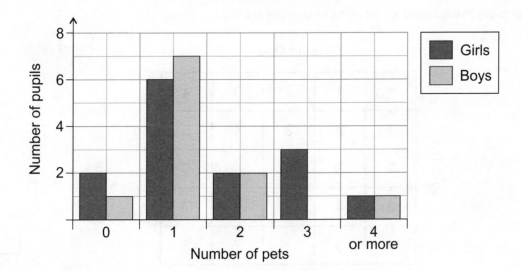

(a)   2 boys in the class have 3 pets.
      Use this information to complete the bar chart.

1 mark

(b)   How many more girls in the class have 1 pet than 2 pets?

....

1 mark

(c)   How many children in the class have no pets?

....

1 mark

9.   Abdul and Rita share a cake.

     Abdul eats 25% of the cake and Rita eats $\frac{2}{5}$ of the cake.

     What percentage of the cake is left?

..................%

2 marks

10. Pat is playing a game with a spinner, labelled 1-4. She spins the spinner twice.
She works out her score by adding together the two numbers that the spinner lands on.

(a) Complete the table to show all her possible scores.

Spin One

	1	2	3	4
1	2	3	4	5
2	3	4	....	6
3	4	5	6	7
4	5	....	7	8

Spin Two

1 mark

(b) Use your table to work out the probability that Pat scores 7.
Simplify your answer if possible.

....

2 marks

11. Shape A is shown on the coordinate grid below.

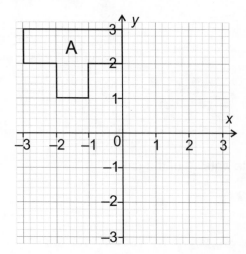

Rotate shape A 90° clockwise about (0, 0). Label the image shape B.

2 marks

12. (a) Write $1\frac{9}{10}$ as an improper fraction.

....

□ 1 mark

(b) Find $\frac{3}{5} + \frac{1}{6}$.

....

□ 2 marks

13. (a) Simplify $p + 4q + 3p + 2q$.

....

□ 1 mark

(b) Expand and simplify $2(x + 10) + x(x + 4)$.

....

□ 2 marks

14. The prices of some of the souvenirs in a seaside gift shop are shown on the right.

Postcard	£0.60
Mug	£2.90
Bookmark	£1.45
Fridge magnet	£1.65

(a) A customer paid for a fridge magnet with a £5 note. How much change did they get?

£............................

□ 1 mark

(b) How much would it cost to buy two bookmarks and a postcard?

£............................

□ 2 marks

15. The first part of a train timetable is shown below.

Deer's Town	Jollygrove	Pharton Moor	Lindun
08 54	09 12	09 35	11 01
09 24	09 42	10 05	11 31
09 54	10 12	10 35	12 01
10 54	11 12	11 35	13 01

(a) Sunita catches the first train of the day from Deer's Town.
She gets off the train at Pharton Moor.

How many minutes does she spend on the train?

.... minutes

1 mark

(b) Kyle lives a 10 minute walk away from the train station at Jollygrove.
He wants to catch a train and arrive in Lindun before 12.30 pm.

What is the latest time that he can leave his house?
Give your answer in the 24-hour clock.

....

2 marks

16. Here are the numbers of films that five pupils watched in the last two months.

6,   12,   3,   7,   2

(a) Calculate the range of the number of films watched.

....

1 mark

(b) Find the median of the numbers.

....

1 mark

(c) Calculate the mean number of films watched.

....

2 marks

17. The population of the town of Greenley Bay is 84 501.

(a) What is the population of the town to the nearest thousand?

....

1 mark

(b) The town fair was attended by 2293 people.
     Round this number to 3 significant figures.

....

1 mark

18. The map below shows a region of England.

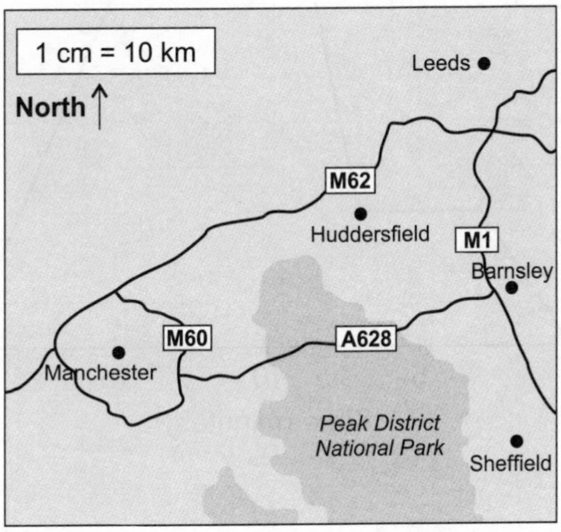

(a) What is the real-life distance between Manchester and Barnsley?

.... km

2 marks

(b) Huddersfield and Leeds are 24 km apart.
     Using 5 miles ≈ 8 km, find the distance between
     Huddersfield and Leeds in miles.

.... miles

2 marks

19. Express $3^{10} \div 3^4$ as a power of 3.

....

1 mark

20. Ian goes out for a run one evening.
This travel graph shows his distance from home while he was on his run.

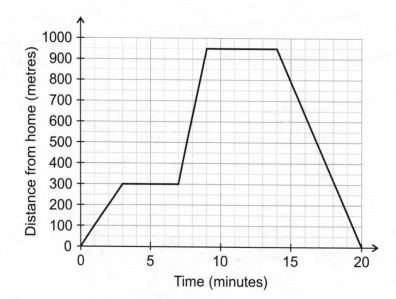

(a) Ian stops twice for a rest. How long does Ian rest for in total?

.... minutes

1 mark

(b) At which of these times was Ian running the fastest? Circle your answer.

2 minutes   5 minutes   8 minutes   10 minutes   15 minutes

1 mark

(c) After how many minutes does Ian begin heading home?

.... minutes

1 mark

21. Dylan has a pencil case containing 24 pens.
    14 pens are black, 8 are blue and the rest are red.

    Dylan is going to pick a pen at random from the pencil case.

    (a) Complete these sentences.

        (i) The probability that the pen will be .... is $\frac{1}{3}$.

        1 mark

        (ii) The probability that the pen will be red is ....

        1 mark

    (b) Before Dylan picks his pen, his cousin Salma borrows two blue pens
        and a red pen from the pencil case. If Dylan now chooses a pen at
        random from the case, what is the probability that it will be black?

        ....

        2 marks

22. The recipe on the right can be
    used to make four mushroom pies.

    | Butter | 20 g |
    | Mushrooms | 350 g |
    | Single cream | 100 ml |
    | Pastry | 400 g |
    | Plain flour | 30 g |

    (a) How many grams of mushrooms would you need to make 16 pies?

        .... g

        1 mark

    (b) What is the ratio of butter to pastry in its simplest form?

        ....

        2 marks

    (c) If you used 150 ml of single cream to make a batch of pies,
        how much plain flour would you need to use?

        .... g

        2 marks

END OF TEST

Key Stage 3 Mathematics Foundation Level Practice Exam

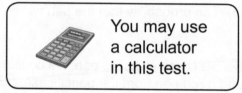

You may use a calculator in this test.

Paper 2
Calculator allowed

Instructions

- The test is one hour long.
- Make sure you have these things with you before you start:
  - pen
  - pencil
  - rubber
  - ruler
  - angle measurer or protractor
  - pair of compasses

  You may use tracing paper.
- The easier questions are at the start of the test.
- Try to answer all of the questions.
- Don't use any rough paper — write all your answers and working in this test paper.
- Check your work carefully before the end of the test.

Score: ⬚ **out of 60**

1. Put these numbers in the correct order, starting with the largest.

$$-12 \qquad 1 \qquad -1$$

....

1 mark

2. This pictogram shows the number of runs scored by three players during a game of cricket.

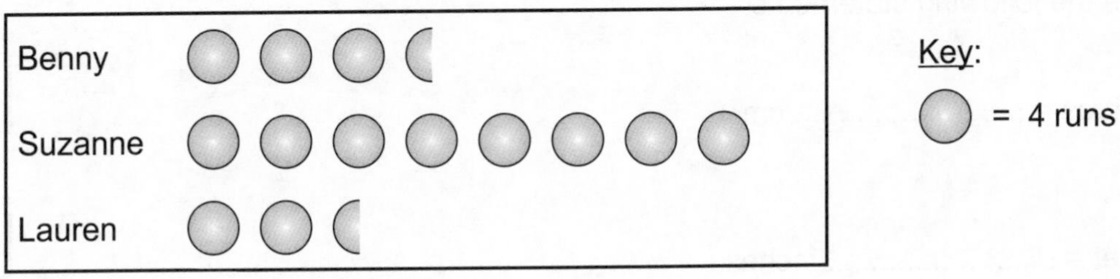

Benny	⬤ ⬤ ⬤ ◖
Suzanne	⬤ ⬤ ⬤ ⬤ ⬤ ⬤ ⬤
Lauren	⬤ ⬤ ◖

Key:

⬤ = 4 runs

(a) How many runs did Lauren score?

.... runs

1 mark

(b) Kristof scored twice as many runs as Suzanne.
How many runs did Kristof score?

.... runs

2 marks

3. A sequence of patterns is made using circles. The first three patterns are shown below.

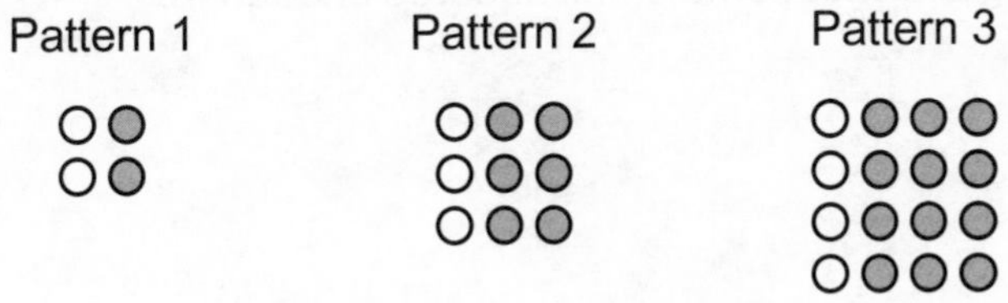

Pattern 1   Pattern 2   Pattern 3

How many of each colour circle will there be in the fourth pattern?

.... white circles   .... grey circles

2 marks

4. For the numbers 6 and 9, find:

(a) the highest common factor,

....
1 mark

(b) the lowest common multiple.

....
1 mark

5. Complete the following statements.

(a) 31 litres = ... cm³

1 mark

(b) 2 feet = ... inches

1 mark

6. (a) This diagram has four small squares shaded in.

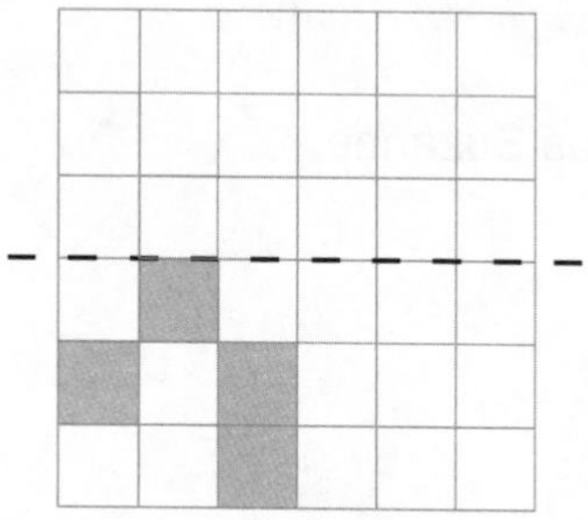

Shade in four more small squares to make a grey pattern that has a line of symmetry along the dotted line.

1 mark

(b) Here is another diagram with some small squares shaded in.

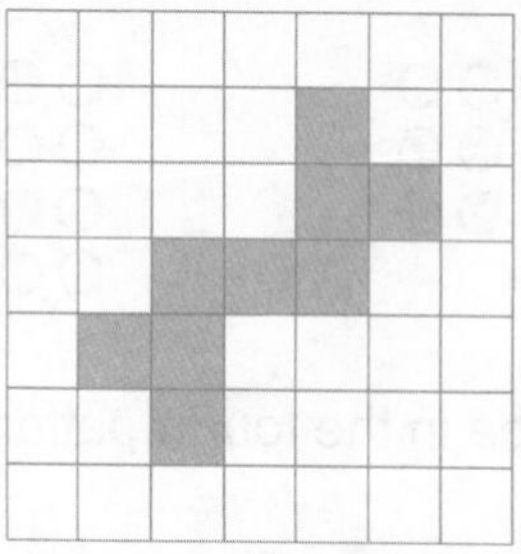

What is the order of rotational symmetry of this diagram?

....
1 mark

7. The pie chart shows the proportions of different sports played by members of a leisure club. Each member only plays one sport.

(a) What is the angle of the "Basketball" sector of the pie chart?

....................°

1 mark

(b) What is the angle of the "Rugby" sector of the pie chart?

....................°

1 mark

(c) The leisure club has a total of 180 members.
     How many play hockey?

....

2 marks

8. Solve the following equations:

(a) $x + 6 = 17$

$x =$ ....

1 mark

(b) $\frac{x}{4} = 12$

$x =$ ....

1 mark

(c) $4x + 18 = 6x$

$x =$ ....

2 marks

9. (a) Complete this factor tree.

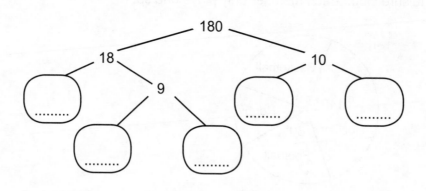

2 marks

(b) Using your answer to part (a), write the number 180 as a product of its prime factors.

....

1 mark

10. (a) On the grid below, plot the points A(0, 1), B(2, −3), C(−2, −1) and D(−2, 1). Join up the four points with straight lines to create the shape ABCD.

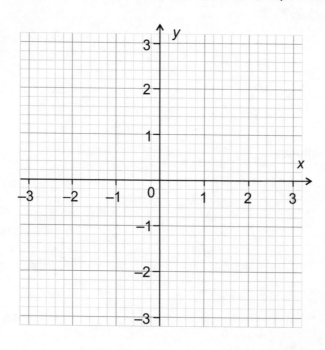

2 marks

(b) What is the name of the shape that you have drawn?

....

1 mark

11. A quarter of 8000 is halved and then multiplied by a mystery number to give 3000.
What is this mystery number? Show all your working.

....
□
2 marks

12. The diagram below shows a regular hexagon.

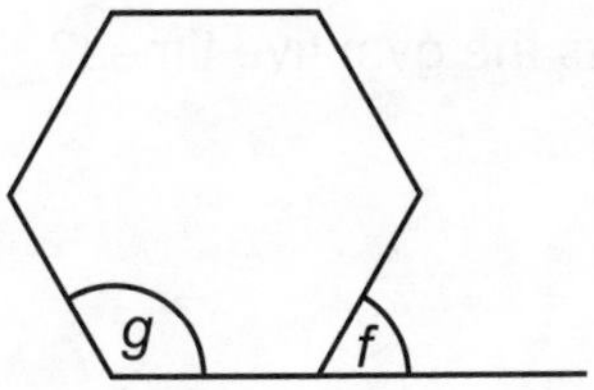

(a) Find the value of the exterior angle *f*.

..................°
□
1 mark

(b) Find the value of the interior angle *g*.

..................°
□
1 mark

13. Joe has a circular pond with a diameter of 2 m.

(a) Calculate the circumference of the pond to 2 decimal places.

.... m
□
2 marks

(b) Joe wants to put some edging around the pond.
It is sold in 1 m pieces and each piece costs £3.20.
What will it cost Joe to buy enough edging to go around the pond?

£ ....
□
2 marks

14. The cost of joining a local gym is £34 plus £2 each time you visit it.
Let C be the total cost in pounds, and n be the number of visits to the gym.

(a) Write a formula to show the cost of joining and using the gym.

....

2 marks

(b) What will be the cost if Amber visits the gym five times?

£......................

1 mark

15. (a) Find the area of the shape below.

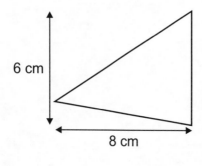

6 cm

8 cm

.... cm²

2 marks

(b) This prism has the shape from part (a) as its cross-section.

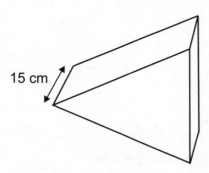

15 cm

Find its volume.

.... cm³

1 mark

16. At a concert, the ratio of adults to children was $3:5$.
120 people were at the concert.

How many adults and how many children went to the concert?

.... adults

.... children

3 marks

17. Write down the letters of all the shapes that are similar to shape X.

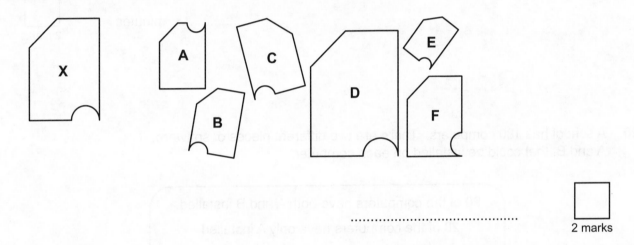

....

2 marks

18. A school tuck shop sells three different types of sweets. Taj worked out the probability of a pupil choosing each type of sweet, based on sweet sales from the last three months. The incomplete table below shows the results.

Chocolate	Mints	Fudge
....	0.1	0.25

(a) Complete the table.

1 mark

(b) What is the probability that a pupil does not choose fudge?

....

1 mark

19. Monique travels 115 miles to visit her grandmother.

(a) One day the journey took 2 hours.
What was her average speed in miles per hour?

.... mph

(b) If she drove at an average speed of 46 miles per hour, how long
in minutes would it take her to get to her grandmother's house?

.... minutes

2 marks

20. A school has 180 computers. There are two different pieces of software,
A and B, that could be installed on each computer.

> 90 of the computers have both A and B installed.
>
> 20 of the computers have only A installed.
>
> 15 of the computers have neither A nor B installed.

Complete this Venn diagram to show the number of
computers with each piece of software installed.

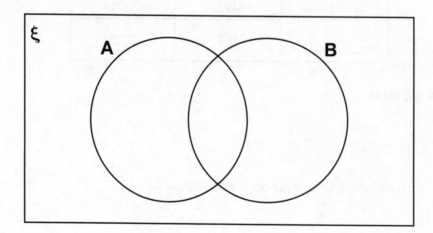

3 marks

21. An ice cream parlour sells ice cream tubs in three different sizes.

    A: 500 ml tub for £1.80

    B: 1 litre tub for £3.20

    C: 750 ml tub for £3.00

Which tub of ice cream represents the best value for money?
Show your working.

....

3 marks

22. Elliot has two bank accounts, A and B. He has £245 in account A and £300 in account B.

    (a) He makes a withdrawal from account A that reduces the amount in the account by 13%.
    How much is in account A now?

    £ ....

    2 marks

    (b) Simple interest is paid on the money in account B at a rate of 1% per year.
    Assuming Elliot makes no deposits or withdrawals, how much money will be in
    the account after 6 years?

    £ ....

    2 marks

END OF TEST

Practice Paper 2

Answers

Section One — Numbers

Page 15 (Warm-Up Questions)

1 72

2 a) Nine million, nine hundred and five thousand, two hundred and eighty-five.

   b) Six million, fifty-four thousand, two hundred and three.

3 a) $34 < 47$ b) $-2 > -6$
   c) $1.4 > 0.8$ d) $-1.2 < 0.44$

4 0.004, 0.032, 0.55, 1.23, 3.42, 8.63, 13.54

5 a) 63   b) 84

6 a) 797   b) 852

7 £19.62

8 a) 490   b) 17290   c) 0.333
   d) 0.08521

9 a) 990   b) 3300   c) 17570

10 a) 16   b) 72   c) 46

Page 16 (Practice Questions)

2 a) $5 + 6 \times 2$ *[1 mark]*
      $= 5 + 12 = 17$ *[1 mark]*
      [2 marks available in total — as above]

   b) $\dfrac{60}{20 - 10}$ *[1 mark]* $= \dfrac{60}{10} = 6$ *[1 mark]*
      [2 marks available in total — as above]

3 a) 7, 48, 309, 517, 572, 6479
      [2 marks available — 2 marks for all numbers in the correct order, lose a mark for missing out a number or putting one number in the wrong place.]

   b) 0.043, 0.303, 0.31, 0.4, 0.43, 0.44
      [2 marks available — 2 marks for all numbers in the correct order, lose a mark for missing out a number or putting one number in the wrong place.]

4 a) 25.00
      + 6.37
      ‾‾‾‾‾
      31.37
      £31.37
      [2 marks available — 1 mark for the correct method, 1 mark for the correct answer]

   b) $^{2\ 10\ 13}$
      31.37
      −08.90
      ‾‾‾‾‾
      22.47
      £22.47
      [2 marks available — 1 mark for the correct method, 1 mark for the correct answer]

Page 22 (Warm-Up Questions)

1 a) 5   b) −15   c) 18   d) −3

2 14 °C

3 53, 61, 123, 7305

4 1, 64

5 73, 83

6 a) 9, 18, 27, 36, 45, 54, 63, 72
   b) 1, 2, 3, 4, 6, 9, 12, 18, 36

7 $2 \times 2 \times 3 \times 5$ or $2^2 \times 3 \times 5$

8 21

9 16

Page 23 (Practice Questions)

2 a)

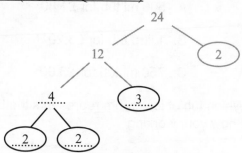

[2 marks available — 1 mark for correct factors of 12, 1 mark for correct prime factors of 4]

   b) $2 \times 2 \times 2 \times 3$ or $2^3 \times 3$ *[1 mark]*

3 a) Trybridge Tigers *[1 mark]*
   b) $-6 + 3 = -3$ *[1 mark]*
   c) $12 - -3 = 15$ *[1 mark]*

Page 29 (Warm-Up Questions)

1 a) $\dfrac{4}{5}$ b) $\dfrac{3}{10}$ c) $\dfrac{1}{25}$ d) $\dfrac{3}{20}$

2 a) 30%   b) 50%   c) $\dfrac{17}{25}$

3 a) $\dfrac{5}{7}$ b) $\dfrac{1}{4}$

4 $\dfrac{4}{5}$

5 a) $\dfrac{2}{30} = \dfrac{1}{15}$ b) $\dfrac{24}{35}$ c) $\dfrac{10}{8} = \dfrac{5}{4}$
   d) $\dfrac{4}{5}$ e) $\dfrac{7}{8}$ f) $\dfrac{7}{12}$

6 a) 196.95   b) 51

7 a) 30%   b) 250%

Page 30 (Practice Questions)

3 a)

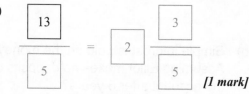

[1 mark]

   b)

[1 mark]

4 a) $(6 \div 15) \times 100 = 40\%$ *[1 mark]*
   b) $(20 \div 100) \times 15 = 3$ *[1 mark]*

5 $\dfrac{2}{7}$ of $21 = 21 \div 7 \times 2 = 3 \times 2 = 6$ blue marbles.

   $\dfrac{1}{3}$ of $21 = 21 \div 3 = 7$ red marbles.

   $21 - 6 - 7 = 8$ green marbles.
   [2 marks available — 1 mark for finding the number of blue or red marbles correctly, 1 mark for correct answer]

Page 36 (Warm-Up Questions)

1 a) 16.8   b) 6.648

2 a) 7.70   b) 11.800

3 a) 3000   b) 37   c) 0.0558

4 a) 18   b) 64600

5 a) 0.048   b) −230

6 E.g. $80 \times 10 = £800$

7 a) 72   b) 56
8 a) 4^{16} b) $7^2 = 49$
9 7^{12}
10 a) 3 and –3   b) 11 and –11   c) 13 and –13
11 a) 4.36   b) 8.63   c) 4.44

Page 37 (Practice Questions)

2 $5^5 = 5^6 \div 5 = 15\ 625 \div 5 = 3125$ *[1 mark]*
3 a) 11.92 *[1 mark]*
   b) 4.34 *[1 mark]*
4 E.g. $\frac{614}{154} \approx \frac{600}{150} = 4$ *[1 mark]*

   No, Harry is not right — £40 is far too much. *[1 mark]*
   [2 marks available in total — as above]
5 a) 4 *[1 mark]*
   b) 1024 *[1 mark]*

Page 38 (Revision Summary)

1 a) 9   b) 8   c) 10
2 a) One million, six hundred and
        forty-five thousand, one hundred
   b) Eight million, seven thousand,
        one hundred and eighty-two
3 12, 19, 81, 87, 98, 564, 874, 911
4 0.001, 0.02, 0.09, 0.51, 0.9, 1.8, 2.91
5 a) 121   b) 180
6 a) 611   b) 596   c) 2.673
7 a) 122.3   b) 15120
   c) 0.675   d) 0.0062
8 a) 414   b) 34
   c) 2489   d) 96
9 a) –2   b) –14
   c) 56   d) –9
10 a) Even numbers are whole numbers that divide by 2.
    b) Odd numbers are whole numbers that don't divide by 2.
    c) Square numbers are the numbers you get when whole
         numbers are multiplied by themselves.
    d) Cube numbers are the numbers you get when whole
         numbers are multiplied by themselves and then by
         themselves again.
11 a) 41, 43, 47   b) 83, 89
12 a) 11, 22, 33, 44, 55
    b) 1, 2, 3, 4, 5, 6, 10, 12, 15, 20, 30, 60
13 a) 2×5^2 b) $2^2 \times 3^2$ c) $2 \times 3^2 \times 5$
14 a) 24   b) 16
15 a) $\frac{6}{10} = \frac{3}{5}$ and 60%

    b) $\frac{35}{100} = \frac{7}{20}$ and 0.35
16 a) E.g. $\frac{6}{10}$ and $\frac{9}{15}$ b) $\frac{4}{30} = \frac{2}{15}$ c) $\frac{1}{3}$
17 a) $\frac{8}{9}$ b) $\frac{1}{12}$

    c) $\frac{20}{33}$ d) $\frac{35}{60} = \frac{7}{12}$
18 a) 120   b) 210
19 a) 11.7   b) £132.44   c) £98.01
20 4.42%
21 a) 164.4   b) 76 000   c) 765440
22 –45

23 a) E.g. $40 \times 30 = 1200$
    b) E.g. $(60 \times 10) + 100 = 700$
    c) E.g. $\frac{20 \times 50}{20} = 50$
24 a) 1 000 000   b) 555   c) 49
25 a) 6^{13} b) $3^4 = 81$ c) 2^{18}
26 a) 16   b) 1.77   c) 4

Section Two — Algebra and Graphs

Page 46 (Warm-Up Questions)

1 a) $3a$ b) $8d$ c) $8 - 2x + 2y$
   You can write the terms in part c) in any order.
2 a) $2x^2 + 3x$ b) $3x^2 + 15x$ c) $x^2 + x - 15$
3 a) 15   b) 13   c) 1
4 $c = 50s + 40$
5 a) $x = 3$ b) $x = 11$ c) $x = 3$
6 a) $x = 6$ b) $x = 4$ c) $x = -5$ d) $y = 4$

Page 47 (Practice Questions)

2 a) $7x - y$ *[1 mark]*
   b) $4x^2 + 4x - 5$ *[1 mark]*
3 a) $8x^2 + 16x$ *[1 mark]*
   b) $10x - 2 - 7x$ *[1 mark]*
      $= 3x - 2$ *[1 mark]*
      [2 marks available in total — as above]
4 a) $7k = 14$ *[1 mark]*
       $k = 2$ *[1 mark]*
      [2 marks available in total — as above]
   b) $2t + 6 = 12$ *[1 mark]*
         $2t = 6$ *[1 mark]*
          $t = 3$ *[1 mark]*
      [3 marks available in total — as above]
5 a) $T = 50n + 20$ *[1 mark]*
   b) $50 \times 3 + 20 = 170$ minutes
      [2 marks available — 1 mark for substituting n = 3,
      1 mark for the correct answer]

Page 50 (Warm-Up Questions)

1 a) 20 — Subtract 6 from the previous term.
   b) 64 — Multiply previous term by 4.
2 a) $3n + 2$ b) $-5n + 8$
3 15
4 a)

   b) 11 squares
5 a) $-4n + 2$ b) -30

Page 51 (Practice Questions)

2 –1, 4, 9, 14
   [2 marks available — 2 marks for all correct,
   otherwise 1 mark for at least 2 correct]
3 a) $2n + 5$
      [2 marks available — 1 mark for 2n, 1 mark for +5]
   b) $-4n + 15$
      [2 marks available — 1 mark for –4n,
      1 mark for +15]

4 a)

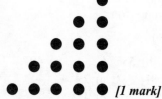

[1 mark]

b) In the 5th pattern (above) there are 15 and the number you add increases by 1 each time.
6th pattern 15 + 6 = 21,
7th pattern 21 + 7 = 28,
8th pattern 28 + 8 = 36
[2 marks available — 1 mark for realising that the number you add increases by 1 each time, 1 mark for the correct answer]

Page 57 (Warm-Up Questions)

1

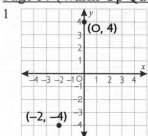

2

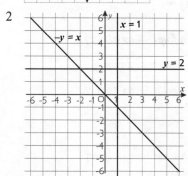

3 a) yes   b) yes   c) no
   d) no   e) yes

4

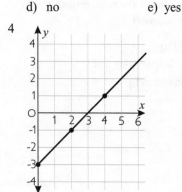

5

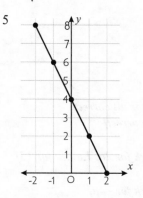

Page 58 (Practice Questions)

2 a) $y = 2$ *[1 mark]*   b) $x = 4$ *[1 mark]*
   c) $y = -2$ *[1 mark]*   d) $x = -4$ *[1 mark]*

3 a)

x	0	3	6
y	8	5	2

[1 mark]

b)

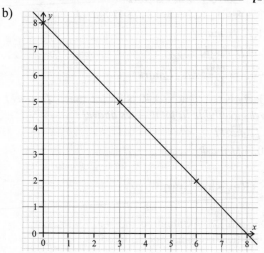

[1 mark]

c) (8, 0) *[1 mark]*

Page 62 (Warm-Up Questions)

1 a) 2.5 metres

   b) About 0.125 seconds and 1.625 seconds

2 The travelling object is stationary (has stopped).

3 The speed the object is travelling.

4 Distance

5 Approximately 43 miles

Page 63 (Practice Questions)

2 a) 3 km *[1 mark]*   b) 30 minutes *[1 mark]*
   c) 14:45 *[1 mark]*   d) 3 + 5 + 2 = 10 km *[1 mark]*

3 a) 11 gallons *[1 mark]*

   b) 7.5 gallons = 34 litres *[1 mark]*
       50 litres − 34 litres = 16 litres *[1 mark]*
       [2 marks available in total — as above]
       You can also subtract 7.5 gallons from 11 gallons, then convert the difference into litres.

Page 64 (Revision Summary)

1 a) $5a$ b) $9b$

2 a) $6d + e$ b) $-2f + 9$

3 a) g^4 b) $9mn$

4 a) $3v + 24$ b) $-14w - 35$

5 a) $3x^2 + 10x$ b) $7y^2 + 8y - 15$

6 a) $P = 29$ b) $P = -1$

7 −4 °F

8 $P = 8s + 15t$

9 a) $x = 7$ b) $x = 22$ c) $x = 12$ d) $x = 80$

10 a) $x = 3$ b) $x = 4$ c) $x = 2$

11 a) 26 — Add 6 to the previous term.

   b) −7 — Subtract 3 from the previous term.

   c) 243 — Multiply the previous term by 3.

12 $2n + 3$

13 A: (2, 2), B: (3, −2), C: (−2, −3), D: (−2, 1)

14 a) no   b) yes   c) yes   d) no

Answers

15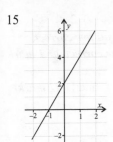

16 a) He rode faster on his way back.   b) 15 minutes

17 Draw a straight line from the value you know on one axis
to the graph. Then draw a straight line from that point on
the graph to the other axis, and read off the value.

Section Three — Ratio, Proportion and Rates of Change

Page 69 (Warm-Up Questions)

1 a) 1 : 3   b) 6 : 5   c) 2 : 7
2 a) 20 litres   b) 15 litres
3 39 trees
4 600 g = 0.6 kg
5 1 litre of the juice for £3
6 £3400
7 £16

Page 70 (Practice Questions)

2 1 calculator costs £28 ÷ 14 = £2 *[1 mark]*
so 22 calculators cost £2 × 22 = £44 *[1 mark]*
[2 marks available in total — as above]

3 Total number of parts = 5 + 2 = 7 *[1 mark]*
1 part = 35 ÷ 7 = 5 DVDs *[1 mark]*
Shaun gets 5 parts = 5 × 5 = 25 DVDs *[1 mark]*
[3 marks available in total — as above]

4 1 − 0.15 = 0.85
£120 × 0.85 = £102
*[2 marks available — 1 mark for a correct method,
1 mark for the correct answer]*
*Instead of finding the multiplier, you might have found the
amount the phone decreased by (0.15 × 120 = 18) and then
subtracted it from the original amount.*

5 250 ÷ 500 = 0.5p per ml
420 ÷ 700 = 0.6p per ml
1.2 litres = 1200 ml, then 540 ÷ 1200 = 0.45p per ml
So the 1.2 litre bottle is the best value for money.
*[2 marks available — 1 mark for finding all three costs
per ml (or amount per penny), 1 mark for the
correct answer]*

6 In one year Raul earns 0.015 × £2000 = £30 *[1 mark]*
In 10 years Raul earns 10 × £30 = £300 *[1 mark]*
So after 10 years, he'll have a total of
£2000 + £300 = £2300 *[1 mark]*
[3 marks available in total — as above]

Page 75 (Warm-Up Questions)

1 a) 100 cm   b) 12 inches   c) 16 ounces
2 a) 5.6 litres b) 98 pounds
3 5 pounds
4 300 kg
5 180 cm, 2 metres, 7 feet
6 1.32 pm
7 a) 2 hours 25 minutes   b) 10:40 pm

Page 76 (Practice Questions)

2 a) 220 × 300 = 66 000 ml *[1 mark]*
b) 1000 ml = 1 litre, so 66 000 ml = 66 000 ÷ 1000
= 66 litres *[1 mark]*

3 a) 3.35 pm *[1 mark]*
*Don't forget to include am or pm in your answer if you're
giving it in the 12-hour clock.*
b) The lesson lasts 2 × 50 = 100 minutes
= 1 hour 40 minutes *[1 mark]*.
9.05 am plus 1 hour is 10.05 am, then
10.05 am plus 40 minutes is 10.45 am *[1 mark]*.
[2 marks available in total — as above]

4 a) 8.20 am *[1 mark]*   b) 12 minutes *[1 mark]*
c) 6.33 pm *[1 mark]*

Page 82 (Warm-Up Questions)

1 50 km
2 7 cm
3 1 cm by 3 cm
4 200 metres
5 10 km/h

Page 83 (Practice Questions)

3 a) Distance on map = 3 cm *[1 mark]*
Multiplying by scale gives 3 × 5 = 15 km *[1 mark]*
[2 marks available in total — as above]
b) Dividing by scale gives 20 ÷ 5 = 4 cm *[1 mark]*
c)
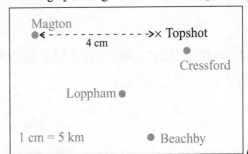
[1 mark]

4 a) Speed = distance ÷ time = 6 km ÷ 4 hours
= 1.5 km/h *[1 mark]*
b) Distance = speed × time = 3 km/h × 5 h
= 15 km *[1 mark]*

5 a) Drawers measure 1.5 cm by 1 cm *[1 mark]*
Multiplying by scale gives 1.5 × 0.5 = 0.75 m
by 1 × 0.5 = 0.5 m *[1 mark]*
[2 marks available in total — as above]
b) E.g.
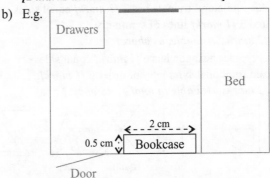

*[2 marks available — 1 mark for the correct width,
1 mark for the correct length]*
*The bookcase can be positioned anywhere between
the bed and the door.*

Answers

<u>Page 84 (Revision Summary)</u>

1 a) 1:5   b) 7:8   c) 3:2
2 21 nails
3 250 g
4 30 cars
5 84p
6 90 olives
7 750 g for £3
8 £6.90
9 £780
10 £156
11 See p.71
12 600 cm
13 10 yards
14 22 pounds
15 a) 50 miles   b) 75 cm
16 100 minutes
17 4 cm
18 50 m by 25 m
19

Home
×
⋮1 cm
×⋯⋯**2 cm**⋯⋯×
Cinema   Bus station

20 6 m/s
21 75 km

Section Four — Geometry and Measures

<u>Page 90 (Warm-Up Questions)</u>

1 1
2 2
3 Kite
4 20 lines of symmetry, order of rotational symmetry = 20
5 A: same shape, same size
6 Any regular hexagon is similar to shape E.

<u>Page 91 (Practice Questions)</u>

2 a) A parallelogram has 2 *[1 mark]* pairs of equal sides
       (which are parallel). It has 0 *[1 mark]* lines of
       symmetry and rotational symmetry of order 2 *[1 mark]*.
       [3 marks available in total — as above]
   b) An equilateral triangle has 3 *[1 mark]* equal sides
       and 3 *[1 mark]* lines of symmetry.
       [2 marks available, as above]
   c) A regular hexagon has 6 *[1 mark]* equal sides
       and rotational symmetry of order 6 *[1 mark]*.
       [2 marks available in total — as above]

3 a)

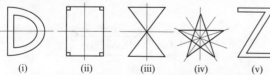

(i)   (ii)   (iii)   (iv)   (v)

*[3 marks available — 3 marks for all five shapes
correct, otherwise 2 marks for three or four shapes
correct, otherwise 1 mark for two shapes correct]*

b) (i) 1   (ii) 2   (iii) 2   (iv) 5   (v) 2
    *[3 marks available — 3 marks for all five correct,
    otherwise 2 marks for three or four correct, or 1 mark
    for two correct]*
4 a) A and C *[1 mark]*   b) A, C and D *[1 mark]*

<u>Page 97 (Warm-Up Questions)</u>

1 20 cm
2 18 cm
3 40 cm²
4 28 m²
5 45 cm²
6 26 cm
7 Circumference = 62.8 mm (1 d.p.)
   Area = 314.2 mm² (1 d.p.)
8 1253.50 m² (2 d.p.)

<u>Page 98 (Practice Questions)</u>

2 a) Area = $\pi \times 9^2$ = 254.469... = 254.47 m² (2 d.p.)
       *[2 marks available — 1 mark for using the formula,
       1 mark for correct answer]*
   b) The amount of fence needed is
       the circumference of the pond.
       Circumference = $2 \times \pi \times 9$ = 56.548...
                     = 56.55 m (2 d.p.)
       *[2 marks available — 1 mark for using the formula,
       1 mark for correct answer]*
3 a) Perimeter = $5 + 5 + 5 + 5 + x$ *[1 mark]*
       So $20 + x = 28$, so $x = 8$ cm *[1 mark]*
       [2 mark available in total — as above]
   b) area of rectangle – area of triangle
       $= (8 \times 5) - \left(\frac{1}{2} \times 8 \times 3\right) = 40 - 12 = 28$ cm²
       *[3 marks available — 1 mark for finding the area
       of the rectangle, 1 mark for finding the area of the
       triangle, 1 mark for the correct answer]*

<u>Page 103 (Warm-Up Questions)</u>

1 a) Tetrahedron (or triangular-based pyramid)
   b) Faces = 4, edges = 6, vertices = 4

2

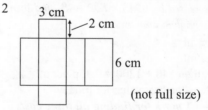

3 cm
↕2 cm
6 cm
(not full size)

3 96 cm²
4 24 cm²
5 168 cm³

<u>Page 104 (Practice Questions)</u>

2 a) 6 *[1 mark]*
   b) 6 *[1 mark]*
   c) 10 *[1 mark]*
3 Surface area = $2(5 \times 3) + 2(8 \times 3) + 2(5 \times 8)$
                = 30 + 48 + 80 = 158 cm²

   *[3 marks available — 1 mark for attempting to find the
   area of each rectangle of the net, 1 mark for putting the
   numbers in correctly, 1 mark for the correct answer]*

4 a) Radius = 6.2 ÷ 2 = 3.1 cm
       Area = $\pi r^2 = \pi \times 3.1^2$
           = 30.1907... = 30.19 cm² (2 d.p.)
       [2 marks available — 1 mark for using the correct formula, 1 mark for the correct answer]
   b) Volume = cross-sectional area × length = $\pi r^2 \times h$
           = 30.1907... × 10 = 301.907...
           = 301.9 cm³ (1 d.p.)
       [2 marks available — 1 mark for using the correct formula, 1 mark for the correct answer]

Page 112 (Warm-Up Questions)

1 a) obtuse   b) reflex   c) acute
2 See p.106 for method.
3 $x = 25°$
4 54°
5 $y = 102°$
6 Exterior angle = 72°
   Interior angle = 108°

Page 113 (Practice Questions)

2 a) Corresponding angles are equal, so $a = 101°$ *[1 mark]*
   b) Vertically opposite angles are also equal, so $b = 101°$ *[1 mark]*
3 a) Angles in a quadrilateral add up to 360° *[1 mark]*
       so $p = 360° - 147° - 85° - 80° = 48°$ *[1 mark]*
       [2 marks available in total — as above]
   b) Angles on a straight line add up to 180°, so
       $q = 180° - p = 180° - 48° = 132°$ *[1 mark]*
   c) The sum of interior angles in a pentagon is
       $(5 - 2) \times 180° = 540°$ *[1 mark]*
       $r = 540° - 110° - 122° - 88° - 132° = 88°$ *[1 mark]*
       [2 marks available in total — as above]
4 Angles on a straight line add up to 180°, so
   angle ABC = 180° - 115° = 65° *[1 mark]*
   Angles in a triangle add up to 180°, so 65° + 75° + x = 180°.
   This means $x = 180° - 75° - 65° = 40°$ *[1 mark]*
   [2 marks available in total — as above]

Page 117 (Warm-Up Questions)

1 Translation by the vector $\begin{pmatrix} 2 \\ -7 \end{pmatrix}$

2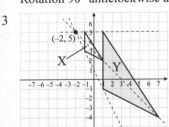

   Rotation 90° anticlockwise about point (-2, -1)

3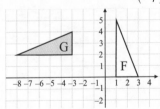

   Enlargement of scale factor 3, centre (-2, 5)

Page 118 (Practice Questions)

2 a) (i) $\begin{pmatrix} -3 \\ -2 \end{pmatrix}$ *[1 mark]*   (ii) $\begin{pmatrix} -1 \\ -5 \end{pmatrix}$ *[1 mark]*

b) Rotation 180° *[1 mark]* about point (0, -1) *[1 mark]*
    You can rotate clockwise or anti-clockwise —
    you will get the same result.

3 a)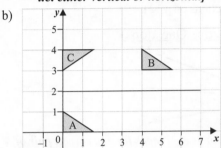

       [2 marks available — 2 marks for the correct position, otherwise 1 mark for one correct translation — i.e. either vertical or horizontal]

   b)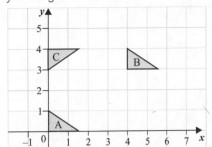

       [1 mark]

   c)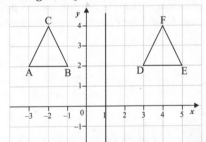

       [2 marks available — 1 mark for enlarging by the correct scale factor, 1 mark for the correct centre of enlargement]

4 a)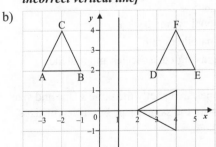

       [2 marks available — 2 marks for fully correct reflection, otherwise 1 mark for a reflection in an incorrect vertical line]

   b)

       [2 marks available — 1 mark for a rotation of 90° anti-clockwise, 1 mark for using the correct centre of rotation]

Answers

Page 122 (Warm-Up Questions)

1 E.g.

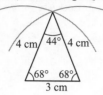

2 E.g.

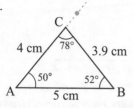

3 See constructions on p.121
4 See constructions on p.121

Page 123 (Practice Questions)

2

[2 marks available — 1 mark for one correct pair of compass arcs, 1 mark for bisector accurately drawn]

3

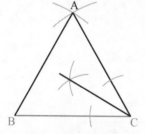

a) *[2 marks available — 1 mark for correct arcs, 1 mark for drawing straight lines joining B and C to the point where they cross and labelling this point A]*

b) *[2 marks available — 1 mark for one correct pair of compass arcs, 1 mark for bisector accurately drawn]*

4

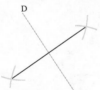

[2 marks available — 1 mark for one correct pair of intersecting arcs, 1 mark for perpendicular line]

Page 124 (Revision Summary

1 Lines of symmetry = 2
   Order of rotational symmetry = 2
2 Rhombus and parallelogram
3 Equilateral, right-angled, isosceles and scalene
4 Heptagon
5 Congruent shapes are exactly the same shape and size.
   Similar shapes are the same shape but different sizes.
6 Perimeter = 32 cm,
   Area = 55 cm^2
7 48 cm^2
8 30 cm^2
9 Circumference = 50.3 cm (1 d.p.)
   Area = 201.1 cm^2 (1 d.p.)

Answers

10 4 complete rotations
11 Faces = 5, edges = 9, vertices = 6
12 Surface area = 62 cm^2
    Volume = 30 cm^3
13 See p.101
14 400 cm^3
15 a) E.g. 72° (any value from 0°-89°)
    b) E.g. 111° (any value from 91°-179°)
    c) E.g. 260° (any value from 181°-359°)
16 See method on p.106
17 See p.107
18 Alternate angles
19 a) $x = 70°$ b) $y = 70°$ c) $z = 40°$
20 Exterior angle = 36°
    Interior angle = 144°
21 720°
22 The angle of rotation, the direction of rotation and the centre of rotation.
23 (5, 3), (14, 3) and (11, 12)
24 E.g.

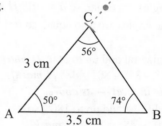

25 See method on p.121

Section Five — Probability and Statistics

Page 128 (Warm-Up Questions)

1 0 (it is impossible)
2 0.6
3 a) $\frac{1}{10}$ b) $\frac{5}{10} = \frac{1}{2}$ c) $\frac{4}{10} = \frac{2}{5}$
4 $\frac{8}{15}$
5 8
6

	Coin	
	Heads	Tails
1	1H	1T
2	2H	2T
3	3H	3T
4	4H	4T
5	5H	5T
6	6H	6T

(Dice)

Page 129 (Practice Questions)

2 E.g.

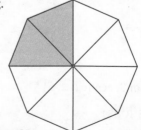

[1 mark]
It doesn't matter which 2 triangles you shade as long as only 2 are shaded.

3 a) $P(5) = \frac{1}{6}$ *[1 mark]*

b)
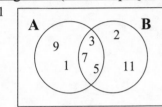

[1 mark]

4 a) There are 4 vowels out of 11 letters,
so P(vowel) $= \frac{4}{11}$ *[1 mark]*

b) There are no Xs, so P(X) = 0 *[1 mark]*

5 P(on time) = 1 − P(not on time) = 1 − 0.22 = 0.78 *[1 mark]*

6 Number of blue balls $= \frac{1}{8}$ of 8 = 1

Number of red balls $= \frac{1}{4}$ of 8 = 2

Number of green balls = 8 − 1 − 2 = 5

*[2 marks available — 1 mark for a correct method,
1 mark for the correct answer]*

Page 134 (Warm-Up Questions)

1
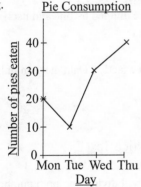

2 n(P) = 5, n(Q) = 4

3 X = {1, 3, 5, 7, 9, 11, 13, 15, 17, 19}
Y = {1, 4, 9, 16}

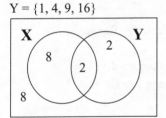

4 a) Discrete   b) Qualitative
c) Discrete   d) Continuous

5 E.g.

6 23 doughnuts

Page 135 (Practice Questions)

2 a)
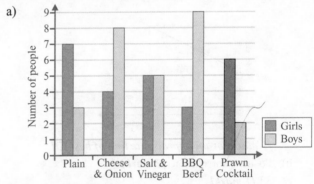

[1 mark]

b) March *[1 mark]*

c) 24 − 20 = 4 more runs in July than in September
[1 mark].

d) 14 − 4 = 10 more swims than runs *[1 mark]*

3 a)
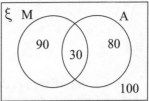

*[3 marks available — 3 marks for all four numbers
correct, otherwise 2 marks for three numbers correct
or 1 mark for two numbers correct]*

*Don't forget that the number of students studying music
includes those who study both art and music so you need to
subtract 30 from the number you are given. Do the same
for the number of students studying art.*

b) Number of students studying music or art
= 90 + 30 + 80 = 200 *[1 mark]*

Page 139 (Warm-Up Questions)

1 a) Blue   b) 8 students

2 The bar chart with shoe sizes along the horizontal axis
has gaps between bars because the data is discrete.

3 a) 60°   b) 20 people

Page 140 (Practice Questions)

2 a)

[1 mark for both bars correct]

b) 3 + 9 = 12 children chose BBQ Beef and 5 + 5 = 10
children chose Salt & Vinegar *[1 mark for both]*
12 − 10 = 2 children *[1 mark]*
[2 marks available in total — as above]

3 a) Multiplier = 360° ÷ 45 = 8°

Destination	Frequency	Angle of sector
UK & Ireland	12	12 × 8° = 96°
Europe	23	23 × 8° = 184°
USA	7	7 × 8° = 56°
Other	3	3 × 8° = 24°

*[2 marks available — 2 marks for all four angles
correct, otherwise 1 mark for a correct method]*

b)

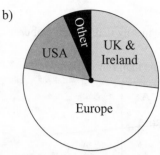

[2 marks available — 2 marks for all sectors drawn correctly, otherwise 1 mark for two sectors correct]

Page 145 (Warm-Up Questions)

1   Median = 11, mode = 12, mean = 11, range = 7
2   15
3

Food	Sausage rolls	Crisps	Pork pies	Quiche	Sandwiches
Frequency	5	3	5	3	4

4   a) Mean = 1.54 (2 d.p.)   b) Mode = 1
5   (Strong) positive correlation
6   About 2.7 years
    Any answer between 2.5 and 3 years is allowed.

Page 146 (Practice Questions)

2   42 + 49 + 44 = 135 *[1 mark]*
    135 ÷ 3 = 45 *[1 mark]*
    [2 marks available in total — as above]

3   a) E.g.

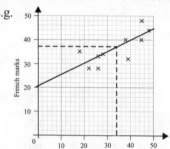

[1 mark for an appropriate line of best fit]
    b) Positive correlation *[1 mark]*
    c) 37 *[1 mark]*
        Any answer between 35 and 38 is allowed.
    d) Range = 48 – 28 = 20 *[1 mark]*

Page 147 (Revision Summary)

1   A probability of 1 means that something is certain to happen.
2   P(lose) = 0.9
3   $\frac{5}{12}$
4   a)

	Second spin	
	Black	**White**
Black	BB	BW
White	WB	WW

First spin

    b) $\frac{2}{4} = \frac{1}{2}$ or 0.5

5   a) X = {2, 3, 5, 7, 11}, Y = {1, 2, 4, 8}
    b)

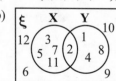

6   Primary data is data you've collected yourself.
    Secondary data is data someone else has collected.

7   Qualitative
8   Continuous
9   E.g.

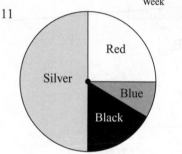

January	📖📖 📖📖
February	📖📖 📖📖 📖
March	📖📖 📖📖 📖
April	📖📖 📖

    Key: 📖 = 2 books

10 E.g.

Number of camels sold vs Week bar chart (Week 1: 4, Week 2: 8, Week 3: 18, Week 4: 22)

11

Pie chart showing Red, Silver, Blue, Black sectors

12 $\frac{30°}{360°} \times 120 = 10$ people
13 Mode = 5, Median = 5, Mean = 6, Range = 9
14 a) 12 houses
    b) Mode = 2, Mean = 2, Range = 4
15 E.g. people's height and shoe size

Section Six — Exam Practice

Page 148 — Mixed Practice Test 1

1   A number that can only be divided by one and itself.
2   D   3   D
4   (0, 0)   5   C
6   Data that can be recorded exactly / Data that can only take certain values
7   80   8   B
9   5   10 4

Page 149 — Mixed Practice Test 2

1   0   2   C   3   B
4   The biggest number that will divide into both numbers
5   C   6   24 pints   7   A
8   C   9 $x = 7$
10 Sum of interior angles = $(n - 2) \times 180°$

Pages 150-151 — Mixed Practice Test 3

1   (4, 3)   2   8
3   B   4   1, 2, 4, 8, 16
5   D   6   9.8
7   0.2   8   D
9   C   10 A

Answers

Page 152 — Mixed Practice Test 4

1 $A = \frac{1}{2} \times b \times h$ (or Area = $\frac{1}{2} \times$ base $\times$ height)

2 C   3 1   4 C

5 360°   6 27   7 B

8 North-west   9 $10x + 25$ 10 A

Page 153 — Mixed Practice Test 5

1 80   2 B

3 $5m + 3n$ 4 5

5 C   6 A

7 8   8 B

9 2   10 24

Pages 154-155 — Mixed Practice Test 6

1 9 and –9   2 7

3 42%   4 A

5 A   6 B

7 C   8 D

9 1.5 m/s   10 $2^4 \times 7$ (or $2 \times 2 \times 2 \times 2 \times 7$)

Page 156 — Mixed Practice Test 7

1 C   2 –5

3 The total area of all the faces of the shape added together.

4 C   5 B

6 360°   7 8.37 pm   8 300

9 B   10 $\frac{3}{10}$

Page 157 — Mixed Practice Test 8

1 828 000

2 Data that can take any value over a certain range.

3 28   4 D

5 1329 (or 1.29 pm)   6 B   7 B

8 12 cm   9 A   10 3

Pages 158-167 — Practice Paper 1

1 a) $56 - 9 = 47$ *[1 mark]*   b) $7 \times 9 = 63$ *[1 mark]*

2 a) 1 cm = 10 mm, so 120 mm = 120 ÷ 10

        = 12 cm *[1 mark]*

   b) Area = $\frac{a+b}{2} \times h$

       = $\frac{15+9}{2} \times 12$ *[1 mark]*

       = 12 × 12

       = 144 cm² *[1 mark]*

     [2 marks available in total — as above]

3 (Regular) octagon *[1 mark]*

4 $\frac{6.2 \times 29}{8.9} \approx \frac{6 \times 30}{9}$ *[1 mark]* $= \frac{180}{9} = 20$ *[1 mark]*

   [2 marks available in total — as above]

5 a) $s + 150° = 180°$, so $s = 180° - 150° = 30°$ *[1 mark]*

     Angles on a straight line add up to 180°.

   b) $t = 65°$ *[1 mark]*

     Corresponding (F-shaped) angles are the same.

   c) $t + s + u = 180°$, so $u = 180° - 30° - 65° = 85°$ *[1 mark]*

     Angles in a triangle add up to 180°.

6 $\frac{1}{4} = 0.25$, so the order is: 0.05, 0.15, $\frac{1}{4}$, 0.4

   [2 marks available — 2 marks for all four numbers in the correct order, otherwise 1 mark if only one number is missing or out of order]

7 a) 21, 26 *[1 mark]*

     The sequence is given by the rule 'add 5 each time'.

   b) 49, 64 *[1 mark]*

     The terms are all square numbers. You could also define the sequence by the rule 'add 7, then add 9, then add 11, then add 13, etc.' — i.e. the number you add on increases by 2 each time.

8 a)

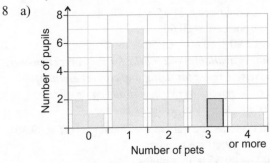

     [1 mark for bar for boys with 3 pets correctly added]

   b) 6 girls have 1 pet and 2 girls have 2 pets.
     So the answer is 6 – 2 = 4 more girls. *[1 mark]*

   c) 2 girls and 1 boy have no pets, so 2 + 1 = 3 children have no pets. *[1 mark]*

9 $\frac{2}{5} = \frac{40}{100} = 40\%$ *[1 mark]*, so the percentage that's left is $100\% - 25\% - 40\% = 35\%$ *[1 mark]*.

   [2 marks available in total — as above]

10 a)

Spin One

Spin Two	1	2	3	4
1	2	3	4	5
2	3	4	5	6
3	4	5	6	7
4	5	6	7	8

     [1 mark for both entries correct]

   b) There are 2 ways to score a 7 *[1 mark]* out of 16 results.

     So the probability is $\frac{2}{16} = \frac{1}{8}$ *[1 mark]*.

     [2 marks available in total — as above]

11

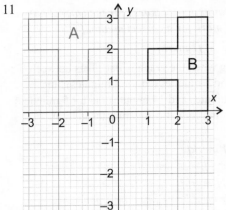

   [2 marks available — 1 mark for shape A rotated 90° clockwise, 1 mark for the correct position on the grid]

12 a) $1\frac{9}{10} = 1 + \frac{9}{10} = \frac{10}{10} + \frac{9}{10} = \frac{19}{10}$ *[1 mark]*

   b) $\frac{3}{5} + \frac{1}{6} = \frac{18}{30} + \frac{5}{30}$ *[1 mark]* $= \frac{23}{30}$ *[1 mark]*

     [2 marks available in total — as above]

13 a) $p + 4q + 3p + 2q = p + 3p + 4q + 2q = 4p + 6q$
[1 mark]

b) $2(x + 10) + x(x + 4)$
$= 2 \times x + 2 \times 10 + x \times x + x \times 4$ *[1 mark]*
$= 2x + 20 + x^2 + 4x = x^2 + 6x + 20$ *[1 mark]*
[2 marks available in total — as above]

14 a) £5.00 – £1.65 = £3.35 *[1 mark]*

b) E.g. 2 bookmarks: £1.45 × 2 = £2.90
1 postcard = £0.60
£2.90 + £0.60 = £3.50
[2 marks available — 2 marks for the correct answer, otherwise 1 mark for using any correct method]
You could have done this by just adding up all three prices instead — that would be fine too.

15 a) Sunita catches the train at 08:54 and gets off at 09:35.
08:54 → 09:00 = 6 minutes
09:00 → 09:35 = 35 minutes
So she is on the train for 6 + 35 = 41 minutes. *[1 mark]*

b) The latest train that Kyle can catch arrives in Lindun at 12:01. This train leaves Jollygrove at 10:12.
To catch this train, he must leave his house 10 minutes before this: 10:12 → 10:02
[2 marks available — 1 mark for identifying which train he needs to catch, 1 mark for the correct answer]

16 a) Range = 12 – 2 = 10 *[1 mark]*

b) In order, the list of numbers is: 2, 3, <u>6</u>, 7, 12
So the median is 6. *[1 mark]*

c) 6 + 12 + 3 + 7 + 2 = 30 *[1 mark]*
Mean = 30 ÷ 5 = 6 *[1 mark]*
[2 marks available in total — as above]

17 a) 85 000 *[1 mark]*

b) 2290 *[1 mark]*

18 a) The distance on the map is 5 cm *[1 mark]*.
Using the scale, 1 cm = 10 km, so the distance is
5 × 10 km = 50 km *[1 mark]*.
[2 marks available in total — as above]

b) 8 km ≈ 5 miles and 24 = 3 × 8,
so 24 km ≈ 3 × 5 = 15 miles
[2 marks available — 2 marks for the correct answer, otherwise 1 mark for a correct method]

19 $3^{10} \div 3^4 = 3^{10-4} = 3^6$ *[1 mark]*

20 a) Ian is resting when the graph is flat. This between 3 minutes and 7 minutes (so for 4 minutes), and between 9 minutes and 14 minutes (so for 5 minutes).
So Ian is resting for 4 + 5 = 9 minutes in total.
[1 mark]

b) 8 minutes *[1 mark]*
Ian is travelling fastest when the graph is steepest.

c) 14 minutes *[1 mark]*
Ian begins heading home when the graph starts going downhill.

21 a) (i) $\frac{1}{3} = \frac{8}{24}$
The probability that the pen will be **blue** is $\frac{1}{3}$.
[1 mark]

(ii) Number of red pens = 24 – 14 – 8 = 2
The probability that the pen will be red is $\frac{2}{24}$.
[1 mark]
You could simplify the answer to part (ii) to $\frac{1}{12}$.

b) Salma takes 2 blue pens and 1 red pen, so there are
24 – 2 – 1 = 21 pens left *[1 mark]* and 14 are black.
Probability of picking a black pen = $\frac{14}{21}$ or $\frac{2}{3}$ *[1 mark]*
[2 marks available in total — as above]

22 a) 16 = 4 × 4 so you would need 350 × 4 = 1400 g
of mushrooms. *[1 mark]*

b) $20:400 \xrightarrow{\div 20} 1:20$
[2 marks available — 1 mark for dividing by a common factor, 1 mark for the correct answer]

c) $100:30 \xrightarrow{\times 1.5} 150:??$ *[1 mark]*
So 30 × 1.5 = 45 g of plain four is needed. *[1 mark]*
[2 marks available in total — as above]

Pages 168-177 — Practice Paper 2

1 1, –1, –12 *[1 mark]*

2 a) 4 + 4 + 2 = 10 runs *[1 mark]*

b) Suzanne scored 8 × 4 = 32 runs *[1 mark]*
There are 8 full symbols.
So Kristof scored 2 × 32 = 64 runs *[1 mark]*.
[2 marks available in total — as above]

3 To get the next pattern, you add another row and another column of circles, always keeping the first column white.
So the fourth pattern will be:

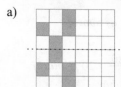

There are 5 white *[1 mark]* and 20 grey *[1 mark]* circles.
[2 marks available in total — as above]
Instead of drawing out the next pattern, you could think about the number of each colour of circle. The white circles increase by 1 each time and the grey circles increase by 4, then 6, then 8, etc.

4 a) Factors of 6: 1, 2, <u>3</u>, 6
Factors of 9: 1, <u>3</u>, 9
So the highest common factor is 3. *[1 mark]*

b) Multiples of 6: 6, 12, <u>18</u>, 24, 30, ...
Multiples of 9: 9, <u>18</u>, 27, ...
So the lowest common multiple is 18. *[1 mark]*

5 a) 31 000 cm³ *[1 mark]*

b) 24 inches *[1 mark]*

6 a)

[1 mark]

b) The shape has rotational symmetry of order 2.
[1 mark]

7 a) 90° *[1 mark]*

b) 360° – 140° – 90° – 80° = 50° *[1 mark]*
Angles around a point always add up to 360°.

c) 180 members is represented by 360°, so 1 member is represented by 2°. The hockey sector has an angle of 140°, so 140° ÷ 2° = 70 members play hockey.
[2 marks available — 1 mark for a correct method, 1 mark for the correct answer]

8 a) $x + 6 = 17$, so $x = 17 - 6 = 11$ *[1 mark]*
   b) $\frac{x}{4} = 12$, so $x = 12 \times 4 = 48$ *[1 mark]*
   c) $4x + 18 = 6x$, so $18 = 6x - 4x = 2x$ *[1 mark]*
       So $x = 18 \div 2 = 9$ *[1 mark]*
       [2 marks available in total — as above]

9 a)

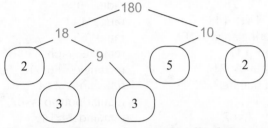

[2 marks available — 2 marks for all values correct, otherwise 1 mark for three or four values correct]
   b) $2 \times 2 \times 3 \times 3 \times 5$ or $2^2 \times 3^2 \times 5$ *[1 mark]*

10 a)

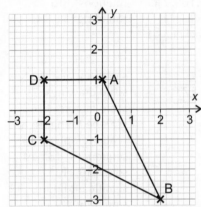

[2 marks available — 2 marks for the correctly drawn shape, otherwise 1 mark for at least two points plotted correctly]
   b) Kite *[1 mark]*

11 A quarter of 8000 is 2000,
   then half of this is 1000 *[1 mark]*.
   $1000 \times ? = 3000$, so the mystery number is 3 *[1 mark]*.
   [2 marks available in total — as above]

12 a) exterior angle $= \frac{360°}{6} = 60°$ *[1 mark]*
   b) interior angle $= 180° - 60° = 120°$ *[1 mark]*

13 a) circumference $= \pi \times$ diameter $= \pi \times 2$ *[1 mark]*
       $= 6.28$ m (2 d.p.) *[1 mark]*
       [2 marks available in total — as above]
       It's fine if you said $r = d \div 2 = 1$, then used $C = 2\pi r$.
   b) Joe will need seven pieces, so $7 \times 3.20 = £22.40$
       [2 marks available — 1 mark for saying that Joe needs seven pieces of edging, 1 mark for the correct answer]

14 a) $C = 2n + 34$
       [2 marks available — 1 mark for each correct term]
   b) $C = 2 \times 5 + 34 = £44$ *[1 mark]*

15 a) Area of a triangle $= \frac{1}{2} \times$ base $\times$ height
       $= \frac{1}{2} \times 6 \times 8$ *[1 mark]*
       $= 24$ cm² *[1 mark]*
       [2 marks available in total — as above]
   b) Volume of a prism = area of cross-section $\times$ length
       $= 24 \times 15 = 360$ cm³ *[1 mark]*

16 $3 + 5 = 8$, so 1 part $= 120 \div 8 = 15$ *[1 mark]*
   $15 \times 3 = 45$ adults *[1 mark]*
   $15 \times 5 = 75$ children *[1 mark]*
   [3 marks available in total — as above]

17 C, D and E
   [2 marks available — 2 marks for all three letters correct only, otherwise 1 mark for two or three letters correct alongside a maximum of one incorrect letter]

18 a) Probabilities add up to 1, so P(Choc) $+ 0.1 + 0.25 = 1$.
       So P(Choc) $= 1 - 0.25 - 0.1 = 0.65$

Chocolate	Mints	Fudge
0.65	0.1	0.25

[1 mark]
   b) P(not fudge) $= 1 -$ P(fudge) $= 1 - 0.25 = 0.75$ *[1 mark]*

19 a) speed = distance $\div$ time
       $115 \div 2 = 57.5$ mph *[1 mark]*
   b) time = distance $\div$ speed
       $115 \div 46 = 2.5$ hours
       $2.5 \times 60 = 150$ minutes
       [2 marks available — 1 mark for a correct method, 1 mark for the correct answer]

20 Work out how many computers have only B installed:
   $180 - 90 - 20 - 15 = 55$

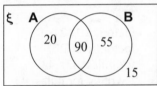

[3 marks available — 1 mark for calculating the correct number of computers with only B installed, 1 mark for any two values in the correct places on the Venn diagram, 1 mark for the remaining two values in the correct places on the Venn diagram]

21 E.g. work out the amount per penny for each tub.
   A: $500 \div 180 = 2.77...$ ml per penny
   B: 1 litre = 1000 ml
       $1000 \div 320 = 3.125$ ml per penny
   C: $750 \div 300 = 2.5$ ml per penny
   So B is the best value because you get the most ice cream per penny.
   [3 marks available — 1 mark for finding ml per penny or price per ml, 1 mark for all three values correct, 1 mark for the correct conclusion]

22 a) 13% of £245 $= 0.13 \times £245 = £31.85$
       So 13% reduction $= £245 - £31.85 = £213.15$
       [2 marks available — 1 mark for a correct method, 1 mark for the correct answer]
       Alternatively, you could answer this by multiplying £245 by $1 - 0.13 = 0.87$.
   b) Amount of interest earned in 1 year:
       1% of £300 $= 0.01 \times £300 = £3$
       Amount of interest earned in 6 years:
       $6 \times £3 = £18$ *[1 mark]*
       Total amount after 6 years: $£300 + £18 = £318$ *[1 mark]*
       [2 marks available in total — as above]

Index

A

addition 3, 7-10, 17
algebra 39-41
  brackets 41
angles 105-111
  acute 105
  alternate 109
  around parallel lines 109
  corresponding 109
  exterior 110
  in a quadrilateral 107
  in a triangle 107
  interior 110, 111
  obtuse 105
  on a straight line 107
  reflex 105
  right 105
  round a point 107
  vertically opposite 109
area 92-96
averages 141, 143
axes 52

B

bar charts 136, 137
bar-line graphs 136
best buy 67
BODMAS 3

C

calculators 4
circles 95, 96
circumference 95, 96
clocks 74
compass directions 78
congruence 88
constructions
  angle bisector 121
  perpendicular bisector
    121
  triangles 119, 120
continuous data 132
conversion factors 72, 73
converting 71-73, 77, 78
  map distances to real life
    77
  metric to imperial 71, 73
  real life to map distances
    78
coordinates 52
correlation 144
cube numbers 18
cube roots 35
cubes 100
cuboids 100, 102
cylinders 102

D

data 132
decimal places 6, 12, 31
decimals 6, 10, 24
diameter 95
discrete data 132
dividing by 10, 100, etc. 12
division 3, 7, 12, 14
dual bar charts 137

E

enlargements 89, 116
equilateral triangles 87
error 33
estimating 33
even numbers 18
events 125
expressions 42

F

factors 20, 21
factor trees 20
formulas 42, 43
  writing formulas 43
formula triangles 80
fractions 3, 24-27
  equivalent 25
  mixed numbers 27
  ordering 25
  simplifying 25
frequency 136, 142
frequency tables 142, 143

G

grouped frequency tables
  142

H

HCF 21

I

imperial units 71
improper fractions 27
interest 68
intersection 130
isosceles triangles 87, 107

K

kites 86

L

LCM 21
line graphs 133
line symmetry 85

M

maps 77, 78
mean 141, 143
measuring angles 106
median 141
metric units 71
mixed numbers 27
mode 141
money 2, 67
multiples 20, 21
multiplication
    3, 7, 8, 11, 13
multiplying by 10, 100, etc.
    11
multiplying out brackets 41

N

negative numbers 17
nets 100, 101
nth term 49

O

odd numbers 18
ordering
  decimals 6
  fractions 25
  whole numbers 5
origin 52
outcomes 126, 127

P

parallel lines 109
parallelograms 86, 92, 93
percentages 24, 28, 68
  increase and decrease 68
perimeter 92
pi (π) 4, 95
pictograms 133
pie charts 138
place value 5, 6
polygons 87, 110, 111
powers 34
prime factorisation 20
prime numbers 19
prisms 101, 102
probability 125-127
proportion 66, 67
proportional division 65
protractors 106, 120
pyramids 101

Q

quadrilaterals 86, 107
qualitative data 132
quantitative data 132

R

radius 95
range 141
ratios 65
real-life graphs 59-61
rectangles 86, 92, 93
reflections 114
regular polygons 87, 110
remainders 14
rhombuses 86
right-angled triangles 87
rotational symmetry 85-87
rotations 115
rounding 31-33

S

sample space 127
scale drawings 79
scale factors 116
scalene triangles 87
scatter graphs 144
sequences 48, 49
sets 130, 131
significant figures 32
similarity 89
simple interest 68
solids 99
solving equations 44, 45
speed 80, 81
square numbers 18
square roots 35
squares 86, 87
straight-line graphs 53-56
  equations 53-55
  plotting 56
subtraction 3, 7, 9, 10, 17
surface area 100, 101
symmetry 85-87

T

terms 39, 41
timetables 74
translations 114
trapeziums 86, 92, 93
triangles 87, 92, 93, 107,
    119, 120
triangular prisms 101, 102
two-step equations 45

U

units 2, 71
universal set 131

V

vectors 114
Venn diagrams 130, 131
volume 102